Geographical Work in Primary and Middle Schools

Edited by
David Mills
Vice-Principal
Avery Hill College

THE GEOGRAPHICAL ASSOCIATION
343 FULWOOD ROAD
SHEFFIELD S10 3BP

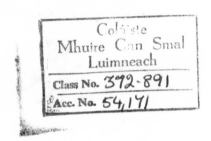
Printed by McCorquodale (Newton) Ltd, Newton-le-Willows, Merseyside, WA12 0DH

Contents

Contributors

JOHN BAINES   Council for Environmental Education, Reading

JOHN BENTLEY   King Alfred's College, Winchester

RACHEL BOWLES   Avery Hill College, London

SIMON CATLING   Southmead Junior School, London

ROGER CLARE   Avery Hill College, London

COLIN CONNER   Homerton College, Cambridge

ROGER CRACKNELL   Itchen College, Southampton

TOM DALTON   Avery Hill College, London

GAVIN FARMER   Avery Hill College, London

TIM FIRTH   Craven Park School, London

GORDON HARRIS   City and Tower Hamlets Teachers' Centre, London

MELANIE HARVEY   Chorleywood County Primary School, Herts.

MICHAEL HELLYER   Canada House, London

PAUL KELLY   Eastbury School, Barking

DAVID MILLS   Avery Hill College, London

DAVID ROWBOTHAM   Kingswood Junior School, West Norwood, London

HERBERT A. SANDFORD   College of St. Mark and St. John, Plymouth

REX WALFORD   University of Cambridge Department of Education

BRIAN WRIGHT   British Broadcasting Corporation, Birmingham

DAVID R. WRIGHT   School of Education, University of East Anglia

JILL A. WRIGHT   *Formerly of* Avery Hill College, London

GERALD YOUNG   Prince Rock Secondary School, Plymouth

Acknowledgements

The Geographical Association would like to thank the following individuals and organisations for permission to reproduce material in this handbook.

Sister Bridget Arscott, for the project on India reproduced on p. 128.

R. A. Beddis, for the diagram on p. 50.

Centre for World Development Education (128 Buckingham Palace Road, London SW1W 9SH) for the extracts from *Involved in Mankind* reproduced on pp. 128-31.

The Headmaster, Dunraven School (Mount Nod Road, London SW16 2LG) for the project on Botswana on p. 130.

The Headmaster, Eastbury School (Dawson Avenue, Barking, Essex, IG11 9QQ) for the syllabus reproduced on pp. 148-9.

Tim Firth, Headmaster, Craven Park School (Castlewood Road, London N16 6DH) for the syllabus reproduced on pp. 162-3.

The Headmaster, Forest Hill School (Dacres Road, London SE23 2XN) for the syllabus reproduced on pp. 168-9, 171-5.

S. D. Howard for the film-making project reproduced on p. 131.

ILEA Learning Materials Service, Publishing Division (Highbury Station Road, London N1 1SB) for the matrix on the study of places in the primary school reproduced on pp. 164-6.

The Headmaster, Shevington County High School (Shevington, Nr. Wigan, WN6 8AB) for the syllabus reproduced on p. 150.

Pamela M. O. Singh for the project on Botswana reproduced on pp. 128-9.

Sarah M. Smith (Farthingsgate Junior School, Scratchface Lane, Purbrook, Waterlooville, Hants.) for the project on 'Time' reproduced on pp. 158-61.

Preface

In a summary of the DES report on Primary Education, amongst many things, we read: 'There was considerable evidence that work in this subject (Geography) would benefit from more careful planning to provide some ordering of the content to be taught and to ensure that children are introduced to essential skills, such as the ability to use atlases, maps and globes.'

This handbook has been designed to help teachers of children of the 5-13 age range to achieve the above desire. The help it offers will provide a measure for teachers in the accountability factor which the profession must vouchsafe.

But it is not a provision simply of tips for teachers. For the instant lesson, like instant coffee, has to undergo a lot of preparation before the final and easy application. Rather it is a genuine attempt to increase competency and in turn to strengthen one's powers of accountability.

Geographical work in our schools is not solely a means of giving information. Professors of Geography, on their own admissions, are ignorant of some parts of the earth's surface. But they know it is of paramount importance that we should train our pupils in the use of atlases and reference books so that, if they need to find out facts on Zimbabwe, they can do so.

A Science adviser admitted to me that geography, not science, was the real core subject of primary and middle school work. All of us have followed the tenets of literacy and numeracy as fundamental in education. Some of us have used the tools of geography - maps, diagrams, models and photographs and spatial awareness. These bases of geography, which may be termed graphicacy, rank it with English and mathematics as a foundation school subject. After forty years teaching service, I know this to be true. And why? - 'What geography, in exchange for the help it receives from other sciences, can bring to the common treasury is the art of not dividing what nature brings together' - said Vidal de la Blache, a French geographer.

The contributors of this book have this essence in mind, to give teachers a tool which has been tempered in the heat of classroom activities and will cut through any barrier to deliver to pupils a logical and reasoned experience of the world around them.

And this world starts at the window or the school door, without recourse to limited capitation grants! We are able to help our pupils learn from reality using the principles of observation, investigation and recording in that order. I well remember the late Professor Wooldridge beginning such an outdoor lesson with this quote from Proverbs Ch. 17 V. 24.

> Wisdom is before him that hath understanding, but the eyes of a fool are in the ends of the earth.

The contents of this book have been written sincerely and professionally to give teachers such an understanding—to support their work, removing doubt and uncertainty and giving confidence and competence.

The Geographical Association is grateful to the contributors of this handbook. I am sure future readers will be grateful also.

RONALD S. BARKER
Ipswich.
Headmaster, and Chairman of the
Primary and Middle Schools Section
of the Geographical Association.

Introduction

This handbook succeeds the previous publication *Geography in Primary Schools* and has been enlarged to incorporate suggestions for work for pupils who are in middle schools. There is also a somewhat greater emphasis on work with younger children than has previously been the case. I have attempted to ensure that there is not an overlap with the handbook *Geographical Education in Secondary Schools,* also published by the Geographical Association. This division of handbooks is appropriate for there is a tendency for geographical work to be organised in a different way in primary and middle schools than in secondary ones. Although there is still much to commend what was to be found in *Geography in Primary Schools,* particularly in relation to techniques, there have necessarily been changes in content and methodology over the last ten years. In particular, I have been concerned with the lack of a development structure in the subject and it is hoped that the ideas put forward in this handbook will be of assistance.

The aim of the handbook is to help teachers, particularly those who have had no particular training in geographical work. Whether this aim has been met will have to be judged by each teacher; but it is hoped that everyone who reads the handbook will gain some assistance.

Originally, an editorial committee was formed to devise the structure of the book and once this work was done the writing was left to the contributors. As editor, I would particularly like to thank them for all the thought and work which has gone into this handbook. In many cases, the ideas are original and have developed the frontiers of teaching the subject with the age group. As with all publications which are edited there are variations in style, but hopefully, these have been kept to a minimum.

I am also very grateful to Ron Barker, the Chairman of the Primary and Middle Schools Committee of the Geographical Association, and his team for guidance as the handbook began to take shape. I am also anxious that the work of Ann Barham of the Geographical Association's staff should not go unnoticed. She has been extremely helpful in making the handbook suitable for publication.

DAVID MILLS

1. Geographical work for the 5-13s

1.1 Introduction

Simon Catling, Colin Conner, Michael Hellyer and David Mills

The teaching of geography to pupils of this age range is regarded as an essential part of their education. However, two major changes have occurred within recent years. The first is that the subject is now being taught within some form of integrated or interdisciplinary approach as well as a separate subject. Secondly, considerable changes have recently taken place in the way in which geographers are looking at their own subject and this is reflected in the new methods of analysis, and an emphasis on ideas rather than facts.

The aim of this book is to interweave the strands of theory and practice. However, a strong emphasis is placed on practical advice on what to teach and suggestions on how to teach it. Nevertheless, the teaching of the subject cannot be seen in isolation but must be fitted in with current views on the nature of learning and curriculum development.

Why teach Geography at all? The pressures on the school timetable, particularly for the older age ranges under consideration, are such that any subject must be able to justify its place. It is our contention that:

1. *Geography has important ideas which can help the pupil to gain an insight into the nature of the world in which he lives,*
2. *Geography contributes to the development of the individual's attitudes towards the society and environment in which he finds himself.*
3. *Geography develops skills which are of value to the learner.*

At the centre of the geographer's study is the relationship between man and his environment, and the interaction between man and man within that environment. The study of landscapes and their evolution in both rural and urban areas, also an important part of geographical teaching, can be studied within areas or regions, and clearly children should become aware of the similarities and differences between their own localities and contrasting ones both in Britain and the rest of the world. Likewise, children should:

> come to realise, through the study of distant places, that the world contains great variety in its landscapes and climates and in the ways by which people come to terms with their environment, and realise that some peoples have greater wealth and technical resources than others. (Morris, 1972.)

Geographical studies also lead to the discussion of important issues which are relevant to society. For example many planning problems within cities or associated with motorway development or creation of open space can be used as a starting point or develop from studies of particular environments.

School geography in the past has often lacked developmental structure and in recent years there has been an increasing emphasis placed on basic concepts, ideas and generalisations which can be introduced at different stages in a course and also re-visited in greater depth as the course develops. Some key ideas are given in a section later in this chapter. It is not intended that the list should be regarded as comprehensive, but it is hoped that the lists given will provide a beginning from which teachers can develop their own syllabi.

The teacher of geography, besides being concerned with ideas also develops certain skills and study methods. Many of these are also relevant to other fields of knowledge but they have been included in order to provide checklists on methods of work. The specific objectives of geography teaching for these age ranges may be regarded as follows:

1. To develop *concept/idea formation* in the areas of:
   (a) the inter-relationships of people and their environment;
   (b) recognition and classification of objects on the earth's surface;
   (c) the nature of processes, e.g. those on the physical landscape;
   (d) spatial relationships, e.g. distributional patterns;
   (e) location, distance and accessibility.
2. To develop the *skills* of:
   (a) first-hand observation and measurement;
   (b) recording observed data by the use of maps, spoken and written words, photographs, field sketches and diagrams;
   (c) map making, map reading and map expression;
   (d) reading and interpreting photographs of environmental phenomena;
   (e) presenting ideas by appropriate means;
3. To initiate children (working as individuals or groups) into the following *study methods:*
   (a) the inductive method of scientific enquiry, including the use of direct personal observations in the accessible environment;
   (b) the use of second-hand sources, such as reference books, atlas maps, statistics, diagrams, literature, pictures, tapes, films, T.V. and radio;
   (c) experience of games, simulation and problem-solving situations as a means of understanding the process of decision-making.
4. To encourage *attitude formation:*
   (a) to foster the interest of children in their local environment, including the people living and working in it;
   (b) to develop a sympathetic understanding of people from different environments and of different cultural and ethnic backgrounds;
   (c) to help towards an understanding of the inter-dependence of people, communities and areas of the world.

In summary, geography has much to contribute in the teaching of certain ideas, attitudes and skills which must take an important place in the curriculum of children in the 5–13 age range.

1.2 The current place of geography in first, junior and middle schools

Colin Conner and David Mills

First and Infant Schools

There is limited information available concerning the type of geographical work undertaken in infant and first schools. Various research reports concerned with this age range suggest that much of the general experience presented to children might be seen as geographical, but it is often difficult to separate the geographical from the non-geographical, for as Education Pamphlet No. 59 argues:

To children up to the age of eight or nine the concept of place even in an area as large as a parish, a sizeable village, or the district of a

town served by the school may be hard to grasp as a whole. (Department of Education and Science, 1972, p.11.)

As such, it is generally agreed that this early period is the time during which children's minds are being enriched and vocabulary being learned. Children's interests in things geographical are stimulated through visits to the locality, the park, the church, the shops. During such visits curiosity is aroused and moves from one thing to another, and with this arousal teachers are able to enlarge and refine the vocabulary with the differentiation, for example, of trees into various species, vehicles into lorries, cars, bicycles etc., and building types into banks, shops, offices, etc.

A report by the Bedford Board of Studies isolated the following as the major directions of geographical work with children of first school age. They believed that work in the first instance should aim to teach children how to observe, to guide their observations and then teach them how to record their observations in a variety of ways. Young children should be encouraged to observe within their own environment and locality and be encouraged to ask questions. This approach is well documented in the Plowden Report, which argues that geographical work with young children,

> is concerned with indiscriminate examining and observing of objects, events and phenomena, and learning the vocabulary needed to communicate about them. Weather, people and their actions, growing plants, inanimate objects, scenes in a road or street are all matters of curiosity and comment. (Department of Education and Science, 1967.)

Junior Schools

For many years geography has been accepted as one of the main subjects in the primary school curriculum. In recent years however, its place as a separate subject, in common with other disciplines, has been increasingly challenged, and geographical learning is now widely pursued in various forms of combined studies.

In the early 1950s geography in most primary schools followed a traditional syllabus, commencing with children and family life in other lands, products such as cocoa, tea, rice, followed by an introduction to the British Isles and Herbertson's natural regions during the final year. Much of the study was textbook orientated using out-of-date resource material. The survey conducted by the Inspectorate (Morris, 1972) confirmed a move away from this approach, and revealed some significant changes. Of the schools in the sample only 19% retained geography as a separate subject, 61% of the schools absorbed geography into a combined studies course, and the remaining 20% retained geography as a separate element within a combined course; i.e. perhaps by allocating one term of the year for mainly geographical studies, and other terms for history or scientific studies etc.

The research found that the most successful geography was found in those courses which gave it recognition as a subject in a combined studies programme. The weakest achievement was found when geography was wholly absorbed in combined studies.

A further surprising factor was the apparent lack of organisation within the courses. Only 31% of the schools had what the Inspectorate would accept as adequate schemes of work, 18% had poor schemes, and the remaining 43% had no schemes at all. (The qualification of a good scheme was that it outlined objectives both for the course and the development of the subject, and translated this into the learning experiences through which these might be achieved. Such courses equated this information to the changing development levels of the children, and had researched relevant experiences and resource material.)

Good courses were rarely static, always adapting to the changing situation, and changing demands of the children. The comparative success of schools with good or adequate schemes of work emerges clearly. The poor schemes either imposed too rigid a control over the teacher or were merely a list of topics or ideas with no integrating theme or clear objectives, nor any statement about how progression in learning was to be achieved. One striking factor to emerge was that a poor scheme was worse than no scheme at all.

The survey indicated a clear understanding of the difficult task facing primary school teachers, having to teach completely across the curriculum. As such it was difficult for all teachers to keep abreast with current developments in all subjects. There was a close relationship between the enthusiasm of the head teacher for geography, and the importance attached to geographical work in the curriculum.

In a smaller, but comprehensive survey undertaken by Cracknell (1974), many of the Inspectorate's findings were substantiated. Cracknell concluded that whilst geographical experience still clearly exists within primary school topic/project work, there may be cause for concern about the quality of this experience. He found that little fieldwork was undertaken in the schools, few teachers used large and small-scale maps, and that the geography taught lacked any real conceptual stucture.

Finally, the survey *Primary Education in England* published in 1978 made it clear that in many primary schools geographical work still needed to be improved. For example, three-fifths of 7-year-old classes and one-third of the 11-year-old classes were still not carrying out geographical studies in the local environment. Similarly, one-quarter of 11-year-old classes were not using atlases and two-fifths were not introduced to globes. Three-quarters of 9-year-old classes and three-fifths of 11-year-old classes were not using maps of the locality. The survey concluded that 'as with history, much of the work tended to be superficial and there was often little evidence of progression' (Department of Education and Science, 1978).

Middle Schools

Many of the results of the primary school surveys are further substantiated by the findings of surveys into the place of geography in the new middle schools. In a survey by the Bradford branch of the Geographical Association (Coley, 1974), factors emerged which are a cause for some concern. As with the primary schools, geography often becomes subsumed into a multi-disciplinary learning programme. It was argued however that in the courses considered, the geographical work included tends to be the factual kind, and that geographical skills, concepts, and ways of thinking are not being learned except in a haphazard and fortuitous way. In the survey, which admittedly focused on a small sample of 17 schools, it was found that 66% of the teachers responsible for geography had no formal academic qualifications in the subject. Such findings have obvious implications for geography in the middle school, and subsequently implications for the development of geography in upper schools.

The latter point is directly significant, especially since Education Pamphlet No. 59 stated quite categorically that every middle school will need the services of at least one teacher well versed in modern geography and its teaching. In a larger survey of 115 middle schools, Conner (1976) found that teachers with some form of training in geography comprised 12.92% of the total teaching force of the sample schools. Of these teachers, 54% possessed a teaching certificate with geography as main subject and 30% with geography as a subsidiary subject. The re-maining 16% had a degree which included geography as a component. In the schools of this sample 15% included geography as an independent subject, 69% included it as part of combined studies, and the remaining 16% as an independent subject and part of a combined studies course. Where geography was taught separately a trained geographer was responsible, but when geography became absorbed into combined studies non-geographers were often involved in the teaching.

A further point of interest was that 19% of the teachers with a qualification in geography were employed purely as class teachers covering a range of subject matter and only teaching geography incidentally. The most surprising factor to emerge was the range of subjects with which it was felt geography might combine. The major combinations tended to be Arts biased, contrary to the recent changes within the subject itself. The most popular combination was that of history, geography and religious studies under the umbrella title of Humanities. Some combinations consisted of three or four disciplines, whereas others were made up of seven or eight—and several schools even argued for no subject boundaries at all and approached all school work through total integration.

In schools where geography retained its independence, the courses were similar to the traditional syllabus outlined earlier, following a concentric approach of studying the locality before the British Isles, and the British Isles before other lands. There were limited attempts to incorporate recent developments in the subject into course work.

When geography was included in combined studies, much geographical material was included, but it could often occur intermittently. On some occasions geography could be the major aspect of a topic, whereas in others another subject might dominate. There was little evidence to suggest that balance over a period of time between the contributory disciplines had been attempted. As with the Inspectorate's primary school survey, the greatest benefit of combined studies was in the flexible allocation of time, often in morning or afternoon blocks, which allowed frequent use of the locality for study courses. (It was not possible, however, to assess the proportion of such time which might be spent studying geographical elements).

1.3 The nature of geography

David Mills

It is often said that there are as many definitions of geography as there are geographers. In common with many other subjects changes have taken place recently in the way in which the subject is both studied and taught, and some of the points which are considered to be fundamental have been made at the start of this book. However, it is not without interest that geographers have at times emphasised different aspects of the subject. A paper which clearly makes these points was written by Pattison (1964), in which he states that geography has four main traditions: (1) a spatial tradition, (2) an area studies tradition, (3) a man-land tradition, and (4) an earth science tradition.

The word spatial may bring a sinking feeling to non-geographers but it is a term increasingly used in geography courses. When children draw maps they are dealing with space. The research worker who uses a computer to map distributions is concerned with space. Spatial patterns and distributions, geometry and movement, are seen by some as being all-important in the study of geography. Although it may seem somewhat arid in its approach, this tradition of geography clearly has its place in school geography and some of the concepts associated with it are given later on in this chapter. Teachers familiar with Cole and Beynon's *New Ways in Geography* (1969) will be aware of the kind of work which children in the seven-plus age range can do in order to gain an insight into spatial tradition.

The area studies tradition, largely through the regional study approach, was extremely popular in many schools in the UK for a long period until about the mid-1960s when it began to lose its appeal mainly because of the fact that a syllabus based on this approach alone was not sufficiently rigorous or developmental. Nevertheless, area studies still have an important part to play in the geography syllabus for the characteristics of a place or area are recognised as being basic to the subject. It is recognised that the area studies approach is closely tied to other traditions but this understanding of places and areas does enable the synthesis of factors affecting these to take place, this being an important education process.

The man-land tradition is concerned with the relationship of man and his environment, and in particular his physical environment. In primary school geography for many years there has been an emphasis on teaching about the natural environment and in particular the important differences between the forested lands, grasslands, deserts, etc. The physical environment obviously affects man and the way he lives and works. However, it is important to realise that man also affects the environment, e.g. in altering atmospheric conditions by creating 'heat islands' over large cities, by re-afforestation, by creating pollution, etc. If one alters 'man–land' to 'man-environment' then it is possible to extend the concept to environments other than physical; e.g. economic environments, cultural and social environments and even behavioural environments in which the behaviour of man is related to the environment which he believes he inhabits.

The earth science tradition includes the study of the earth, its waters and atmosphere. The study of physical geography continues to be regarded as an important aspect of the subject for it enables pupils to understand the physical environment in which they live, and gives them an understanding and an appreciation of the physical landscape. Elementary studies in geology are not uncommon with younger pupils and can lead to a life-long interest in the study of rocks and fossils.

Pattison (1964) in his conclusion states that: 'the four traditions though distinct in logic are joined in action. One can say of geography that it pursues concurrently all four of them'. This is a view to which many would subscribe.

1.4 The Influence of Learning Theory on the Teaching of Geography

Simon Catling and Colin Conner

Some factors contributing to effective learning for 5-13-year-olds

The nature of geographical work in schools relates not only to the character of the subject-matter, but to current insights into how children learn. Learning starts from 'where the learner is'. He brings to the situation the sum total of his experience to that moment. Effective teaching starts at this point and builds upon its foundations. Because of this, learning is a highly individual process. Group activities may be the means of learning, but it is the individual who learns. Individual differences need to be taken into account and allowed for in learning situations. Children at different stages of cognitive development differ in their learning needs and interests and teaching procedures should take account of this.

The development of children's understanding

Ever since the turn of this century research has continued to analyse the way the child comes to understand his world, in all its varied aspects. This ongoing research has had much influence on the way children learn in school, the way teachers teach, and the sorts of ideas, skills and study methods teachers set out to get over to children. Geography teaching has been as subject to this evolution as any other subject. Indeed it has been recognised that there is a structure to the way children learn, and that the structure of our knowledge needs to be related to the development of children's understanding. This is as true in geographic learning as it is in mathematical, musical, or any other learning situations. The works of Piaget and Bruner have been fundamental in their influence here, the former in his research findings and the latter in the way he has applied these findings to curriculum structures. Though many have quibbled with Piaget's findings, none has seriously challenged his general interpretation. In summary, Piaget postulates three distinct phases of development with the approximate ages at which these stages occur:

1. Sensori-motor (0–2 years).
2. Pre-Operations (2–7 years).
   (a) Pre-Conceptual (2–7 years).
   (b) Intuitive (4–7 years).
3. The Operational Period (from 7 years).
   (a) Concrete Operations (7–11 years).
   (b) Formal Operations (from 11 years).

The significance of these divisions for the teacher lies in the fact that Piaget identifies the type of thinking characteristic of children for each particular phase. He recognises that what might appear as logical inconsistencies to an adult are not so typical for children of a particular age group. These stages should not be linked too closely to the ages suggested by Piaget, for he admits that they are approximate, and subject to cultural variation. The important factor to remember however, is that the sequence of stages is invariant, so that no matter what age each succeeding stage emerges, the course of development remains unaltered. It is also important to recognise that not every child attains the last of Piaget's stages, that of thinking abstractly and dealing with hypothetical deductive relationships, nor are all adults capable of thinking at this level in all areas; this must depend on intellectual capacity, experience and adaptability.

The most significant aspect of Piaget's work for the teacher, and more particularly for the planning of work of a geographical nature, lies in the implications which are drawn by educators from his researches, which, through systematic questioning, have covered the child's conception of moral judgement, the world, causality, time, space, number, geometry, perception and many other areas. For Piaget it would seem that education for the 5-13-year-olds will involve the use of the child's own experiences which have largely happened in the immediate local environment and the presentation of situations to the child which eventually demand experiment and the seeking of his own answers. The teacher's role in such a scheme would be one of structuring the environment and helping the child to make his own discoveries rather than the presentation of direct verbal learning.

'Children's desire to learn can be strengthened by teachers who not only impart instruction, but are ready to follow up questions and suggest that hypotheses are tested and information sought out by the child himself.' The presentation of such learning situations stems directly from the work of Bruner in the United States who has argued for the introduction of problem solving in school rather than didactic, and direct verbal teaching methods. By setting up learning situations which require children to collect their own information, present their own solutions, and test out their own ideas, Bruner argues that learning will become more meaningful, there will be greater retention, and the active involvement stressed by Piaget would lead to improved motivation.

This approach is open to a great deal of question, particularly by teachers of younger children, yet Bruner resists such opposition and believes that certain types of subject matter or certain teaching styles should not be thought of as outside the intellectual scope of children on the grounds of insufficient intellectual ability or sophistication. Instead he emphasises that rather than wait for a child to achieve the necessary cognitive readiness for certain types of curriculum content, the learning content should be adapted to suit the patterns of thought of the child. It seems essential, however, that some indication be given as to the right sort of curricular material of a geographical nature which might be more suitable to particular age groups or developmental levels. Indeed Bruner (1963) suggests that such a structure is essential since for him 'knowledge one has acquired without sufficient structure to tie it together is knowledge that is likely to be forgotten'. What Bruner envisages is a spiral curriculum in which certain key concepts, ideas or generalisations are revisited at increasing levels of complexity as the child progresses through the education system. As far as geography is concerned this would imply isolating the key ideas of the subject and organising learning experiences such that increasing sophistication is introduced as the child develops the intellectual maturity to be able to cope.

1.5 Graphicacy

David Mills

The term 'graphicacy' was first used in an article by Professor W. G. V. Balchin and Miss A. M. Coleman in 1965. They argued then and since that there are four main orders of communication—Literacy, Numeracy, Articulacy and Graphicacy. Balchin has defined graphicacy as the art of communicating spatial information that cannot be conveyed by verbal or numerical means; e.g. the plan of a town, the pattern of a road or rail network, a picture of a distant place. Later, he suggested that the content of this field of communication might include:

appreciation of direction and distance
appreciation of size, shape and area
linear and angular measurement
space relations and map forms
appreciation of scale
conventional signs
colour distinctions, pattern recognition
mathematical graphs and their interpretation
use of coordinates
map projection and art projection
perspective in field sketching and photography
perspective in area reproduction
map making and map interpretation
networks and distributions
ground and air photo interpretation
photogrammetry
colour, radar and infra-red photography
computer graphics
remote sensing devices.

Quite clearly not all these concepts and skills are appropriate for the primary and middle age range, but equally clearly many are appropriate, particularly in the sphere of mapping. The importance of including map reading and map drawing within the syllabus must be emphasised at this point, and it is maintained that the teacher should nurture the graphicate ability of children right through the school career so that the skills may be used in adult life. Later in this handbook a number of suggestions are given to enable the teacher to help his pupils to become graphicate.

1.6 Geography and Integrated schemes of work

David Mills

It is well known that much geography is now taught within an integrated framework. In first and junior schools the timetable commitment is usually termed 'Project' or 'Topic work' or 'Environmental Studies', whereas in middle schools geographical ideas may be taught under the heading of 'Social Studies' or 'Humanities' or, as with younger children, 'Environmental Studies'.

Curriculum integration is frequently contrasted with the compartmentalisation of knowledge which is often stated to be characteristic of 'traditional' syllabi. It is stated that the child often cannot see the division between subjects and that subject-based courses often confine study. It is also argued that a division of knowledge into subject areas in the school curriculum is artificial. It is much more important that 'enquiry' or 'discovery' methods should be used and these can be more readily adapted to the integrated curriculum than to one which is dominated by subject. It is also argued by supporters of integration that school work can be related much more readily to the needs and interests of the child and these are often expressed in terms of theories or issues which cross the subject barriers. In the school, however, a wide array of approaches have been used and these have affected the way in which the school timetable is constructed and also the teaching methods. Hence the development of the integrated day or blocked timetables, team teaching, topic-based teaching etc. When cross-subject courses are constructed it is possible for the subjects to still retain a unit within the scheme or it is possible for all subject identity to be submerged.

Despite the development of this approach a number of questions can be asked.
1. Are the contents of courses conceived within an interdisciplinary enquiry scheme as worthwhile as the contents of the separate courses which might otherwise be taught?
2. Is the method of exploring a topic in its various aspects better than that which explores the principles, skills, and concepts of the individual subject?

N. J. Graves has stated that

it is clear, however, that developing a worthwhile course on interdisciplinary lines must be an extraordinarily difficult task, since the topics chosen must not only enable the dovetailing of various disciplines in some coherent pattern, but each succeeding topic chosen must build upon the previous topic in such a way that principles and concepts learnt are gradually unveiled and developed.

Clearly, therefore, there are difficulties in adopting an integrated approach, but they are not insurmountable. There is a case for showing the relationship between subjects and most teachers of this age range apparently do not wish to teach subjects in isolation. In the primary school and perhaps the middle school there is a case for a predisciplinary approach providing the structure of courses is well thought out.

In the planning of courses of an interdisciplinary nature is is urged that a geographer must be involved in the planning so that the aims and objectives, concepts/ideas, enquiry and presentation skills are included. Otherwise there is a tendency for geographical work to be reduced to factual learning. Geography must play an important part in any integrated scheme of work.

1.7 The Study of Local Environments

David Mills

The importance of direct personal experience in the accessible environment cannot be overstated at this stage of the child's education. Fieldwork is not only a basic geographical study-method it is an educationally sound means of teaching and learning. Preparation for fieldwork provides ample opportunities for valuable activities such as discussing expectations—what do you think we shall find? This prepares the mind for the experience, exposes conceptions and mis-conceptions which the teacher can build upon or modify during the work, and provides an interesting basis for a 'before and after' discussion in which the children can be helped to see what they have learned. Local maps and photographs can be used which will become more meaningful once the child has related them to the reality he has experienced. Observation, enquiry and recording can be fostered as study methods in the local environment.

Follow-up work in the classroom can both reinforce and extend the learning that has taken place 'in the field'. Talking, writing, recording on graphs and in drawings and maps, comparing situations, making models—that is, using basic skills of oracy, literacy, numeracy and graphicacy—not only develops skills valuable in themselves but contributes to greater understanding and helps to formulate attitudes toward society and the environment itself.

Ideas, skills and study methods, introduced in the context of work in the accessible environment can, in the middle years, in addition be explored and extended through secondary sources, providing they convey as realistic a picture as possible about other places. A good introduction to such work can be for the teacher to use his experience of a place outside the experience of his class. He can bring it alive with words enriched by his personal reminiscences, slides, photographs and postcards, brochures, maps, posters, pieces of rock, and mementoes, thus providing a visual 'second-hand' or 'indirect' personal experience of what is, for the children, at the time an inaccessible environment. Their ability to relate to the place through their personal association with the teacher provides an important emotional setting which can ease the transition from working in the accessible environment itself to learning about the inaccessible through secondary sources, particularly if he concentrates on similarities and differences between what they have experienced and the second-hand experience he is attempting to provide. The important link in this transition is the initial search for common features of personal experience and the areas of second-hand study, leading on to an analysis of the differences.

1.8 Skills

David Mills

In the teaching of geography it is felt that the teacher should be aware of and plan to use certain skills. There have been a number of attempts in recent years to list skills which should be considered when a syllabus is constructed. The *Teachers' Guide* to the Schools Council Environmental Studies Project (1972c) listed skills under the following headings:

Basic
1. Using reference books
2. Factual writing
3. Imaginative writing
4. Mathematics
5. Modelling and pictured representation
6. Conduct of class discussion
7. Respect for the environment

Study Skills
8. Use of maps and plans
9. Collecting and classifying
10. Experimenting
11. Questionnaires

The Project considered that the development of the study skills was the main objective of environmental studies although there were other objectives as well. The importance of mapping skills has already been outlined. On classifying it was stated that:

Another group of skills are those associated with collecting, classifying and identifying material and data. Different types of physical material and abstract data require different collecting processes. Specialised equipment, though often of a simple nature, may be required to gather insects and trap small creatures. Questionnaires, tables and maps are necessary for the accumulation of social statistics; outline sketches may be needed for recording architectural or historical remains; and bags and other containers will be necessary for collecting flowers and stones. The construction and use of this equipment, simple and complex, covers a wide field. Random collections of leaf specimens will precede quadrat counts; simple lists of survey questions will come before sampling methods of collecting social data; and large scale plans and models of small areas will anticipate small scale transects of large areas. All of these activities are geared to careful observation, collecting and recording of the raw material upon which children can practise classification and identification.

The processes of grouping the material are many and varied, and must be related to the ability of the children. Simple activities using apparatus such as hoops to separate the physical specimens may be followed by the drawing of Venn-diagrams using descriptive criteria. More difficult groupings based on multiple criteria requiring a list of specified tests and examinations on the material can follow later. The building of simple keys and the later use of more advanced identification tables are important to these activities, though the need to name specimens should not be over-emphasised. (Schools Council, 1972 c)

On experimenting it is made clear that the formulation, conduct and interpretation of simple and complex experiments are desirable, though difficult, activities for young children.

The posing of questions requiring lists in order to provide answers is frequently encountered in work of this type, though the questions often arise as a result of leading by the teacher. Few variables can be involved in tests though the number will increase as the children's experience develops. 'Through practical involvement in experiments children begin to develop control, the powers of criticism, the need for measurement and the supervision of judgement'.

The importance of the basic skills cannot be overestimated as they form part of nearly all work undertaken. Similarly social attitudes involving the development of individual and group behaviour are also very important. Another Schools Council Project, *Place, Time and Society* (1975) listed skills as follows:
1. Observational, recording and classification skills.
2. The use of scientific methods of enquiry including the use of measurement and quantification.
3. The ability to understand and use pictures, charts, graphs and maps (these include the graphicacy skills).
4. Problem solving, testing and generalisation and decision taking.
5. The physical skills involved in e.g. model making.
It can be seen that most of these skills can be applied to the teaching of a variety of subjects including geography. However, there are a number of skills which have become particularly linked with the teaching of geography. There is clearly much overlap with the skills suggested by the Environmental Studies Project, though problem solving, testing and generalisation and decision taking are skills which have been added. These skills are more appropriate for the older age ranges being considered in this handbook.

In constructing and using syllabi it is important that teachers should check that the various skills are being used in their work. Not every skill will be used in every piece of work but over a period of a year all relevant skills should have been developed.

1.9 Attitudes and Values

Gavin Farmer

The importance of attitudes and values within geography teaching has only recently become well clarified with the publication of Sister Annette Buttimer's important contribution on the subject (Buttimer, 1974). Like all teaching, the teaching of geography is inextricably bound up with values (Smith, 1978), yet many teachers have failed to admit that their subject is value-laden (Cowie, 1978) and realised the implication of the reality of such a position and the teaching problems which follow from it. It has been observed that every teacher affects the value system of his pupils, even if he tries conscientiously to avoid doing so (Fenton, 1966).

Attempts to specify values in geographical education have generally followed Fenton's classification which identifies three classes of values: behavioural, procedural and substantive. He believes that teachers have the right to teach the first two of these, but not the third. Behavioural values are concerned with procedures in the classroom: if the teacher does not teach such values associated with patterns of behaviour he cannot teach effectively. But this does require the teacher to justify that these values are good or worthwhile within the context of certain accepted rules of order in the classroom and society.

Similarly procedural values enable the teacher to teach in a meaningful way according to the validity of the methodology of the discipline. This is more difficult at a time when many accepted methodological practices in geography are under close scrutiny, but we would not expect the scientist to accept that commonsense approaches are preferable to critical analysis or experimentation, nor the historian to ignore the nature of evidence. Substantive values, however, are often related to personal beliefs—for example, 'Democracy is better than totalitarianism'. Such values are best left outside the classroom.

If we cannot or should not avoid values altogether we still need to decide the limits to which we have a right to go into them in the classroom. In this sense we need to distinguish between teaching values and teaching about values. Although Blachford (1972) believes that all values are derived ultimately from substantive

values, Cowie (1978) has suggested that it is necessary to re-investigate the nature of the values that enter geographical education through the content and methodology of the subject itself and the choices made in the classroom by teachers. This has important curriculum implications for the teaching of geography in the primary age range, as with the upper age ranges.

In what form then might such a re-investigation take place? Jessie Watson in her article in *Geography* (1977) has outlined some of the possible ways in which the teacher can approach this task. She makes it clear that geographers should not be entirely objective when studying problems for the most impersonal construct of an area or problem has to take account of the values that have affected this area and shaped the problems. Further she believes that geographers cannot ignore personal, class or national bias and that there is a need for a geography which will help pupils to study opinion and values in order to evaluate issues for themselves and to try to create a geography that might bring about a better state of affairs. There is now considerable interest in teaching about the problems of developing countries, pollution and poverty and these subjects will require the pupil to look closely at other peoples' values.

A paragraph in a recent working paper of the Geography Committee of H.M. Inspectorate also states the position in a clear fashion:

Geography offers the opportunity of situations where responsible efforts can be made to help pupils understand the nature of values and attitudes and their importance in making decisions. This is because social issues and matters of environmental concern, which constitute much of the subject matter of geography, are clearly value-laden. Despite the fact that the influence of the school may be slight compared with that of the home environment, television, and society in general, geography teachers should be endeavouring, along with others, to encourage worthwhile attitudes towards learning such as a respect for evidence, an awareness of biased reporting and intolerance, a suspicion of simplistic explanations, and a willingness to engage in rational discussion. Furthermore, geography teachers should be trying to ensure that their pupils develop an interest in other people and other places; have an appreciation of and sympathy for the life styles and culture of others, including minority groups in our society; develop a concern for the quality of the environment, both urban and rural; are willing to consider other points of view and reach compromise solutions relating to proposed changes in the environment; are concerned with efforts to conserve scarce and valuable resources of all kinds (animals, plants, minerals, landscapes).

Pupils can be helped to reflect on their own attitudes and to develop values through the many opportunities given in the subject to acquire relevant knowledge about important issues, to diagnose problems, to discuss the values and attitudes relevant to the situation and to weigh the advantages and disadvantages of alternative responses. (DES 1978a, p.3)

Clearly, the teaching of value geography lies more properly with upper age ranges. Nevertheless the teacher of geography will need to keep in mind the importance of teaching about attitudes and values with all age ranges.

1.10 A suggested structure of geographical work

David Mills

Figure 1.1 indicates some key ideas which the teacher should consider as basic to the structure of a geographical syllabus. The list is not comprehensive and the teacher can easily add to it. However, it is suggested that the key ideas should be grouped under general headings which are appropriate for all age ranges except for the infants. These broad headings are:
1. Physical studies
2. Local environment
3. Distant areas
4. Other topics
Clearly there can be overlap between physical studies and the local environment. The structure suggests that all these four groupings should be considered for study with all age ranges. Following the consideration of the key ideas some themes are suggested for study and these have been set out under two headings: some geographical themes or some general ones, so that it is

possible to adopt the appropriate heading according to whether a geography or combined syllabus is being followed. Finally, some particular activities are suggested and within this heading are to be found the skills and study methods which are appropriate to each theme. The teacher will clearly attempt to give as great a variety as possible within this heading with some skills and study methods being used more commonly under certain headings than others. No attempt has been made to classify the areas of study where appropriate attitudes and values should be considered. These should arise naturally from the matters under discussion.

Finally, it must be emphasised that the suggested structure is not intended as one to be followed blindly, but one which can be altered or amended or developed. However, it does provide the guidelines for a structured syllabus.

A suggested structure for geographical work

GEOGRAPHICAL WORK FOR THE 5-7s

SOME KEY IDEAS	SOME SUGGESTED TOPICS/THEMES	SOME PARTICULAR ACTIVITIES
Physical studies Weather affects us	Weather studies (stress relationship with children's activities)	Using simple weather instruments Simple recording
Local Environment Plans, Shape, Texture, Movement Growth and change Water and land	Local work on houses, shops, streets; traffic in street, movement of pupils in school, local gardens, parks and open spaces	Observation Measuring, Recording Collecting, sorting Making models Use map of local area
Distant areas Other places in UK are different from local environment Other places in the world are different from the UK environment	Work based on visits Homes of children/animals of other lands	Reading Looking at photographs Writing Simple plans Making Models
Others (examples) Differences between day and night Differences between the seasons	What animals/plants/people do by day and night Spring, Summer, Autumn, Winter	Make graphs/charts Classification Collage and model making Collecting

KEY RESOURCES
Globe.
1:2500, 1:10 000 maps for teacher

SUMMARY
By the end of the infant school the children should have:
1. undertaken some work in the local environment, e.g. local streets, shops, houses, park, water;
2. drawn simple maps of classroom and local area;
3. made simple weather measurements in order to understand that weather changes from day to day;
4. undertaken studies to show that different areas of the UK and the world look and are different from their own home area.

GEOGRAPHICAL WORK FOR THE 7-9s

SOME KEY IDEAS	SOME GEOGRAPHICAL TOPICS/THEMES	SOME GENERAL THEMES	SOME PARTICULAR ACTIVITIES
Physical studies			
Weather varies during each month and year	Weather studies	Weather studies	Observation and recording of temperature, rainfall, clouds; Use compass directions
Landscapes vary (valleys, hills, mountains)	Simple landscapes/river studies	Mountains, Rivers	Observation and recording; Study pictures; Make models and maps
Rocks and soils vary	Simple rock and soil studies	Rocks and Buildings; The Sea Shore; Soils and Land use	Collecting; Experimenting with rocks - hard, soft, colour, texture; Simple classification; Introduction to sampling
Local environment			
Buildings are of different ages and used for different functions	Houses, streets, shops	Local environment	Observation and recording; Classification; Use local 1:10 000 maps, make own map; Simple house, street models
Shops provide different goods, shops are grouped			
Distant areas			
Farms vary in type	Farm Studies	On the Farm; Food	Make plans of farms; Case studies (visit farm)
Areas of world have different climates	Climates of different areas of world	The Cold Lands; The Hot Lands	Study pictures, readings
Animals/people adapt to different environments	Area Studies	Africa, Australia	Study world and continental maps; Models; Collage; Graphs

KEY RESOURCES
1:2500, 1:10 000 O.S. maps of local area
Wall map of world, Globe
Weather instruments

SUMMARY
By the end of the second year in the primary school the pupils should have:
1. undertaken field work in local area using appropriate recording techniques;
2. completed a log of weather changes;
3. made use of globe and local maps;
4. undertaken some simple landscape studies;
5. studied some environments different from their own area.

GEOGRAPHICAL WORK FOR THE 9-11s

SOME KEY IDEAS	SOME GEOGRAPHICAL TOPICS/THEMES	SOME GENERAL THEMES	SOME PARTICULAR ACTIVITIES
Physical studies			
Weather patterns (temperature and precipitation, variations over the year, general weather patterns)	Weather studies	Weather studies	Detailed weather observations and recording over a period of time using recording sheets
Rocks vary in age and type Landscapes change over space and time	Study of rocks and fossils Man and water	The physical world around us	Classification of rocks and fossils Distribution maps Study of pictures Diagrams and models Experiments with water and soil Hypothesis testing Sketching Field recording Detailed sampling
Local environment			
Location ideas	Local road systems Distribution of housing/open space/industry/services Distribution of high/low ground	Local environment	Use of 1:50 000 and road maps Make local land use maps
Distant areas			
Settlements vary in size Settlements have different functions (houses, services, industry)	Hamlets and villages Towns and cities	Settlement studies	Use country and national maps Case studies
Land use varies over area and time in each area	Farms vary in type	Farming	Farm studies in field Case studies of farm Identify different crops and animals
Industries vary in type	Introduction to major industries of UK - power, capital, extensive, consumer industries	Industrial studies	Distribution maps Case studies
People are interdependent Human and physical factors affect people	Europe/North America/Asia/ other countries of world	Area studies	Use of visual material Atlas and globe study Games and simulations Diagrams Case studies

KEY RESOURCES
Local 1:10 000, 1:25 000
1:50 000 O.S. maps
Wall maps of world and British Isles Atlases
Examples of fossils, rocks, soils
Weather instruments and recording sheets
Photographs/Pictures/Charts

SUMMARY
By the age of 11 the pupils should be able to:
1. read maps of different kinds, use an atlas and interpret a globe;
2. read the basic weather instruments, draw temperature and rainfall graphs and be aware of the different kinds of clouds;
3. identify different kinds of rocks and landforms;
4. understand the differences in urban and rural landscapes and know some of the causes.

The pupils should have undertaken:
1. studies of aspects of the local environment;
2. studies of farms in the UK and abroad and be aware of some of the reasons for the differences;
3. some industrial studies and be aware of simple ideas of location of industry;
4. some studies of countries outside Britain showing the variations between industrialised/advanced countries and the Third World.

GEOGRAPHICAL WORK FOR THE 11–13s

SOME KEY IDEAS	SOME GEOGRAPHICAL TOPICS/THEMES	SOME GENERAL THEMES	SOME PARTICULAR ACTIVITIES
Physical studies			
Theories of formation of the earth	Introduction to geology/landscape development/weathering/soil studies	Earth as a planet	Diagrams, models
	Water	Man and water; Man and coast;	Measuring, recording; Field work on rivers, coasts, slopes
Introduction to theories of continental drift and plate tectonics	Ice	Man and land	Land form sketching
Erosion/deposition affect landscape development	Slopes	Hazards, earthquakes, landslides	Photo interpretation
Weathering			Field work on soils
Distribution of soil types varies			Soil classification
Soil horizons vary			Transects
Weather patterns (summer/winter, wet/dry periods)	Continuation of weather observation/recording	Weather	Recording; Graph construction
Climates vary and affect human activities	Introduction to world climates	Climate and Man	Interpretation of climatic data, and photographs

Local environment (urban)			
Towns/cities grow or decline over time Occupations vary	Extended environmental studies	Living in towns and cities	Fieldwork in towns Construction of urban land use maps
Service centres are hierarchical Variations in density of population and housing Variations in journey to school/work patterns Land use conflicts			Interpretation of urban statistics Use of questionnaires Town trails/transects
Distant Areas			
Towns/cities show similarities in growth, functions and problems	Studies of town/cities elsewhere in UK and abroad	Living in towns/cities	Comparative case studies
Agricultural land use varies	Agricultural studies from distant areas	Farming across the world	Study agricultural land use maps
Farming may be intensive/extensive			Agricultural land use games
Industrial location varies for different industries	Industrial location analysis of selected industries - capital/labour intensive, consumer industries	Manufacturing Industry	Use of case studies
Area Studies			
Regions in countries/continents vary	Area Studies	Southern continents, North America	Atlas studies Synthesis of regional and national characteristics Use of visual aids
Others (examples)			
Food supplies/Health vary throughout the world Cycle of poverty	Geography of poverty	Poverty	Analysis of statistics Distribution maps Study appropriate visual material
Patterns of population Migration	Geography of populations	Population	Classification of population data Construction of diagrams and maps
Recreation facilities and use vary from area to area	Geography of recreation	Recreation	Use of questionnaires Study recreation demand, recreation provision in local/distant areas

KEY RESOURCES
1:25 000, 1:50 000 O.S. maps. Selection of oblique aerial photographs, film strips/slides. Range of wall maps of the continents
Stevenson screen and weather instruments
Local statistical data
Examples of 2nd Land Use Survey Maps

SUMMARY

By the age of 13-14 the pupils should have undertaken:

1. physical studies - so that they have some knowledge and understanding of elementary climatology and geomorphology. They should have undertaken some field work linked with physical geography, and continued weather recording and analysis;
2. more detailed studies in their own local area. Further field work should have been carried out and use made of appropriate statistics e.g. census material. An introduction should have been made to local issues;
3. introductory studies in agricultural and industrial geography making use of case studies and geographical games;
4. area studies in at least two continents leading to a synthesis of regional and national geographical characteristics;
5. studies in a selection of geographically based themes to illustrate current world problems and the interdependence of people;
6. further mapping skills.

FIGURE 1.1 A suggested structure for geographical work

2. Resources for learning : weather studies and physical geography

2.1 Weather Studies

Tim Firth

WEATHER 5–7s

Children of this age need to know 'how weather affects us'. Knowledge is best gained through young children's own first-hand personal experiences, i.e. to make use of what they already know or understand of the weather, and the fact that weather changes from day to day.

An introduction can be made through finding out what they know of heat, cold, wind, shade, shelter, shadow, moisture, dryness and ice etc. There is no formal order in which to take these themes. Instead use can be made of variations in weather as they occur from day to day throughout the year, by way of the child's direct observation and experience guided and led by the teacher. The emphasis is not on record keeping or under-standing seasonal patterns, but children will become familiar with the terms for the seasons.

An example of how this might be done in practice by a teacher using a 'Spring theme' is given below, together with how the topic might be expanded in the classroom.

A Spring Experience

A tree that is about to burst into leaf could be taken as a starting point, particularly a horse chestnut, but any tree found in the street or park would do. Children can be questioned to find out what they can see for themselves. 'Where are the new leaves coming from?' 'What colour are these leaves?' 'Where have they been during the Winter?' 'What clothes do we need to wear outside today?' 'Is it windy, sunny, cold or warm?'

Back in the classroom, it would be useful, though not always desirable or possible to have twigs in water coming into leaf. The 'sticky buds' of the horse chestnut make an excellent study of a bud breaking into leaf. Language work based on what is observed by children is important, i.e. their words and expressions to say what they see and notice. Words can be noted which describe the colours of the leaves, the sky, other children's coats and so on.

Artwork can be based on the study of the shapes of the twigs, leaves and even the tree itself. An important feature of the classroom could be a display of material that children have brought in themselves, such as bark, twigs, bird's nest, daffodils, crocuses or anything which emphasises Spring. Sentences contributed by children about these items or their visit can be written out by the teacher and added to the display. Pictures, and books depicting springtime, e.g. farming scenes and lambs, give an important source of stimula-tion. Children should be encouraged to bring their own contributions which might include photographs, pictures, bulbs, sheep's wool etc. Work in mathematics can be encouraged, partic-ularly in sorting and sets: groups which are yellow; those which are plants, those which belong to birds or animals and so on.

This theme can be returned to at the different

19

ages or each year in a vertically grouped class, and different aspects stressed, or more detail taken in as the children grow older; a five-year-old may not understand where the leaves of trees go to in Winter, whereas a seven-year-old may want to know more about this.

Other first-hand experiences can be explored using the same general approach in the classroom, once the initial experience has been felt. Some examples follow.

Snow and Ice

Much can be made of the dressing-up that is required to go out in frosty weather; i.e. items of clothing necessary—boots, coats, scarves, gloves and hats and the excitement generated by a visit to see some snow. Children should be directed to answer what it feels like to touch snow; what happens to the eyes when you look at snow; what it feels like to walk on; what the sky looks like when it is snowing and what snow is like.

Rain

What equipment and clothing is required to go out in rain? Questions can be asked about rain— What happens to rain after it has fallen? What is a puddle? Where does a puddle go to? What does being wet feel like?

Shade

Try taking children out on a sunny, summer day. Let them stand in the sun, and then in the shade of a building. What do they notice? Do plants like the shade? How hot are objects made of different materials in the sun, e.g. metal railings, bricks, wooden benches and asphalt playgrounds?

Wind

Children should observe the effects of wind. What happens to their hair and their clothes on a windy day? What do they notice about things around them, such as pieces of paper, leaves on trees, telegraph wires etc.? Let them feel what it is like to walk against a strong wind. Let them feel the power of wind. Use any local resource; smoke from factory chimneys, reservoirs with sailing boats, even wind pumps or windmills.

Shelter

People and animals need shelter in winter for survival; buildings for people, rabbit hutches for rabbits, stables for horses, barns for cows. What shelter do lambs born in the fields need? What shelter do plants need? What do we shelter from; e.g. cold, frost, sun, wind? How do buildings shelter us and what are the shapes of roofs etc.?

Sun

Clothes can again be related to this topic in listing what clothes are necessary on a hot summer day compared with those needed on a frosty day. Questions can be asked about the effect of the sun—What happens to the skin exposed to the sun for long periods? What happens to the soil? What happens when the sun 'goes in' and what does it feel like?

At this age simple instruments can be used, e.g. a bucket to collect rain and seven bottles to show how much fell on each day. No formal records of the weather need to be kept until later stages, although pictures and symbols can be devised to show the different elements. These can then be drawn to show weather over short periods, such as a week or a fortnight taken at different times of the year to illustrate seasonal change, in addition to daily change.

WEATHER 7–9s

Children of this age will have already gained first-hand experience of the basic elements of the weather at the earlier stage. They should now be able to make more detailed observations and to record their findings more formally. Observation and experiences will continue to be of major importance.

The emphasis at this stage is to understand that weather not only varies from day to day but also during each month and year. The seasons have their own broadly typical characteristics, although one year taken with another can show considerable change. For example, a given place may have little snowfall one winter, but may experience lengthy periods of freezing weather with snow the next. Or, drought may be a problem to a farmer one summer and the next year too much rain may be the problem.

The key to understanding these monthly and seasonal changes lies in observation and recording. Hitherto, recording has been mainly of a pictorial manner; a picture of the weather as the child sees it. Now, recording becomes more

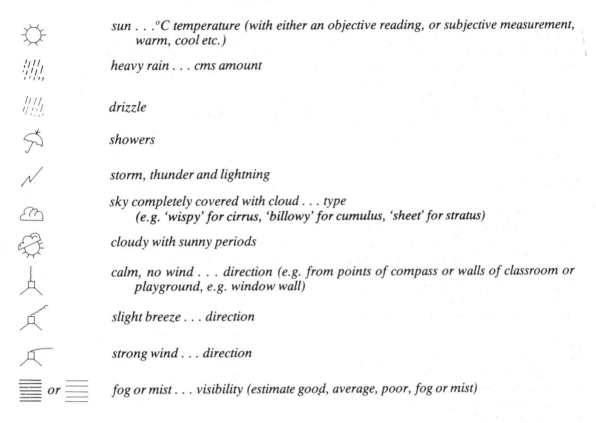

sun . . .°C temperature (with either an objective reading, or subjective measurement, warm, cool etc.)

heavy rain . . . cms amount

drizzle

showers

storm, thunder and lightning

sky completely covered with cloud . . . type
(e.g. 'wispy' for cirrus, 'billowy' for cumulus, 'sheet' for stratus)

cloudy with sunny periods

calm, no wind . . . direction (e.g. from points of compass or walls of classroom or playground, e.g. window wall)

slight breeze . . . direction

strong wind . . . direction

fog or mist . . . visibility (estimate good, average, poor, fog or mist)

FIGURE 2.1   Symbols for weather record

detailed as more abstract symbols begin to be used, and new elements of the weather, such as visibility, included. Children and teachers together can devise their own symbols at this stage. An example of the type and number of symbols is given in Fig. 2.1 and can only be considered as a guide. This record can be kept for a longer period; e.g. from 2 to 4 weeks during each term of the year. This is preferable to one long continuous record which will be difficult to maintain, both in terms of application and interest.

The degree of sophistication and number of symbols used can be increased according to the understanding, ability or age of the children. Children will show great enthusiasm and invention in designing their own. In addition, as they learn how to use symbols, actual readings can supplement this record.

Recording is only the end result of earlier work on observation and measurement. The following are some examples of experiment and recording in practice.

The Sun
Work can again be linked with first-hand experience; e.g. how hot different materials become in direct sunlight; in what parts of the playground snow, ice or frost remains unmelted for the longest time.

Temperature and duration of sunshine
A centigrade thermometer may be used by some older or more able children at this stage, to record outside, shade temperatures. Before this, subjective estimates about the heat of the sun can be made; e.g. hot, warm, cool, and its duration;

e.g. all day, half the day, less than half the day.

Shadow and direction
A shadow stick may be used to record the changes in direction and length of shadows. This is a vertically-held pole approximately 2m high. The length of its shadow can be marked in the playground at hourly intervals for one day. Observations can be made about what time the shortest shadow occurs and which direction it faces. Alternatively, the length of shadow could be marked at noon every sunny day for one month, or once every month throughout the year, and the changes noted.

Compass points
Compass points can be learnt with the aid of the shadow stick and in relation to the positions of the sun in the sky in the morning, at noon and in the afternoon. There are many activities and games to be followed concerning direction. For example, the following ones which involve finding north or south without a compass:
1. Boy Scout Method: Point the hour hand of a watch to the sun. South will be a line radiating from the centre of the watch midway between the hour hand and the figure 12.
2. The Shadow Stick: Casts a shadow pointing south at midday.
3. North Pole Star: North can be found on a clear night by finding the North Pole Star as early adventurers, sailors and explorers used to do.
4. Lichen on trees: The north side of trees may have a powdery green lichen growing on the shady parts, usually facing north, where the sunlight does not strike them.

Precipitation (Rain and Snow)
A simple rain gauge can be made and used as follows. Collect rain in a cylindrical container about 15cms in diameter. Pour 2.5cm of water from the container into a measuring bottle, medicine bottle or similar and mark the height on the side. With a strip of paper stuck onto the side, further subdivisions can be made to give centimetre marks. Daily amounts can be recorded on a graph.

Questions on children's observations can be asked. What hapens to rainwater that falls on roofs? What happens to rainwater after it has fallen on the ground, on the road etc.?

Let the children hold a piece of tissue paper out

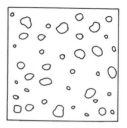

FIGURE 2.2   Raindrops

in the rain for a short time and then hold the paper up to the light. What can be seen? Are the spots the same size? Try to measure them (Fig. 2.2).

Clouds

Cloud cover
A simple estimate of cloud cover is all that is necessary at this stage. It can start with pictorial symbols as shown earlier, or it can be shown as a simple fraction of the sky covered by cloud; e.g. sky wholly covered, more or less than half covered.

Cloud type
The older children could attempt a simple classification as suggested earlier:

billowy	= cotton-wool type cloud	= cumulus cloud
wispy	= high streaks and wisps	= cirrus cloud
sheet	= layer of cloud	= stratus cloud
dark	= dark bank or layer	= nimbus cloud, when it rains

Children can be asked to make further observations about clouds including drawing their shape and saying whether they are 'high' or 'low', and what shade they are; e.g. white, grey, dark grey. A simple record could be kept as shown in Figure 2.3.

DATE	DRAWING OF CLOUDS	WEATHER	NAME OF CLOUD
7th July		Sunny spells, dry	Cumulus

FIGURE 2.3   Cloud record

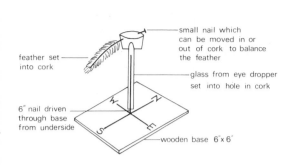
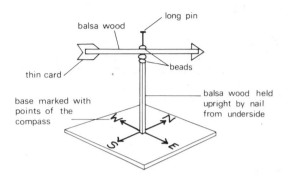

FIGURE 2.4   Wind vanes

Wind

Wind direction can be seen from a wind vane, often on a tall building or church spire. A wind vane can also be made in a variety of ways as shown in Figure 2.4. The model vane can be set up with a magnetic compass to make sure that the north arrow points in the right direction. Wind vanes show the direction that the wind is coming from. They should be used in open space where buildings cannot easily deflect the flow of wind.

Wind velocity at this stage can be estimated, especially if smoke from a chimney can be seen, as shown in the diagram of symbols earlier (Fig. 2.1). Other criteria can be drawn up for this purpose, such as movement of tree branches, holding out light fabrics like a flag, licking a finger, or throwing grass into the air.

Activities which can lead to further observation about the behaviour of wind include the flying of kites or balloons. The differences in behaviour of a kite at different levels can be noted, as can the influence that tall trees, buildings or slope may have. A wind-sock, as seen at airfields, could be made by threading thin wire through the top of a stocking to hold it open (Fig. 2.5).

The flight of a kite or balloon could even be mapped by the more able child.

Visibility

Judgment of visibility is purely subjective at this stage. For example, a suitable vantage point can be found from an upstairs window or roof. A number of objects can be located at varying distances to represent long, middle, and short distances and foreground. These objects could be chimneys, trees, church steeples, pylons or buildings etc. How easily these can be seen will give an indication of visibility. For example, if the furthest away can be seen clearly, visibility can be said to be 'excellent', if only a middle-distance object can be seen, visibility will be 'fair' or 'average'; if only the nearest objects can be seen, visibility will be poor. Fog or mist will be recorded if no short-distance or foreground objects only yards away can be seen.

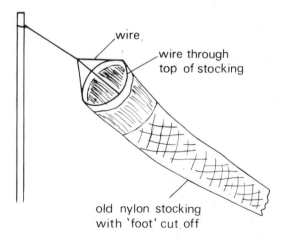

FIGURE 2.5   Wind sock

Measuring and recording weather should not be an end in itself. Hand in hand with this activity should go projects centring on 'how weather affects us', as a starting point for work across the curriculum. Some examples of the way work can be related to weather is shown in the Nuffield Junior Sciences approach. With this approach, 'weather' is taken as the main topic, and a 'development web' of related work is then drawn out similar to the headings shown below.

People who work outside
A study of jobs that are directly affected by the weather, eg. the postman, milkman, dustman, builder, sailor etc.

Weather lore
A collection of sayings about the weather; e.g. 'a red sky at night is the shepherd's delight'. These can be discussed and their origins discovered, if possible, or the extent to which they are true, debated.

The wind is dangerous
A visit could be made to a coastguard station, or an airfield. Sketches can be made, and newspaper cuttings collected, especially of winter news items such as those of ships stranded on beaches during gales, promenades breached etc. Children could record their experiences on a beach, cliff or country walk on a windy day.

Events at school which need good weather
A number of activities can be discussed where good weather plays a vital part; e.g. playtimes, sports days, fairs and fêtes, school journeys, visits, a walk to the library, a football or games lesson. The extent to which good weather is essential can be examined, as can what we mean by 'good weather'.

A holiday experience
Reports of holidays that have been 'made' or 'broken' by outstanding or poor weather, and why. These can include the adventures of a child's family on a camping holiday in the rain or a holiday by the Mediterranean in burning sunshine.

Poems, paintings, field sketches, creative writing, work with graphs and model-making are all ways in which information gained from first-hand experience can be recorded. This is in addition to observations recorded formally on a weather log. Different forms of presentation should illustrate the main emphasis for this age, which is that weather varies during each month and from year to year.

WEATHER 9–11s

At this stage, children are usually in their last two years at primary school. They should achieve an understanding of the general pattern of weather for a year, and that one year's pattern can vary with the next. This will be achieved largely by keeping a weather record throughout the year by the end of this stage. More accurate recordings will be made than hitherto and instruments used that are designed for this purpose. These will be particularly important for the older and more able children.

In addition, the general, yearly weather pattern for the area of the country in which the child lives should emerge; e.g. for South East England, the Lake District, etc. The idea of other lands being hotter/colder, drier/wetter can be developed, which can lead to the introduction of the concept of 'climate', as opposed to 'weather' being a phenomenon influencing a given place at a given time.

The more dramatic and unusual aspects of weather also provides a popular and useful area of study at this age; e.g. the effect of storms, floods and droughts etc.

Keeping a Weather Record
Central to work on measurement and recording at this age is the development of a 'weather station'. This is best achieved with a Stevenson Screen housing most of the required instruments, with others situated nearby; e.g. wind vane and rain gauge. The Stevenson Screen is basically a ventilated 'box' constructed about 1½m above the ground in which instruments such as thermometers can be placed. This enables shade temperatures to be read, with other readings relating to temperature and humidity of the atmosphere, which can freely circulate through slots in the screen's walls. The direct disturbance caused by sunlight, rain, wind or frost is thus kept to a minimum.

This screen should ideally be placed in the

open away from the obtrusive effects of buildings, areas of concrete or asphalt, or trees, which could give distorted readings. A location above grass is usually very satisfactory. Suitable locations are often difficult to find and many school weather stations are set up on a roof, playground, or small area of playing field or garden.

Improvised screens can be made from slotted packing cases, protected with overlapping wooden (not metallic) roofs, raised to leave a gap with the walls. Other essential instruments such as a wind vane and rain gauge can be set up nearby—again in an open space where buildings or trees etc. are unlikely to give an unrealistic record.

Observation by the child is again of paramount importance; the final result being more scientific than that given by earlier subjective methods involving estimating. The elements of the weather can be observed, measured and recorded under their headings as follows.

Temperature

Children by the age of eleven years should be able to obtain a temperature reading from a thermometer using a Centigrade scale, and possibly a Fahrenheit scale also. They should be taught what the divisions of the scale mean in each case, and that thermometers usually contain mercury or alcohol.

To demonstrate how a thermometer works fix a drinking straw upright in the neck of a bottle of cold water coloured by ink, using plasticine, so that the water appears above the top of the bottle. Mark the level of the water on the straw. Heat the bottle slowly in a jug of hot tap water and notice the changing level of water in the straw. Note the value of using thermometers to take records under a wide range of conditions. For example, take the temperature of one's own hands, and the room temperature. Take temperatures in the sun and shade; of soil; of grass and of ice cubes and water; i.e. to find a range of temperatures, so that children know the temperature at which water freezes and boils. Results could be entered on a graph.

Simple experiments

These can be set up as the following examples show:

1. Two similar tins should be filled with water and soil respectively, and placed in the sun.

Their temperatures are then recorded at hourly intervals from 9 a.m. to 6 p.m. A graph can then be made of the results and a discussion can follow on why the sea feels so cold to your feet on a day when the sand feels hot.

2. Another experiment involves temperature readings taken at different heights above the ground surface, as shown in Figure 2.6. The most noticeable temperature differences will be achieved if readings are taken when it is calm and sunny although comparisons can be made when it is cloudy or windy. The thermometer stand should be placed on a short grass area and the readings taken at about 1.0 p.m.

3. Another exercise involves taking temperatures on the various outside walls of the school building; some will be sunny, others in shade; some with soil and plants nearby, others may be part of the boiler house or near kitchen ventilators etc. Foil-wrapped tubes can again be used to obtain shade readings.

In all these experiments, results can be shown graphically, sometimes by a line graph, sometimes with block graphs. Work with a Maximum and Minimum thermometer will also prove rewarding and average daily readings for weeks or months can be worked out and compared with different periods in the year.

The Sun

Work on shadows was introduced in the section for 7–9s, and further work involving the sun can be undertaken now.

Sundials

These can often be seen on churches, and sometimes in a vertical position. A sundial can be made using a flat board 30 cms square, covered with white paper. The 'gnomon' or pointer (a right-angled triangle) has to be inclined to the horizontal at an angle equal to the latitude (between 50° and 60°). Use a spirit level to test that the board is horizontal. The gnomon must be vertical.

Hours of sunshine

Few schools will have access to a sunshine recorder, which looks like a gipsy's crystal ball. Records of hours of sunshine can be seen in newspapers, usually for seaside resorts. Children's own records can be compared with these. An improvised recorder can be made using a large,

THERMOMETER STAND

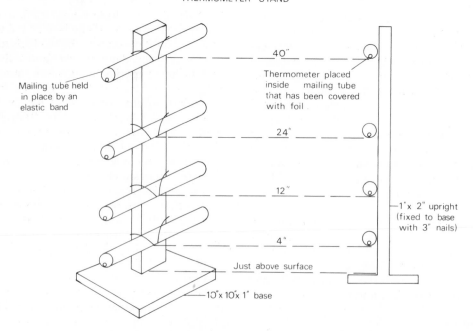

FIGURE 2.6   *Temperature measurements at different heights*

cylindrical tin. Punch a small hole (about 2 mm in diameter) half-way up the vertical sides of the tin. Leave the hole uncovered and line the inner cylindrical part of the tin with blue-print paper. At 9 a.m. place the tin with the hole facing south. Leave until 3 p.m. and remove the paper and fix in water. Try the effect of inclining the base of the tin at an angle to the horizonal. When this angle is equal to the latitude, the sun's 'path' on the flat paper will be a straight line. If the record from 9 to 3 is continuous, the paper can be calibrated.

Rainbows

Discussion can take place about when rainbows are seen; when rain or moisture is in the air, while the sun is shining. Children might comment that they have seen 'rainbows' in pieces of thick glass, such as glass stoppers or bevelled edges of plate glass mirrors. Experiments can take place to show what happens when light passes through a prism.

Precipitation (Rain and Snow)

Rainfall totals can be measured daily using a manufactured rain gauge at this stage, although

an improvised one could still be made. Water is collected in a container set inside a larger one which has a funnel of the same diameter fitted to make a watertight seal. A measuring cylinder is also provided with the kit so the rain water is simply poured into it to obtain a reading (see Fig. 2.7). An improvised rain gauge could be made by

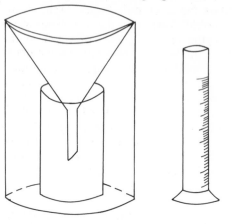

Rain gauge   Measuring cylinder

FIGURE 2.7

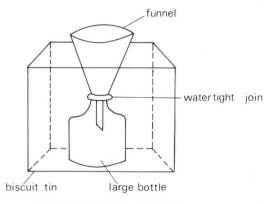

funnel

watertight join

biscuit tin large bottle

IMPROVISED RAIN GAUGE

FIGURE 2.8

using a plastic funnel fitted with a waterproof collar around the stem where it enters a collecting can or bottle. Calibrate a separate measuring bottle by using a tin the same diameter as the funnel, pouring in 2.5 cms. of water and then pouring this into the measuring bottle. Record the height on a stuck-on piece of paper. Further subdivisions into millimetres can be made (Fig. 2.8). A block graph of monthly rainfall can be constructed from daily readings. Average weekly or monthly rainfall amounts can also be worked out. Rain gauges should be placed away from buildings or trees, in open places. They are often placed on flat roofs near the Stevenson Screen. Experiments involving more than one rain gauge can be undertaken to see how amounts vary in different situations; under a tree, nearly under the tree and in the open. Or again, gauges can be placed under different types of tree or bush to see how much rain gets through.

Snow

This is a form of precipitation, and work can be done with snow and ice at this stage as well. Discussion can take place about what snow is; what the sky looks like when it is about to snow; why snow becomes deeper in some places rather than others; how snow is cleared from roads; why trains are often delayed in icy weather and why the sea rarely freezes etc.

A snowflake can be caught momentarily on a piece of dark paper or cloth. Let the children look at some under a magnifying glass. They should

try to make a sketch and count the number of sides to the snowflake. Try this with other snowflakes to see whether they are all the same shape, or have the same number of sides. Observe what happens when snow is squeezed between the hands, or trodden in the playground. Experiment with buckets of water and saline solution left outside on a frosty night. Then take some ice for flotation tests to see how ice floats. This could lead on to discussion on icebergs and dangers to shipping.

Clouds

Children made observations about clouds at the earlier stage and made a simple threefold classification; whether they saw clouds as billowy, wispy or layer-form. By the age of eleven years, children should be able to attempt a daily recognition of clouds based on the cloud characteristics summary in Table 2.1.

Initially, collecting pictures and photographs of the different cloud types would help familiarise children with them and make identification easier 'in the field'. Many topic books on weather or clouds contain good pictures and the Meterological Office can provide sets of photographs.

Children should be encouraged to draw cloud forms which they see, as they did at the earlier stage, and to try to work out what sort of weather is usually associated with them. Discussion can also centre on how moisture gets into the air. Children can be asked to think of their own examples of this. The following might be mentioned:
1. from wet clothes, puddles, wet pavements, ponds, soil, as water evaporates;
2. from a boiling kettle;
3. from our breath;
4. from plants, since they have to be watered.
Equally, moisture comes out of the air:
1. on to a plate covering hot water;
2. where 'rain' is made by playing steam from a boiling kettle on to the side of a tin jug full of cold water;
3. condensation on windows in cold weather.
The water cycle and formation of rain can be introduced to those children able to understand it.

Cloud Cover

Estimates of the proportion of the sky covered by cloud can be made. If the sky is completely

TABLE 2.1   Summary of Cloud Characteristics

Name of cloud	Usual Abbre- viation	Range of height of cloud base in Gt. Britain in feet	Vertical thickness of cloud	Significant features
Cirrus	Ci	20 000-40 000	Often a few thousand feet	Usually indicates an approaching frontal system
Cirrostratus	Cs	20 000-40 000	Often a few thousand feet	Usually indicates an approaching frontal system. Is accompanied by haloes around the sun
Cirrocumulus	Cc	20 000-40 000	Fairly thin	
Altocumulus	Ac	8 000-20 000	A few thousand feet	Bands are often seen ahead of fronts. The castellated types are associated with thunder
Altostratus	As	8 000-20 000 Base often merges into nimbo-stratus	Thick - may be up to 12 000 feet	Indicates closeness to precipitation area of frontal system
Nimbostratus	Ns	300-2 000	Thick - may be up to 15 000 feet	Associated with precipitation. Top merges with altostratus
Stratus	St	500-2 000	Thin - from 100 to 1 000 feet	May cover high ground
Stratocumulus	Sc	1 000-4 500	Thin - from 500 to 3 000 feet	
Cumulus	Cu	1 000-5 000	May be thick - 5 000 to 15 000 feet	Is some indication of atmospheric stability. Strong vertical currents in large types
Cumulonimbus	Cb	2 000-5 000	Very thick - may be 10 000 to 30 000 feet	Very turbulent cloud, accompanied by heavy showers, perhaps of hail, lightning and thunder

obscured by cloud it will be ⁸/₈ covered. The sky is divided into 8 equal parts in estimating cloud cover. Use ½ and ¼ as a general guide; ³/₈ cover would mean just over ¼ of the sky covered. A fraction in eighths forms the record.

Humidity

At this stage it is possibly better to discuss the 'dampness' of the atmosphere as a preparation for the term 'relative humidity'. Activities referred to in the section on clouds, e.g. evaporation examples form a good basis for understanding that the atmosphere holds 'water vapour' and that it has a given capacity according to its temperature. Discussion on what makes good drying days would be useful.

These activities are useful:

1. Suspend sheets of wet blotting paper 10cm x 10 cm outside in the playground in shade, in sun, on the window sill, and indoors, by an open window, near a radiator. Compare times of drying and degree of dryness after a given time.
2. Watch the behaviour of certain things on a wet day; seaweed, fir cones, rope—such as a clothes line which goes taut.

Simple instruments can be bought to measure humidity which monitor how paper or hair react to moisture in the air; they are called hair and paper 'hygrometers' (dampness indicators). Figure 2.9 shows how two hygrometers can be made using hair and catgut. To calibrate the catgut hygrometer, suspend the catgut (degreased) in a jar of calcium chloride to allow to mark 'very dry' on the scale. Then paint with water and mark 'very wet'.

Fun can be had with cobalt chloride solution which is pale pink, like 'invisible ink'. When it is heat-dried it shows blue to reveal the handwritten message on a paper.

Wet and dry bulb thermometer

An ordinary thermometer can be converted into a 'wet' one by using a hollow (football boot) lace and a rainwater-filled ink bottle. The moisture evaporates from the lace around the bulb producing cooling and thus a lower temperature than that given by a dry bulb. The 'wet' and 'dry' readings require conversion by 'hydrographic' tables to give a relative humidity percentage, or percentage of moist to dry air in the atmosphere. However, a difference between the two readings can provide a ready-reckoner for a good drying day; i.e. when the difference is greatest.

Dry bulb	Wet bulb	Difference	Comment
x	y	z	Good drying day
			Bad drying day

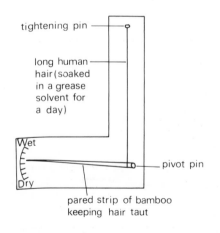
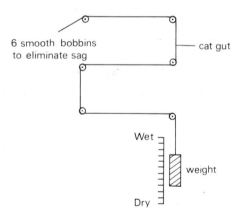

FIGURE 2.9   Hygrometers

WIND ROSE

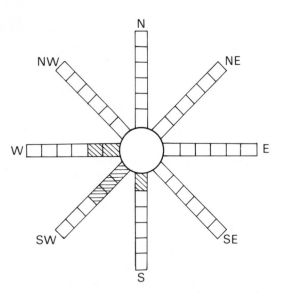

Wind Rose showing wind direction
over 6 days

Wind from SW   3 days
            W   2 days
            S   1 day

FIGURE 2.10

Wind

Direction of the Wind

Wind direction is taken as the direction from which the wind is coming. Observations should now be taken from an accurate wind vane, instead of the home-made models used earlier. A wind vane should be part of any weather station situated on a roof top, or a pole where higher buildings do not alter the wind's flow. Children should also know the points of the compass by now.

     Wind direction for a given period; e.g. week or month, can be shown graphically or by using a 'wind rose', as shown in Figure 2.10. A number of roses for each month in the year will reveal the direction of the prevailing wind over the year. They will also show differences in winter and summer directions, if any. A particular pattern of wind direction for a given season helps in understanding the weather prevailing during that

season, e.g. a bitter, cold and dry winter season may reflect winds coming mainly from the North and East sectors.

MAKING A COMPASS. This is a useful activity to understand more about the working of a magnetic compass. Materials needed are: a needle or a thin nail which is already a magnet; a cork stopper and a container of water. Children will be fascinated to learn that a needle can be made into a magnet by stroking it, as shown (Fig. 2.11), in one direction for a few minutes with another magnet. Place the needle on the cork and float the cork on the water. After settling down the needle and the cork will turn so that the needle points to the north. Keep pieces of iron away from the container so that they do not pull the needle towards them.

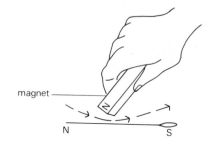

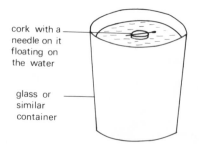

FIGURE 2.11   Making a compass

Wind Speed

The simple estimate of wind speed used at the previous stage (calm, slight breeze, strong wind) can give way to a more precise estimate using the Beaufort Scale of Wind Force shown in Table 2.2. Alternatively, an anemometer can be used.

TABLE 2.2   The Beaufort Scale of Wind Force

Beaufort No.	Descriptive title	Specification for use on land	Speed in miles per hour
0	Calm	Smoke rises vertically	0-1
1	Light air	Direction shown by smoke but not by wind vanes	1-3
2	Light breeze	Wind felt on face; leaves rustle; vane moved by wind	4-7
3	Gentle breeze	Leaves and small twigs in constant motion; wind extends light flag	8-12
4	Moderate breeze	Raises dust and loose paper; small branches are moved	13-18
5	Fresh breeze	Small trees in leaf begin to sway; crested wavelets form on inland water	19-24
6	Strong breeze	Large branches in motion; whistling heard in telegraph wires; umbrellas used with difficulty	25-31
7	Moderate gale	Whole trees in motion; inconvenience felt when walking against wind	32-38
8	Fresh gale	Breaks twigs off trees; generally impedes progress	39-46
9	Strong gale	Slight structural damage occurs (chimney pots and slates removed)	47-54
10	Whole gale	Seldom experienced; trees uprooted; considerable structural damage	55-63
11	Storm	Very rarely experienced; accompanied by widespread damage	64-75
12	Hurricane	As above	

This is often a hand-held instrument which has three arms, attached to which are three cups, as shown in Figure 2.12. Wind strikes these cups, making the arms rotate, which gives a reading of wind strength on a dial. These instruments of varying sophistication can be seen at athletic sports meetings, at weather centres and on ships etc. There are simpler instruments available which are cheaper. Two are illustrated in Figure 2.13. 'A' has a light disc which is blown up or down a central spindle and 'B' has a light plastic ball which is blown up or down a central tube. The harder the wind blows, the higher the disc or ball rises to give a reading on the scale marked on the side of the instruments.

MAKING AN IMPROVISED CUP ANEMOMETER.
This can be achieved by fastening together two slats of wood 45 cm x 2.5 cm so that they are at right angles. Drill a 5 mm hole through the centre to take a biro pen top and glue firmly. Punch horizontal slits in 4 small light metal jelly moulds (cardboard egg boxes can be a temporary measure using the small 'cups') and pass slats through with the moulds facing the same way. Paint one 'vane' red. Place the pen top, with slats attached, on a stout vertical wire filed to a point. Try out in the wind and count the number of times the red vane passes in a minute. Compare with estimate using the Beaufort Scale. A conversion graph can be made; i.e. the wind vane's rotation speed with the Beaufort Scale.

CUP ANEMOMETER

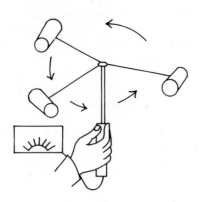

FIGURE 2.12

Some discussion can take place about what causes the wind to blow, although precise answers are best left until later stages. Part of the answer can be found in finding out about the currents set up when hot air rises. This can be seen in the experiment where strips of metal foil (i.e. metal foil spiral mounted on a vertical needle) are suspended above a candle. Other examples of convection currents can be discovered by children. Questions can lead on to whether air behaves as water when heated.

Visibility

Similar work can be achieved as in the section for 7–9s in the selecting of objects at set distances to gauge visibility. Two refinements can be added at this stage:

1. Use a local large-scale Ordnance Survey map to locate the chosen objects and work out the precise distance from the viewing point. This will give visibility measured in miles or metres.
2. A Sighting Tube as shown in Figure 2.14 could be used.

Air Pressure

This is a new concept introduced at this stage, and is not always easy for children to grasp, that air exerts a pressure. Children should be made aware of 'air' through discussion on wind and draughts etc.

Simple experiments will help understanding of air pressure.

1. Fix a small funnel in the top of a milk bottle with clay or plasticine to make an airtight joint. Pour water into the funnel and note what happens.
2. Place a drinking straw in a glass of coloured water (orange squash). Place a finger over the end of the straw and remove the straw from the water. Remove the finger and discuss the result.
3. Take an airtight tin (e.g. syrup or drinking chocolate tin) and punch 2 holes, one in the

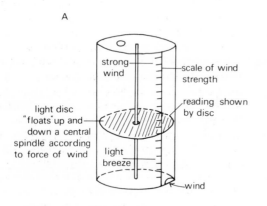

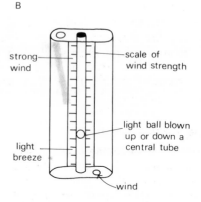

FIGURE 2.13   Instruments for measuring wind speed

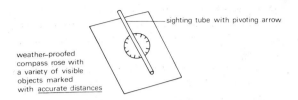

weather-proofed
compass rose with
a variety of visible
objects marked
with <u>accurate distances</u>

sighting tube with pivoting arrow

FIGURE 2.14 Sighting tube

top and one in the bottom. Fill with water and replace the lid. Place a finger firmly over the hole in the top and observe what happens.

4. Fill a glass or beaker to the brim with water. Press a sheet of paper firmly on top. Invert. Remove your hand from the paper and discuss the result.

5. Home-made barometer 'chicken feeder'. Take a milk bottle partly filled with water and invert in a tumbler of water. Variation in the level of water in the bottle can be noted on a scale of graph paper glued to the bottle. Find out if damp air is heavier or lighter than dry air.

6. Lower a glass or beaker mouth downwards in a basin of water—discuss the result.

Children will enjoy looking at instruments that record air pressure, namely the different varieties of barometers. Most children will be familiar with the round aneroid type which has a glass front which they 'tap' to see which way the needle moves; i.e. to show weather change from 'Rain' to 'Change' to 'Fair'. A reading can be obtained from a scale that usually accompanies these words. The scientific Fortin's Barometer with mercury column may have to be found in a weather station or local secondary school. This is also true of the Barograph, which records air pressure as a continuous line marked on graph paper attached to a revolving drum. If any of these instruments are available, then readings from them can be used.

Applying Weather Data

The object of keeping an accurate daily weather record is to be able to interpret it, and find patterns of weather which can be said to be typical of the time of year, or for a given area during the different seasons. For example, the connection between temperature and the seasons; the incidence of frost during spring; identifying the season with the heaviest rainfall or the months with the strongest winds etc. A record helps to quantify impressions that a child may have formed through subjective recording in earlier years. Patterns in weather begin to emerge, over the short period of days or longer periods such as months or throughout a year. A record also helps us to be wary of common generalisations; April may not be a month of showers; March winds may not blow and June may be anything but 'flaming'. A scientific and precise skill is being developed in children to observe carefully, record accurately and to make reasoned deductions.

Linked with this close observation should be work related to the overlying theme for this stage; how the overall patterns of weather through the year and anomalies between years affect our lives. Work may not be undertaken which comes solely under the headings of weather, temperature or humidity etc. For example the topic 'transport and weather' could be studied. This can raise a number of questions; e.g. On wet days what additional use is made of the private motor car to carry people to work? Traffic counts on a number of dry and wet days could be conducted at certain selected locations to provide information. Other questions could include: How many days are lost to air traffic per winter at a given airport? What form of transport is the least disrupted by bad weather—rail, road, water or air?

Other avenues of exploration can include jobs or industries whose success is largely determined by the weather; e.g. people who live in seaside towns; farmers; builders; sport, where, for example, football matches may be postponed through waterlogged or frozen grounds.

The effects of unusual or freak weather conditions is another way of underlining what is taken as 'usual'. These include blizzards, gales, floods, storms, drought, fog or heat-waves etc. They can be taken as they arise. Information can be collected from newspaper cuttings, magazine articles, television reports and personal accounts from friends and relatives. Examples of this may be seen where promenades have been breached by the sea; where a ship has run aground in a storm or where a town has been flooded. Stories can be found of how people coped with disaster; stories of courage, hardship, sadness etc.

Children can also use reports from other countries about man's response to life disrupted by avalanches, floods and storms, and weather-related phenomena. Much can be learnt about the properties of snow and ice and the relationship to temperature if the starting point of an avalanche in an alpine winter holiday resort is taken.

Skills can be used in any area of the curriculum when undertaking work on the weather. For example, a child's own book on clouds can be made incorporating a potato-print of cumulus clouds for the cover; inside, sketches of actual clouds, photographs, poems and creative writing, research into the formation of clouds, graph and number work on the number of days certain cloud types are recorded or averages to show how frequently given cloud types appeared over a given period.

Weather need not be taken in isolation in terms of recording it. Patterns in weather and the implications for man should be looked for.

WEATHER 11–13s

Children at this stage, which approximates to the first two years of secondary school, or the latter years of middle schooling, learn to pick out the more specific patterns of weather through the year. At the previous stage, children became familiar with reading the basic weather instruments. This enabled them to scientifically interpret the differences they had previously experienced in a more subjective way. Children should now be able to use these skills and knowledge to analyse further seasonal and annual weather patterns, and to define characteristics typical of given areas of the British Isles. In short, to begin to define 'climate' as opposed to 'weather', and to begin to understand what is meant by Britain's climate. They will also come to realise that climates vary, although the reasons for this will be understood later.

A realisation should grow that climate in other countries cannot always be defined in terms of our own seasonal differences between summer and winter, autumn and spring. Criteria for distinguishing seasons in other lands may be based on precipitation, for example, giving relatively wet or dry periods of the year, where temperature may be less variable over the year. This may

be seen in some equatorial or monsoon climates.

The role that climate plays in influencing people's activity will also be important; e.g. being able to grow cotton in the southern USA or not being able to grow oranges in Britain. In addition, man's response to climate can be studied in certain instances, such as in the irrigation of a region with low annual rainfall.

Weather Recording
Recording of the weather should continue to be important, but with more detailed instruments, where possible, to give a greater depth of study into the basic elements and how they are formed.

Temperature
Maximum and minimum temperatures can be regularly logged and graphs drawn up to show average daily maximum and minimum temperatures for different months of the year. At this stage, work on discovering the different ways in which air can be heated, e.g. by conduction, radiation or convection, could be undertaken. Other areas of study can include the effect of altitude on air temperature; or the conditions for the formation of frost.

Precipitation
A more detailed distinction between precipitation as rain or precipitation as snow can be made. Elementary principles in the formation of snow and hail can be introduced. Knowledge could be applied to examine and define the wettest and driest parts of the British Isles. Children should become familiar with using rainfall and temperature graphs, which they learnt to draw earlier, as tools for helping to determine the climate of given areas.

Humidity
The term 'relative humidity' can be examined in more detail to enlarge upon the fact that the atmosphere contains water vapour. Regular readings should be taken from a Wet and Dry Bulb thermometer, and converted into a relative humidity percentage with the help of hydrographic tables. Experiments can be devised to examine dew. What is dew? How is dew formed? What is meant by 'dew point'? Work on frost can often be closely related to work on dew.

Visibility

Visibility can continue to be recorded in the manner set out in the previous section. An additional area of study now can include the factors in the formation of fog and mist. What constitutes fog as opposed to mist? What is a sea mist? Why can it form so quickly? Work here can be closely related to humidity. The concept of 'haze' can be introduced, and how haze is different from mist. What exists in the atmosphere that gives rise to haze common in urban or industrial areas? What is 'smog'? What is a 'smokeless zone', and how did they come into being in some of our major towns and cities? What is a heat haze?

Air Pressure

More detailed examination of a Fortin's barometer would be useful, and how it works. This may necessitate visits to a local meteorological office. Discussion could revolve round the fact that atmospheric pressure is not everywhere the same over the surface of the world; there are areas of high and low pressure.

This is a good starting point for examining a weather map. These might be simple ones in the first instance, such as those shown on television weather forecasts, or those seen in the daily newspapers. The terms 'depression', 'anticyclone', 'warm and cold fronts' can be introduced. Children will be familiar with these expressions from television weather bulletins. The theories of formation of these phenomena need not be dealt with in detail at this age, although children can understand the meaning of 'isobar'.

Daily readings can be taken from a number of instruments; aneroid-type barometer, Fortin's barometer or barograph, as outlined in the preceding section.

Wind

Wind can continue to be observed and recorded as discussed earlier. Discussion on wind can progress with finding out what association wind has with areas of high and low pressure; i.e. what characteristics and patterns are observable with winds associated with these different pressure areas. What other factors affect wind?; the terrain over which it blows—plains, deserts, hills or mountains; water over which it blows—seas, oceans, lakes; and the temperature of water relative to the land and vice-versa. What is the part played by wind in the water cycle? This will link in closely with any work on cloud formation undertaken. What are the properties of winds which have blown over vast expanses of sea or land? e.g. the *Mistral* and other named winds. What are sea and land breezes?

Children should find out what symbol is used on weather maps for wind and how wind strength is denoted. From their own recordings children should be in a position to determine from what direction our prevailing winds blows. Further discussion can take place on where this wind has originated: the nature of the surface over which it has blown; the properties it has acquired; and what part it plays in giving us our 'typical' mild, damp climate. When this 'pattern' is interrupted, what sort of weather can replace it, and what clues to wind direction are given?

In a more local sense, experiments can be undertaken to determine how objects affect wind direction. For example:

Experiment 1

On a windy day, choose a building or wall around which a number of wind vanes could be set out. Instructions for making suitable wind vanes were given in the 7-9s section. Place the vanes in such locations as the leeward side, the windward side, at the corners and possibly on the roof. Use stands to keep the wind vanes at a constant height above the ground. Try to place the stands at a uniform distance about a metre from the object you choose. A few vanes might be placed at some distance from the building for purposes of comparison.

Map the area and plot the location of the wind vanes (Fig. 2.15). Use arrows to show the direc-

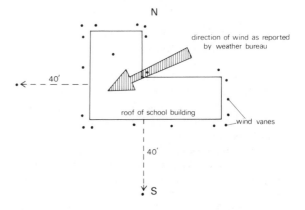

FIGURE 2.15   Measuring wind direction

tion of the wind indicated by each wind vane. Which wind vanes pointed in the same direction? Which seemed to change direction frequently? Which wind vanes agreed with the wind direction reported by the weathermen? Why was it important to locate the wind vanes at the same height and distance from the object? Would similar readings be obtained if the wind vanes were located 10 metres instead of 1 metre from the object?

Experiment 2

Similarly, activities can be carried out to find out how wind direction varies with the height above the ground. For this, a stand should be constructed as in Figure 2.16.

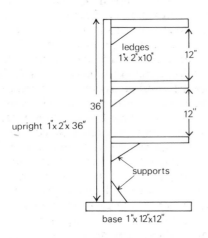

STAND FOR WIND VANES

FIGURE 2.16   Measuring wind direction at different heights

Attach wind vanes to each level of the stand with elastic bands. The help of a partner is necessary to read all the vanes at the same time. A steady breeze should be blowing, and the wind vanes should be observed for about half a minute. Decide in which direction each vane points for most of this period. Which vanes pointed in the same direction at the same time? Which did not? Variations can be tried. Would several stands with wind vanes located near each other in the same area produce the same readings?

Experiment 3

Experiments to find out how wind velocity changes with height above the ground can be carried out. The stand described above could also be used with anemometers, made as shown in the previous section, in the same way as the wind vanes were used. Different floors or roofs of buildings could be used where an anemometer could be placed in the open free of obstruction. Step ladders could also be used instead of a stand. Different questions can be asked. At what height was wind speed the least? In which area was the maximum speed recorded?

Experiment 4

This could show how wind velocity affects temperature. For example, you feel colder on a day when a strong wind is blowing. Use the anemometer and stand to obtain the velocity of the wind. Tape one thermometer to the outside of a cardboard box so that it is in the wind. The second thermometer can be taped inside the box so that it is sheltered from the wind. Compare the temperatures shown by the thermometers. Repeat the experiment when winds of different velocities are blowing. The degree to which a wind appears to lower air temperature is referred to as the wind chill factor.

Clouds

After earlier work on cloud recognition based on the three-fold classification, i.e. clouds seen in the cirrus, stratus and cumulus groups, a more detailed approach can be pursued. At this stage more specific clouds within these groups can be picked out; e.g. nimbostratus storm clouds, 'scud' clouds, herring-bone formations of cirrus clouds. Now the recognition of what sort of weather tends to be associated with each cloud formation can be practised. For example, the sort of weather that is heralded by the progression of certain cloud types seen when a depression approaches can be noted.

Cloud cover can be estimated more precisely, and the method of recording cloud cover on a weather map can be found.

A Local Meteorological Office

A visit to a local meteorological office would be very worthwhile. Children would see a variety of scientific weather recording instruments in use. They would be able to compare how far their own observations and recordings are accurate. The opportunity to examine weather maps should be taken. Children may not understand all that they show; e.g. depressions and anticyclones and how they move, but they will see how much information, which they can record, is mapped. If aerial photograhs can be seen, especially satellite photographs as shown on television weather forecasts, they will be a source of great interest.

Such examination of maps and photographs provides a good starting point for discussion and interpretation of climates. Satellite photographs of other continents may be available. For example, the Sahara Desert in North Africa is often seen clearly when the surrounding area is obscured by cloud. What are the reasons for this? From sources such as this, a discussion on the general climatic zones of the world can take place. Find out, for instance, what children know of the characteristics of climate in the Polar regions as compared with Equatorial zones. What are the features of climate that come between? A simple classification of climate could be defined as follows: Polar, Cool Temperate (Norway), Mid-Temperate (British Isles), Warm Temperate (Italy), Dry Temperate (Desert), Hot Dry Tropical (East Africa) and Hot Wet Tropical (The Amazon).

An understanding will develop that the climate of a given area of the world depends on more than latitude (position between the Poles and the Equator). Factors such as proximity to an ocean; situation in the middle of a large continental land mass; direction and origin of prevailing winds; location in relation to migrating wind belts, and altitude will all be determining factors. At this stage the reasons why these factors influence climate will not be understood in detail, but the realisation that 'a climate' is the result of many factors and processes impinging on each other will emerge.

A useful way of approaching this work is trying to define the factors that are relevant to the formation of Britain's climate; analysing the part played by the Atlantic sea mass, the Westerly Wind Belt and latitude. This will help children arrive at what is considered 'typical' of our climate; cool, moist winters and warm, damp summers. Children already have a knowledge of rainfall and temperature graphs—of how to compile and interpret them. Graphs for different locations in the British Isles should be used to help describe the climate and find variations between regions; e.g. the west and east coasts, southern England and Scotland, highland areas and adjacent lowland areas. After this, a useful study would be to compare graphs of British stations with those of towns and cities typical of other climates in other lands. It is sufficient now for children to realise that climates vary, and that they have an effect on human activities.

Projects can be undertaken to show how man's activity on the earth's surface can often be a response to climate. Examples could initially be taken from the British Isles. Localised examples could include irrigation practice in the drier eastern regions of Britain, the building of reservoirs in the wetter highland areas of Wales and Scotland, or even frost protection measures in orchards and fruit farms. In these cases, visits could link in with this work; to hydro-electric power stations or farms, or wherever a local response to weather and climate is noticed. Even a row of poplar trees forming a wind break is an indication of man's response to climate locally.

On a more global scale, one can pick examples of particular agricultural products, and find out what are their optimum conditions for cultivation on a commercial scale. For example, grapes for wine, sugar cane, citrus fruits, cotton, maize and many other crops. Wider discussion can take place with grapes which would link back to Britain. For example, the re-emergence of a British wine industry, albeit on a very small scale, and the fact that the Romans grew grapes in England for wine. The growth of tourism abroad could also be taken as a response to climate. Examples where this might take place on a national scale, e.g. the movement to south coast resorts in summer, could be extended to examine examples on an international scale; e.g. British holiday-makers moving to the Mediterranean in summer, or further afield still.

Work on weather should be seen to continue to have its roots in observation and recording, even though the means of obtaining data will grow more sophisticated. Patterns will be picked out on a more local scale leaving those on a more large-scale basis covering the British Isles to be examined. In turn, climatic patterns will be introduced and their variety noted. Examples of man's response in terms of human activity can be seen, both locally and further afield, to provide an interesting source of study.

2.2 Physical Geography: Water and Land in the Local Environment

Rachel Bowles

The study of physical geography is basic to geographical studies but has tended to be underplayed in school until the pupils reach the secondary school, where presumably the specialist is available. However, it is contended that all teachers should be able to introduce their pupils to elementary studies in physical geography, mainly through the use of fieldwork and Ordnance Survey and Geological Survey maps. In the section which follows, ideas are given for the main age-range bands under the general title of 'Water and Land' in the local environment. Details of many useful books are given in Appendix 4.

EARLY STUDIES: 5–7s

By the age of five most children are aware that water runs downhill and makes patterns, that a slope means more effort in walking or pushing a pram and bike and that dry sand is quite a different proposition from wet mud. To help collect together this awareness into something more tangible three simple items are useful; a large-scale map of the area, a tray capable of holding a quantity of sand, gravel and pebbles, and a trough suitable for water play.

The map ideally should be a 1:2500 plan of the school area—the local surveyors department may have an old one spare—or an estate agents' plan of the area. In rural areas a 1:10 000 plan may suffice. As this map will be in constant use it should be mounted on hardboard and covered with clear plastic film to preserve it.

Water

Using the plan, the direction of flow of water in the gutters and the direction of slope of the pavement and path can be plotted with arrows (Fig. 2.17). From this the position of valleys and streams and the hills in between can be plotted. In towns not all streams are culverted, parts of the same stream may be seen as a feature in the town centre, along the backs of terraced house

gardens and in the nearby park. With careful preparation beforehand it may be possible to trace the course of the stream before it enters and after it leaves the park. Once it is established where the water flows discoveries of what happens when too little or too much water fills the gutter or stream can be made.

Here the sand tray or water trough partially filled at one end with both sand and gravel and pebbles can be used. Using a washing-machine-type hose near a tap, or a houseplant watering can(s), the work of the river in moving sand and mud 'downstream' and how fast it runs when full or low in water can be seen. Alternatively a pile of ballast and garden hose out in the playground can be used. Some children may even remember seeing the course of the river model on 'Playschool' (BBC TV) or 'Rainbow' (ITV).

Visits to the nearby stream or ditch in dry and wet spells will develop an understanding of narrow, wide, shallow, deep, steep slope, gentle slope, hill and valley and the appearance and disappearance of mud and pebbles. A jam jar of water from the stream allowed to settle on the

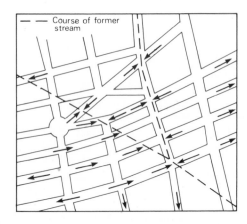

FIGURE 2.17   Street slopes and past river courses

nature table will raise the question 'where does the mud come from?' The shape of pebbles and differences in colour and texture are not beyond a five-year-old and a seven-year-old can begin to consider the source of the materials.

Land

The smallest child is often aware of the difference between sand (pouring when dry, moulding when wet), clay (sticky and wet or squeezable into shapes) and pebbles (shapes, sizes, colours, textures). If necessary a builders' merchant can provide silver sand (best for pouring), rendering sand (moulds well but needs washing to avoid staining) and ballast which gives pebbles, gravel and bits of shell as well as coarse sand, to provide a starting point for looking at rocks. Each child could bring a sample of soil to school—even if they live in a high-rise flat and have to beg from a plant shop or from a nearby park or graveyard. Sufficient variety would then be available to form a basis for comparing the qualities (colour, texture, waterholding) of the different samples and building up a map to show the changes in the area. The mounted base map could be the centre of a display round which are arranged the different samples in screwtop jars or polythene (freezer) bags each with a thread leading to the place where the sample was found.

In northern areas particularly, but also generally north of the Thames Valley, where ice sheets left deposits, the pebbles in the soil show considerable variety of stones. Flints, grey, brown or black with a curved break, predominate in the southern regions but sandstones of every hue increase northwards, varied with fragments of crystalline rocks such as granite. The true nature of the rocks can only be revealed by a happy period of cracking open the pebbles under a piece of cloth (to prevent flying fragments) with a hammer or large pebble. Clear varnish or nail polish or just keeping in an airtight jar of water, helps to bring out the colours.

Not every school is fortunate enough to be near the coast where the effect of water and land on each other can be seen in the cliffs and in miniature on the beach but even at infant level a day visit to the coast is well worth while, not only for the different things that can actually be brought back but also for the stimulation of seeing similar elements, water, sand, pebbles, at a different scale and on return trying to make a model (using chicken wire or boxes and paper to cover for a base) showing what happens to raindrops after they reach the ground and meet up to make a stream and eventually reach the sea as a river.

The water cycle has a fascination for the five-year-olds (one must not forget drains), leading to where one finds water—in clouds, in lakes, in the ground, in the sea and how it is kept for drinking, washing and transportation.

A case study of a class of 6-7-year-olds visiting a local stream is fully described in the Schools Council's *Environmental Studies Project: case studies* (Schools Council, 1972a). Here can be seen the use of a model from which a map was made, work cards which by word and picture gave practice in reading, measuring and writing, the topics discovered at the stream and the group work which developed using the varied abilities of this age group. Vocabulary was added to (source, course, estuary) and developed (cascading, rippling, gurgling), sorting began (big, little; hard, soft; round, irregular), measuring was made of height, depth, width of water and bridge and speed of flow by paper boats. Collecting began of pebbles and plants. Other books in the same series *(Starting from maps; Starting from rocks;* Schools Council, 1972b, 1973) give techniques for initiating skills (e.g. sketching on pre-drawn outlines and plans, p.18 in *Starting from rocks).*

STUDIES IN DEPTH: 7-9s

The young junior is usually used to model making, so if the last model suggested for infants has not been done what better than to start looking at the importance of water and the shape of the land with a model of a river course from mountain to coast, or, if the local area is suitable, a simple model based on the local large-scale map. The question of drawing to scale will depend upon how many of the class can record or measure or are capable of so doing.

Where conditions are suitable for setting up a marked pole, e.g. beside a path over a stream (with the agreement of whoever is responsible for the land, the *Head* park keeper, the vicar (churchyard), local town planner), observations at times of high and low water, high rainfall and drought conditions can show the link between rainfall and stream flow, even the time lag between rainstorm and flood or drought and low water. For certain children in an Edmonton school this meant noticing the height and colour of the water in an open culvert on the way to school to compare with the rainfall measurements of the previous 48 hours.

The kind of measurements possible with juniors is detailed in the next section. The chief difference age makes is in the range and number of observations possible; under nine one would not expect to spend time on more than one site. Repeated visits to the same site in different seasons make a worthwhile study in depth satisfactory to both child and teacher. Change and variation can be observed, leading to a consideration of the effects of different climates, different landscapes and the use of picture study. Colour printing has made available a large range of landscape pictures which can be collected from colour supplements or found in oversize books on nature and the earth (Time Life and St Michael). The question of scale is important and the camera's viewpoint—on earth or above it. Overall one would expect to introduce the concepts of desert, mountain, lowland, plains, valleys, hills, plateau, snowy wastes, streams, rivers and continental waterways (Mississippi, Rhine, Amazon). The engineering instincts of the seven-year-old can be utilised to consider dams and flood barriers, wells and oases. Hardware models can be made (Anderson, 1969) using offcuts of clear plastic, perspex, or marine ply or metal office trays or moulded baking tins. With a 5 cm layer of sand, an inlet and outlet and a hose, seasonal variations can be simulated, as can the effects of interference on flow and the development over a period of time of meanders and features of erosion and deposition.

The lower junior child is fascinated by the variety in the world about him and by collecting the variety available in one product, be it stamps or pebbles. An understanding of landscape often begins with an understanding of rocks and their products. The differences between sand, mud and pebbles are recognised by infants. Where there is variety in the pebbles a simple map of the region could be drawn to show the sources of the pebbles. The Geological Survey publish two sheets at a scale of ten miles to the inch, showing the locality of the major geological series and the associated rocks e.g. chalk, sandstone, clays, granites, slates. The *Readers Digest Atlas of the*

SITE		COLOUR	HARDNESS	TEXTURE	CRACKS OR HOLES	WATER	SLOPE	ROOTS	OTHER
DEPTH	THICKNESS		Soft Hard Sticky	Sandy Gravelly Clayey	Many Some None	Yes, much No Some	Flat Gentle Steep	Many Some None	

TABLE 2.3   Record sheet for soil profiles

British Isles has a simple map of rock outcrops with explanation and block diagrams to show the diversity of landscape in Britain. The same atlas has a map of stone belts of Britain and associated buildings. A collection of stones brought by the children (three each of different colour and texture) would probably show the main materials used for buildings (brick, cement, sandstones, slates) and roads (crystalline rocks such as granite and volcanic rocks). This could be supplemented with rock samples from the local stone mason/gravestone-maker or large builders' merchant. There are several simple books on identification but one should aim to distinguish colour, hardness and texture differences. When related to local buildings it should be possible to show how often the lightest, most porous brick was used for buildings now in the greatest need of repair (or demolished) and the darkest red, finest textured bricks were used for the most important and best-kept dwellings. In rural areas, especially sandstone areas, similar differences can be noticed in the sandstone blocks.

Local museums as well as the Geological Museum in London have displays of local rock types and their uses. Fossils also are usually displayed. Though fossils are more difficult to collect for handling it is possible in favoured areas where quarries are common. Often the quarry foreman can provide enough specimens to consider the habitat of the past and compare with the location of similar habitats today.

Quarries show the gradual change from solid rock to topsoil. In urban areas there is usually a nearby hole deep enough to show made ground, surface soil (A horizon), sub soil, lighter and stickier in nature (B horizons), and then the parent material (C horizon) be it rock or recent deposits of clay, sand or pebbles. Comparison of enough profiles recorded in columns (Table 2.3) enables questions to be raised about the origins of the higher ground and the lower ground (DES, 1972). In rural areas profiles are more likely to be found along streams or beside banked paths. Ditches have to be cleaned out and JCBs are always busy, but on the whole it is generally easier to select one's spot and dig one's own hole.

Another way of recording a soil profile, a soil monolith, allows for study at leisure in the classroom and for more contrasting soils to be collected from further afield by the teacher or interested associates. This also allows for more

flexibility in introducing a study in depth of soils. The monolith can be an actual replica or to scale. Collect a sample of soil from each layer and label it with position, depth from surface and thickness of layer. On a strip of wood or hardboard mark off the layers of the profile, coat with a thick layer of glue, e.g. UHU or Bostik, sprinkle each sample on its appropriate marked area and leave to dry flat until the glue sets.

In the infant school, games of 'I Spy' will have started individual observation. This can be used by the children on their way about the local area. Do the people use the land around the school in different ways? Are the plants/houses/gardens/trees different at the top of the hill to those at the bottom? Using large blank base maps of the district different maps can be built up using symbols (Fig. 2.18).

FIGURE 2.18   Symbols for mapping land use

By adding map tacks of different colours and sizes the vegetation, soil and rock information can be noted with strings to samples around the edge of the map. This can be compared with the model of the local area and information from this added by symbol and contour to the map.

EXPERIMENTS AND HYPOTHESES: 9–11s

In the infant school one hopes that experience in observing and thinking about the patterns in the neighbourhood has been achieved. With the lower juniors studies in depth help to set up a climate of enquiry into how and why and what is where it is on the Earth's surface. Vocabulary should show understanding of such descriptive words as source, stream, river, spring, estuary, deposition, erosion, delta, rapids, mountain, plain, plateau. Where plans or models of the local area have not been made in the past this could be done to give the class experience of the local environment or a frieze can be based upon an enlarged profile across the area or along a major route or river. The urge to compare and contrast and to notice change can be stimulated, earlier ground revised or covered before moving on to experimenting and developing ideas and relationships. The 9-11-year-old not only collects but also collects enough to classify and notice changes both in time, season and space and the effect man can have upon those changes.

Top junior and lower middle school children can measure, observe and record using more sophisticated methods than earlier. Home-made tapes (knotted string), plumb lines (heavy screws on twine), floats (corks, orange peel, ping-pong balls, coloured lolly sticks), ranging poles (garden canes marked with coloured tape into 10 cm lengths) and levels (protractor with plumbline) all help to measure river flow and channel form, valley width and slope. A plan of the channel course can be drawn using a home-made plane table (Scott and Lampitt, 1967) or by compass survey. Simple measuring techniques are shown in detail in *Elementary geographical fieldwork* (Brown, 1976) and with actual examples in Archer and Dalton (1970). Sketching the landscape is not difficult for the young child and most useful for indicating relationships (see Collis, 1974; Archer and Dalton, 1970).

Apart from measuring and recording, collecting in detail from more than one site shows change. Mud and pebbles from the water, stream bed, stream bank, flood plain and valley side extend earlier work on texture and rock types. Vegetation from water, bank, flood plain and valley side can be collected by quadrat sampling (i.e. all the species in an area of similar size e.g. A4 paper/card or wire frame 10 x 10 cm; or to find dominance all the plants counted and one specimen of each kind collected). Add soil samples taken with an auger and a transect diagram of the valley profile can be drawn up on return.

Enough material can be collected in a sufficiently accurate way to make the drawing of graphs and other diagrams mathematically possible; for vocabulary to be extended, and for the children to develop a skill in reporting detail with meaning. Also it is possible to develop simple hypotheses which can be tested further with published data. For children nine years old and over studies in depth achieve more meaning when more than one visit is made to show change. Whether the 'site' be stream, valley, nature trail, garden plot or viewpoint the key to the record is a clear worksheet. This not only helps to develop a data bank for class work but also ensures that the energy expended on devising and completing study has continued momentum, if need be, with other members of staff. Figure 2.19 shows a layout used with 11-year-olds with typical results from a small stream and calculations for classwork. Record forms can be adjusted to topic, interest or ability but the results should be so shown that different people can work on the records back in the classroom if necessary. With classes of mixed ability, group work both in the field and in the classroom is the answer for coping with jobs of differing complexity. Often groups are self selecting, interest in the chosen study carrying them beyond their usual level of attainment. At other times maximum results are best obtained by judicious allocation of work by stage of child development. Instructions should be simple and well laid out, if necessary in diagram or picture form, so that personal interpretation in the field by the teacher is unnecessary. Often this will require good ground work beforehand in instruction in the use of instruments and method of recording, if necessary on a mock-up in the playground (Schools Council, 1972a). Done properly teachers and helpers will have the time in the field to debate and discuss in the field those matters that can only be done in the field; e.g. why a river bank is vegetated in one area and not another.

Legibility on field record sheets, be it sketch, form, rubbing, map or transect can be preserved by using pieces of hardboard with bulldog clip and pencil (rubber-tipped) on string all covered by a polythene bag big enough to allow the cover to remain whilst working on the board in inclement weather. The record form can be a teaching aid in presenting the right vocabulary in a choice situation. E.g. shape of slope: rough/even; convex/concave; rocky/grassed; other............? Soil texture: clay/loam/sand/other..............? It

RIVER	GRID REFERENCE	LOCATION	DATE

Type of Course: Straight/meandering/braided/rapids and falls

Aims 1. To find out if water flows faster in the middle of the channel than at the sides
2. To find out if water flows faster downstream

Method 1. Select straight reach of channel 5 or 10 metres long
2. Throw float(s) in the water above the highest marked point and time between markers of measured length in seconds
3. Repeat and take the mean of 3 readings
   Discard floats which catch on the bank

Velocity (Speed) Profile	No. of observations	Position in stream		
		Edge	Centre	Edge
Length of straight section	1	15 secs	19 secs	14 secs
	2	17 ,,	21 ,,	16 ,,
	3	19 ,,	23 ,,	18 ,,
= 10 metres	Mean	17	21	16
Average velocity in * metres/second		1.8		

SIZE OF FLOW (DISCHARGE) DOWNSTREAM

Measurements	Sites down river at least one mile apart		
	A (Grid ref.)	B (Grid ref.)	C (Grid ref.)
Width of stream (metres)	2	3	5
Depth of stream (metres)	0.5	1	1
Cross - Section (cubic metres)	2 x 0.5 = 1.0	3 x 1 = 3	5 x 1 = 5
Cross - Section x average velocity	1.0 x 1.8	3 x 2	5 x 3
= Discharge in cubic metres per second (*cumecs*)	= 1.8	= 6	= 15

* NB   More accurate velocity figures can be obtained by multiplying the mean velocity of each station by 0.8 thereby accounting for channel side friction

Further calculations in class:

Time to float one kilometre $= \dfrac{1.8}{10} \times \dfrac{1000}{1} = \dfrac{1800}{60} = 30$ mins.

Distance in one hour $= \dfrac{10}{18} \times 360 = 200$ metres

Comparison with a large river, e.g. R. Thames. Annual mean flow:

Eynsham	SP445087 (Witney)	5.04 m³/sec
Days Weir	SO568935 (Oxford)	10.84 ,,
Bray Weir	SU909797 (Henley)	21.35 ,,
Teddington	TQ707713 (Richmond)	25.15 ,,

(Abstract from *Surface Water Year Book 1964-65*, HMSO.)

FIGURE 2.19   Sample river field report form (this can be two small forms)

is useful in preparation of the measuring techniques beforehand to show the degree of tolerance required: viz. working to within one or two degrees or 5 to 10 cms.

Where a stream is not readily to hand the objective should be to find one within striking distance of a half-day visit, shallow enough to enter in wellingtons *or* have a bridge from which the floats can be cast, have a meander form and some evidence of erosion. A stream of this size will usually be in a valley small enough to be traversed across the flood plain at least. On the 1:50 000 Ordnance Survey map these are usually the very smallest streams shown. Hopefully the fieldwork can be accomplished with time for follow-up immediately on return to school where notes and impressions can be tidied, reinforced and future work planned and allocated. Where time is shared with other subjects such visits and follow-up time may be obtained by genial teamwork of the different subjects.

Once the nature of the river has been investigated valley and river courses can be studied on small-scale maps and with photographs (e.g. Rank Film *The Work of Rivers* by Clarke), then extended to look at rivers such as the Mersey, Ouse, Thames, Severn, Rhine, Mississippi and the landforms associated with them.

River work may not be possible, but the coast may be more convenient. Similar measuring, recording, mapping and sampling techniques will show the changes in slope and material on a beach and in time. Here a link can be made with a study of sedimentary rocks and a series of experiments set up. A simple profile survey (pacing and ranging poles/tape and clinometer) linked to a collection of beach deposits (50 cobbles, 100 pebbles, 2 handfuls of gravel, 4 handfuls of sand) taken at lowest ebb tide will on most beaches with a significant slope show a pattern similar to Figure 2.20. With each sample of deposit, sort particles with the aid of meshes of different sizes—garden sieve, colander, mesh sieve, tea strainer, muslin. Glue the particles to a board (6 x 45 cm) in order of size and label according to the sizes in Figure 2.20. Consider the source of the material based on evidence of rock type in the pebbles. Are the smaller particles produced from the same materials? (Evidence of work of waves.) Are the particles from the adjacent cliffs? Where could different particles have come from?

The work of other agencies in breaking down rock can be studied in a series of experiments; e.g. in frosty and very cold spells leave a corked bottle of water or a clay jar in a bucket (to keep the fragments together) overnight. Once the degree of expansion can be seen (about 3 mm) notice can be made of the gardener's use of frost to break down the soil in winter. Do any plants widen cracks?

The importance of water in soils can be shown:
1. By weighing, drying and re-weighing 100g of soil. The loss of weight indicates the amount of water in the soil. Which soil holds most water?
2. Conversely half a litre of muddy stream water can be weighed, evaporated and weighed again to show how silt is carried. Look in gutters and puddles. What is collected at the lowest points?
3. Fill three boxes of the same size (fish boxes or tomato trays) with the same type of soil after drilling holes in one end. Top one box with turf or grow grass seed thickly. When grass covered tilt gently on a small block of wood and put a bucket at the low, drilled end. Tilt one ungrassed box the same amount and the third steeply. Hang buckets below each, pour the same amount of water on each box from the same height.
   (a) Time the percolation rate.
   (b) Measure the amount of soil washed into the buckets by method (2) above.
   (c) How soon does the top soil begin to move in each of the three boxes?

From these experiments one can go on to consider landslides, mudflows, soil erosion, ploughing and digging on steep slopes and how mountainous regions with high rainfall frustrate erosion. Conservation and the Tennessee Valley Project are also developments.

With all the experiments and detailed quantitative fieldwork a qualitative view of the landscape must not be neglected. If the groundwork has been laid earlier in practising picture maps and completing the detail of outline sketches, it is possible to use the field sketch as a means of pulling together the elements of the landscape previously looked at in isolation. The view from the highest window in the school or the nearest high point, be it church tower or open space, usually shows a variety of relief with low rounded hills, wide valleys, perhaps a steep

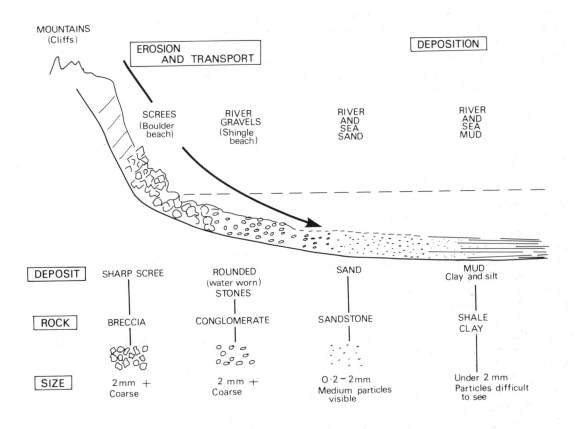

FIGURE 2.20   Beach profile

scarp, usually a ribbon of river or expanse of water. If time is short or skill is doubted a set of slides of the panorama can be used to build up an outline sketch on which further information can be drawn and noted (Beddis, 1968). This can be combined with identifying hills, valleys, spurs, spot heights, re-entrants, rock outcrops, woods and other landmarks on the Ordnance Survey maps with exercises in recognising contour patterns. Again repeated visits to the same viewpoints at different seasons and different times of day will help to develop an eye for landscape in all its guises. This is the time when the ability to stand and stare can be indulged with considerable return. Relationships between slope, vegetation, land use and geology are most quickly recognised after a long time of looking and recording.

THE ELEMENTAL CYCLES: 11–13s

The previous section has been much concerned with the details of outdoor work and indoor experiment. The elements of the physical world about the school should be extended by photographs and television to the elements of the earth, its mountains, deserts, icebergs and ice wastes, volcanoes and rivers, not forgetting the great expanses of forest and grassland between. Reasoning is developing alongside a capacity for abstract thought and the discovery of the inter-relationship of the elements, water, earth, air and man can become more detailed.

The origins of the earth's features, continents, oceans and their major landforms are still most clearly described by Holmes (1976), but the particular theory of continental drift which he

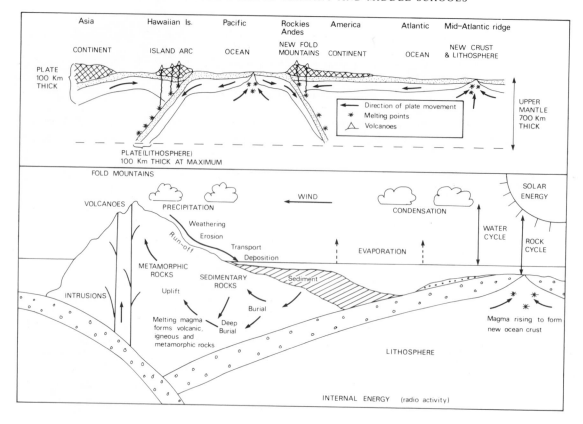

FIGURE 2.21   The structure of the earth's interior and its relationship to the rock cycle

devised, based on a theory of internal convection currents similar to those seen in a boiling pan of jam, has been refined and developed over the last decade in the light of new research into the theory of plate tectonics. Nigel Calder (1972) gives a journalist's view of this Restless Earth; Bradshaw, Abbott and Gelsthorpe (1978) give the most recent simple summary. On first sight an explanation of the internal constitution and mechanics of the earth seem superfluous but once one takes hazards, e.g. earthquakes, or phenomena, e.g. volcanoes, past climates, e.g. ice ages, or merely the distribution of mountains or marsupials (kangaroos), it is clear that some explanation of the earth's configuration is necessary. Moreover it helps to explain the variety in the rocks already studied. Figure 2.21 shows (a) the plates and structure of the outer part of the earth's interior and (b) its relationship to the rock cycle. Figure 2.22 shows the rock and water cycles.

The starting point for considering the earth can arise from any of the geological studies begun earlier or by looking at the hazards man has to contend with. Somewhere in the world there is or has just been an earthquake, landslide, flood, mountain air disaster or volcanic eruption. Nearer at hand the water cycle can be studied by experiment and the use of statistical records. This is well detailed by Weyman and Wilson (1975) from the use of washing up bowls, coffee tins and football pitches to records of river flow and rainfall for major river basins in Britain. Middle-school classes with junior experience of field measurement would benefit from a visit to some branch of the local water authority where the rhythm of the daily work is based upon accurate measurement of rainfall, evaporation and flow above and below ground.

River work can be extended downstream to more sites—at least one mile between each site, preferably two—or to favourable positions on different rivers. The nature of meandering, erosion, deposition, bankful conditions and flooding begin to be understood and the effect of landscape development discussed. Which areas are most dissected by rivers? Sandstone? Chalk? Clay? Using Ordnance Survey maps of different terrain, 'quadrat sampling', i.e. blocks of four or six km squares can be analysed using tracing overlays to show:

1. contour pattern;
2. water distribution;
3. woodland including parks;
4. heathland;
5. cultivated land including orchards and farmland (white).

The Geographical Association series *British Landscape through Maps* covers some 17 or more areas of contrasting nature and gives geographical and geological information, including seven National Park areas.

Where time and colleagues' enthusiasm permit, a transect across country of some 20-50 miles with sample stops for slope measurement, vegetation counts, soil samples, land-use surveys, house-type surveys and rock study using the techniques suggested earlier produces material which can be displayed as friezes, models, maps,

informed exhibitions and from which further experiment and work can arise. The transect can be completed in a day (10 a.m. first stop, 3 p.m. completion of fifth and last stop on a 50-mile transect) or in several short trips using evenings, weekends and half terms with the school either at one end or in the middle of the line.

Not every school is fortunate enough to be near the coast where the effect of erosion by sea and air on the land can be further studied in cliff forms, wave-cut platforms and beach deposits. A useful guide is found in *Teaching Geography Occasional Papers* No. 20 (Kent and Moore, 1974). A repeated study of the same beach either on a monthly or seasonal basis or after or during spells of calm or stormy weather will reveal the importance of the sea as an agent in building up the beach in calm conditions (usually summer) combing the beach down and removing it under storm conditions (usually winter) and lead to consideration of the longshore movement of material, erosion of the coast and how man has dealt with this perennial problem. Even a simple profile of different kinds of sea wall to be found at a resort reflects the kind of work the sea is known to be capable of at that particular seaside settlement.

WATER CYCLE

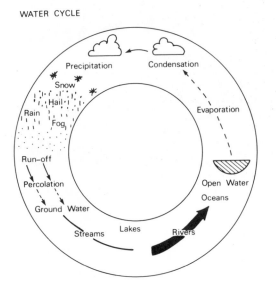

ROCK CYCLE

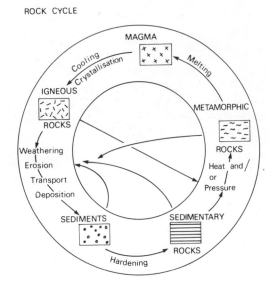

FIGURE 2.22   The rock and water cycles

In severe winters the question of the work of ice is easy to introduce from reality. The patches of snow remaining on the north-east slopes of hollows, the frost which lingers on the north side of the playground where the sun has melted it elsewhere are all good starting points for showing how snow patches develop into ice patches and eventually valley glaciers. Photographs and mapwork on profiles, a comparison of upland and glaciated Britain (the Lake District, Scottish Highlands) with Britain south of the Thames can show sufficient landforms to develop at least some ideas of how corries, horns, arêtes, screes and glaciated valleys come about.

PLATE 1.   Juniors engaged in fieldwork

3. Resources for learning: work outside the classroom in urban and rural areas

3.1 Fieldwork in urban areas

Roger Clare

Urban geography is concerned with where things are located and the geographer studies their distribution patterns looking for order and reason in them, and he examines the links, or lines of communication, between them. He looks for causes, relationships and the changes that occur. Through fieldwork in urban areas, geography gives us a fuller understanding of the highly urbanised society in which we live by investigating the structures, functions and inter-relationships of towns and cities. The structure, or physical form, of a town is seen in the nature of its buildings and its street patterns. By studying these its expansion into the surrounding rural areas may be traced from its original nucleus. Towns are essentially places where people live and work and some areas may be devoted to residential functions or to other functions such as industry, shopping, finance and leisure. The different parts of towns are linked in complex ways as people must move from one area to another, for example to work or to shop, and to enable goods to be distributed. There are also complex links between different towns and with villages and rural areas for both commerce and recreation.

URBAN FIELDWORK WITH CHILDREN

Children respond to, understand and have con-cern for the environment in varying degrees at different ages and at different stages of their development (Fig. 3.1). Fieldwork in urban areas provides them with opportunities to carry out original geographic research and enables them to develop a variety of skills. As well as using secon-dary sources, such as reference books, they also work from primary sources, for example inter-preting different kinds of maps, archive materials, directories, photographs and the evidence found in the streets. It also encourages curiosity and awareness by developing their powers of observation. A wide variety of tech-niques may be acquired, ranging from mapping, drawing and written records to photography and tape recording, and it develops their ability to evaluate and examine underlying hypotheses.

Field studies should be enjoyable and relevant. In the past there has been a tendency to concen-trate on the skills of observation and recording but, without a worthwhile hypothesis to test or an interesting local problem to examine, such work can be dull and unrewarding. Importantly, urban fieldwork encourages involvement in the com-munity as well as in the school and leads to a greater concern for the environment itself and for the people who live in it. Thus assessment of the quality of the environment and positive criticism of it are to be encouraged. Even very young children can be asked for their views on tower blocks or litter while older children may be more concerned with a variety of community issues or with making a positive contribution, for example

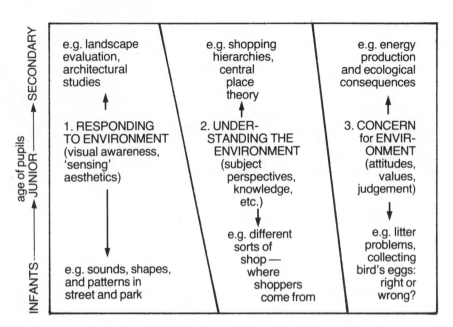

Possible Proportion of Three Elements Changing with Age of Pupils

FIGURE 3.1   Children's relationship to the environment
(after R. A. Beddis, Avon Schools Environment Project)

in establishing a town trail or an urban nature trail for the use of others.

Progressive development

Work should be planned so that there is a progressive development of key concepts and skills. For young children the immediate, generally local, experience provides a foundation for observation, recording, simple classification and interpretation whereby simple relationships in the urban environment can be seen. Vocabulary is constantly extended and the concepts learned are applied to more distant environments, thus introducing them to new places and important world-wide issues. Illustrations might include the overcrowding of tower blocks in Hong Kong, the crush of the journey to work in Tokyo or the seemingly universal use of graffiti and football playing in city streets where there are no other leisure facilities. For older children local and small-scale studies remain important but they can be increasingly extended to include regional, national and global issues.

At an early age training in observation and in skills of importance in geography are likely to be incorporated in a variety of environmental studies. Thus young children examining a building can find a wealth of activity in the building materials with the mathematical shapes of bricks, pipes and gable ends; with the number and arrangements of doors, windows and furniture; with the colours and textures of stone, wood and brick which can be recorded through pictures and rubbings, and with the functions of the different rooms and parts of the building. Many such activities may be carried out in the school itself or at a selected building nearby, but, as with all fieldwork, the prime consideration must be the safety of the child. Indeed, local visits are not permitted by many schools or are hedged with many restrictions. Opportunities to meet bricklayers or plumbers and see them at work or to speak to a shopkeeper, fireman or the school caretaker and see behind the scenes are valuable experiences. It may be possible to obtain an architect's plan and identify individual features of

Victorian terraces
High density

1930's estates
Medium density

Modern suburbs
Low density

FIGURE 3.2   Street patterns and population density

the building or for the children to construct their own large-scale plan.

To introduce streetwork to young children roughly scaled down models of local streets can be constructed in class, at the simplest with arrangements of building blocks. These can be used for a variety of simulations such as postal deliveries, bus services and fire emergencies to develop concepts of direction and distance and to improve mapping skills. Buildings can be classified according to their ages, building materials and uses and progessively more advanced forms of measurement, recording and classification can be used. For example, the slope of the street can be related to its drainage or by visual detective work an approximate population can be ascertained for the street and the population density worked out, as can the proportions of homes with cars and television sets. Simple movement studies of people entering shops or using public transport can be made and the results expressed as graphs or related to large-scale maps or plans. Thus simple relationships can be established, for example between the shops with the most customers and between the local bus stop and the houses in the street, or, by using the local bus timetable, between the street and the centre of the town. Street furniture, such as water hydrants and telephone wires, can be related to the provision of essential services.

It is interesting to compare neighbouring streets or study selected, contrasting, areas of the town. By using old maps it is possible to trace the town's growth. The patterns that roads and streets make on a map often give clues to the age of the buildings. Medieval street patterns in the town centre, Victorian terraces and the sweeping crescents of 1930s housing estates are all distinctive (Fig. 3.2). Interesting studies may take the form of a transect across part of the town to relate the buildings to the slope of the land or to the proximity of the railway. This may lead to more detailed explanations for the siting of factories and industries. Thus the concept that towns have zones of different character may be progressively examined. The results can be compared with theoretical models such as a simple theory of land use in towns (Fig. 3.3).

The movements of traffic and people can be measured and analysed in progressively complex ways and related to relevant issues such as the need for traffic lights at important road junctions or for the provision of better facilities for leisure. Observations of movements may be linked to questionnaires, for example to establish how far people have travelled to shop or to work. Questionnaires need to be brief and carefully vetted

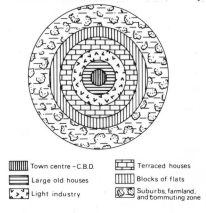

	Town centre – C.B.D.		Terraced houses
	Large old houses		Blocks of flats
	Light industry		Suburbs, farmland, and commuting zone

FIGURE 3.3   Theoretical land-use zones of a town

to ensure they are pertinent and, in many circumstances, it is desirable that the interviews be pre-arranged (Fig. 3.4). Questions relating to finance, in particular, should be avoided.

```
1. Where do you live?
2. How long did it take you
   today by
   bus
   car
   train
   foot
   cycle?
3. Do you come here
   daily
   weekly
   monthly
   not often?
4. Do you shop in
   departmental stores
   food shops
   clothing shops
   furniture shops
   the street market?
5. Do you have a meal
   here
   elsewhere?
6. Is your shopping done
   mainly in this centre
   mainly in another centre?
Time of interview.....................
Place of interview ...................
```

FIGURE 3.4   Questionnaire for shoppers to find the importance of a shopping centre

Selection and guidance

So much material is readily available in towns that the teacher must be aware of what is significant and select that which will lead to a greater understanding of urban areas. The chosen surveys and activities should involve the children in such ways that they respond to and have concern for the urban environment.

Many children have quite limited powers of observation and it may be necessary to point out obvious features. Worksheets too should provide appropriate guidance. Similarly they need guidance in appraising the aesthetic points of the environment before they can make suitably informed value-judgements. Urban fieldwork indicates the different sides of an argument and involves children in decision making. For example, a fine piece of Victorian architecture which has been recommended for preservation may be an appalling place in which to work. Some Local Authorities have seen the value of urban studies in schools and have been keen to support them.

Some of the many textbooks, handbooks and guides to urban fieldwork are concerned with geographical techniques but many are concerned also with comprehensive studies of environmental education. Of these *Let's use the locality* by H. Pluckrose (Mills and Boon) may be found particularly useful for primary schools and *Exploring the environment: a fieldwork handbook* by R. Clare (Geography Colour Units, MacDonald Educational) contains a variety of ideas for surveys using geographical techniques suitable for the middle years. The following

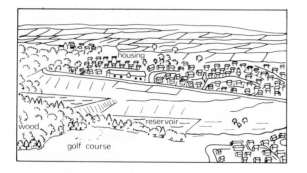
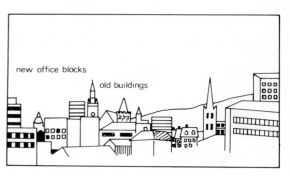

FIGURE 3.5   Completed landscape sketch and drawing of a townscape

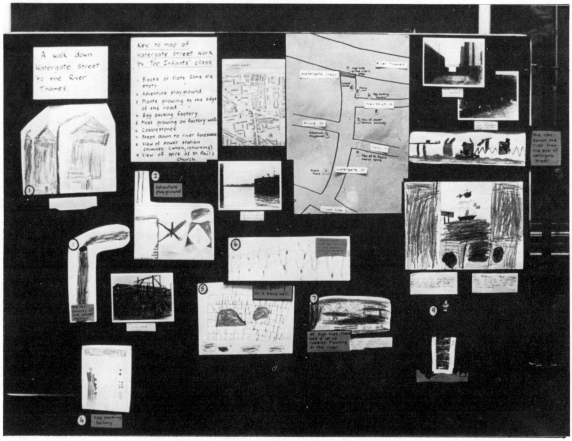

PLATE 2. Work of top infants along local street

suggestions have been selected as an indication of some possible approaches but need adaptation to suit the teacher's own programme, the ages and development of the children and particular local conditions. See *Teaching Geography, The Bulletin of Environmental Education* and *Classroom Geographer* for many detailed examples of work individual teachers have done with their classes. Some of the suggestions for urban fieldwork are expanded in this handbook in the sections on Fieldwork in Rural Areas and Physical Geography.

SUGGESTIONS FOR URBAN FIELDWORK

The following suggestions may be suitable for inclusion in programmes of work by children of most ages when adapted to their appropriate interests and to the level of development of their basic skills and understanding. The interests of 7-9-year-olds, for example, are likely to be based firmly on their own experience with their ideas of place centred on particular rooms, their school, home and local features, whereas with 9-11-year-olds more fruitful work may be done in a broader urban context, collecting and classifying information with increasing opportunities for reasoning.

It is usually possible to identify the original site of a town on the ground or from old maps. Work within the town becomes more meaningful if it is possible to obtain a view of the site from a distance and take photographs, which can later be analysed, or draw sketches of the landscape or townscape to show significant detail. This is not an easy task and most children will need a prepared framework on which to fill in the detail (Fig. 3.5). Buildings can be used to indicate the town's original site and its growth. Studies can be

Age of Building	Field symbol	Map colour
Very old		
Victorian & Edwardian		
1920's and 1930's		
After World War II 1950's — 1960's		
Modern		

A simple chart to use for dating buildings

FIGURE 3.6   Dating buildings (individual features, styles and materials aid the dating of buildings)

made of their age and nature and of their use and importance both today and in the past. The age of buildings is indicated by their shape, style and character. With a pocket reference book on architecture, or with sketches provided on worksheets, detective work may be used to find their ages from the clues in the features of the architecture and in the building materials. Date charts of varying complexity can be completed (Fig. 3.6) and maps made of the building materials (Fig. 3.7). Carefully labelled sketches and photographs of buildings are important methods of recording information. Observations may be entered on base maps of a suitably large scale which, in follow-up work, can be combined on a large map as each section is completed and the results interpreted. An aesthetic appreciation of the buildings is an important consideration and may be linked to proposed planning projects.

The character of a street can be assessed by drawing a streetscape which may indicate features such as interesting angles, building stones, attractive shop signs and street furniture. Attention may be drawn to the nature of the pavements (the footscape), detailing attractive stonework and textures, and to the presence or absence of overhead clutter (the wirescape). To assess the quality of the environment, worksheets (Fig. 3.8) may be devised to draw attention to criteria on which judgements can be made and

|||||	wood
▨	brick
▦	slate
glass	

A brick house with a slate roof. There is a wooden conservatory with a glass roof at the rear.

FIGURE 3.7   A map of building materials

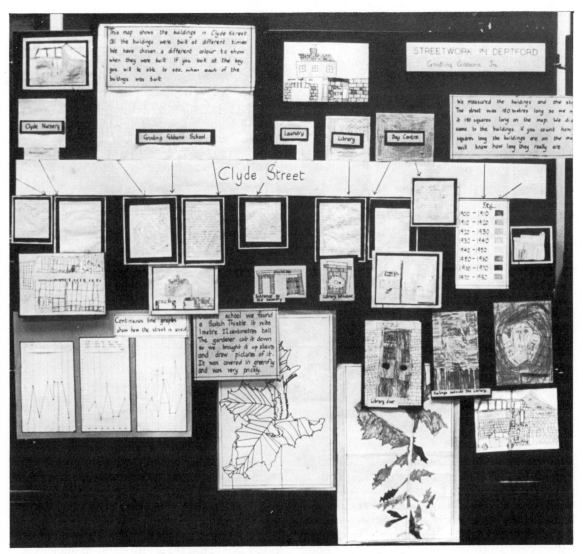

PLATE 3.   *Work of top juniors along local street*

enable some quantification of the results. These may well be linked to significant points on a town trail around selected streets.

Buildings can be classified according to their use and maps compiled which indicate the degree to which different functions are grouped in various parts of the street, or in large areas of the town. A large-scale base map such as the Ordnance Survey 1:2500 is necessary for this, although plans such as that in Figure 3.9a may be found more suitable for recording the uses of the

various floors of a building. A variety of classifications can be selected to relate to different kinds of surveys, for example to indicate the distribution of jobs in the town. Other groupings may be selected to indicate residential, retailing and industrial uses, for example, and further refined to indicate sub-groups in these categories (Fig. 3.9b). Attention is drawn to the Second Land Utilisation Survey which shows how easily identifiable colours can be accorded to a classification so that the zones stand out clearly on a map. The

THE STREETS	THE EFFECT OF TRAFFIC		GOOD	BAD
Score the following points for the appearance of the street along your trail:	Moving	Danger to people		
		Noise		
		Damage to property		
Very attractive 4		Ugliness		
Quite attractive 3				
Attractive 2	Parked	Danger to people		
Not Attractive 1		Parking space available		
Ugly 0		Ugliness		
		Delivery access		

Take into account the following features:	**POPULARITY**
Condition	Do people seem to enjoy the area?
Relationship to surroundings	Can they walk freely?
Scale of buildings	
Trees and shrubs	**OPINION**
Street furniture	What are your own likes and
Tidiness	dislikes?

FIGURE 3.8   The Quality of the Environment
A check sheet for use at selected places

addition of a rural classification is of course appropriate for studies in suburban areas and on the urban fringe. The Central Business District (CBD), or less important suburban centres can be delineated by a simple classification based on the relative importance of buildings. Thus a large department store would rate X and a second-hand clothes shop Y (Fig. 3.10). Similarly, by allocating points to buildings, say 10 for the Town Hall and 9 for Marks and Spencer, streets can be graded in the order of their importance.

An urban transect is an effective way to record the features observed in a journey across a town (Fig. 3.11). The information can be compiled as a chart that relates the various features to each other. For example, the different street patterns may be related to the relief as when rows of terraced Victorian houses are built on steeply sloping land or warehousing is located on flat land alongside a river. The slope of the land can be ascertained by constructing a cross-section from a large-scale Ordnance Survey map, or by simple measuring techniques on the ground. The angle can be obtained with a simple hand-held clinometer or by using a home-made level (Fig. 3.12) and plotting the results directly on the graph paper.

The study of urban ecology is too often neglected. Mapping the distribution of animals is a vital part of the study of urban habitats. This can take the form of a transect whereby the distribution of plants along a line is recorded, using a measuring tape, or piece of suitably knotted string, and graph paper (Fig. 3.13). Alternatively, detailed random samples can be made along the line of the transect using a quadrat which may be constructed of metre-length pieces of wood divided by string to form a grid (Fig. 3.14). Quadrats may also be used to map distributions on opposite sides of trees or walls, or on walls themselves. Studies of lichens can be linked to levels of atmospheric pollution in different parts of the town as shrubby and leafy types will not tolerate pollution. The children should be

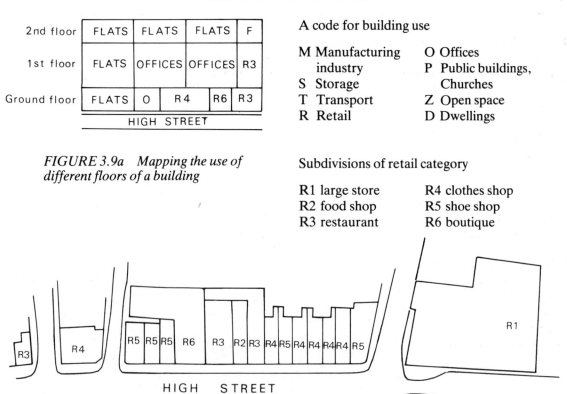

A code for building use

M Manufacturing industry
S Storage
T Transport
R Retail

O Offices
P Public buildings, Churches
Z Open space
D Dwellings

FIGURE 3.9a Mapping the use of different floors of a building

Subdivisions of retail category

R1 large store
R2 food shop
R3 restaurant

R4 clothes shop
R5 shoe shop
R6 boutique

FIGURE 3.9b Mapping building use along a street

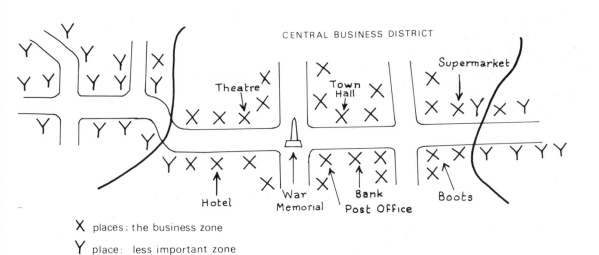

X places: the business zone

Y place: less important zone

FIGURE 3.10 Delineation of central business district

Relief			
Land Use			
Nature of Buildings			
Communications			
Cross Section			
Map			

Cross Section labels: Semi-detached, Park, Shops, Light Industry, Waste land, Rows of terraces, Railway, River

FIGURE 3.11   *Worksheet for an urban transect*

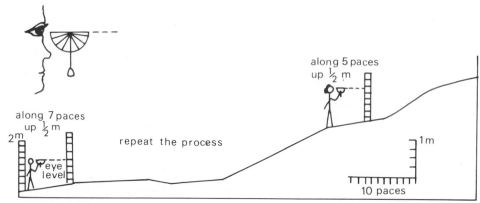

along 5 paces up ½ m

along 7 paces up ½ m

2m

eye level

repeat the process

1m

10 paces

Plot the measurements directly onto graph paper

FIGURE 3.12   *Using a home-made level to measure slopes*

A LINE TRANSECT

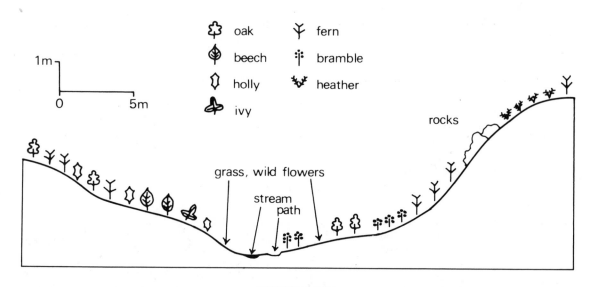

FIGURE 3.13

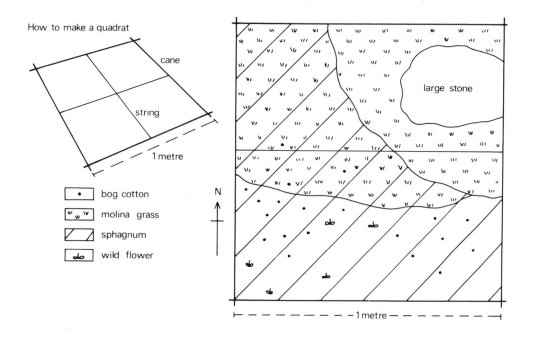

FIGURE 3.14   Quadrat mapping in an area of bogland

HOW TO TEST FOR PARTICLES IN AIR

Place filter paper in neck of milk bottle. Leave out of doors

Pollen and dirt particles collect on filter paper

Add plant nutrient and place a glass dish over the paper to see if algae grows.

FIGURE 3.15
Air pollution measurement

CLEAN AIR SURVEY

PLACE
DATE
TIME
NAME

1   TESTING FOR PARTICLES

How much dirt collected on the paper?
Did algae grow?

2   TESTING FOR ACIDITY

pH of tree bark tested
pH of rainwater tested

3   TESTING FOR LICHEN

What sort of lichen did you find?

4.   What other evidence of air pollution can you see?

encouraged to study lichens, plants and other specimens in situ and to treat everything growing with respect.

Air pollution can also be studied by examining its effects on buildings and by testing surfaces for acidity using litmus paper and mapping the results. Cones of filter paper placed in milk bottle tops can be placed at significant points to catch dirt and pollen, the latter being identified by adding plant nutrient to the papers (Fig. 3.15). Again the results can be mapped and linked to the proximity of roads and perhaps factories. Tests for river pollution may also be made and a useful kit and suggestions for conducting this and other experiments associated with the Sunday Times 'Watch' Club can be obtained from the Advisory Centre for Education (see Appendix 2). Noise levels are worthy of investigation and raise important issues which can be discussed in follow-up work. It may be possible to obtain a noise meter from the local planning office, or the Noise Abatement Society or to obtain, or devise, a scale indicating the effect of noise on people.

For example, it is difficult to use a telephone with a vacuum cleaner in the room (70 decibels). The results can be shown on a map, for example to indicate the differences with distance or with intervening walls from a busy main road.

The geographer needs to consider the links, or communications, that people have established over the years to enable them to move about their territory. Traffic surveys are easy to make. These should not be treated merely as traffic counts, but rather they should be used to identify and analyse particular problems. The results can be analysed in something better than a bar graph, for example by a flow graph to illustrate the movement of traffic through different parts of the town (Fig. 3.16). Congestion is a problem in most towns today and a traffic count can be linked with calculations of passenger car units, shown in Table 3.1, to indicate which streets are officially overcrowded, and the results plotted on a large-scale street map. Important issues such as those of public transport can be analysed from timetables and, as with the provision of parking facilities in

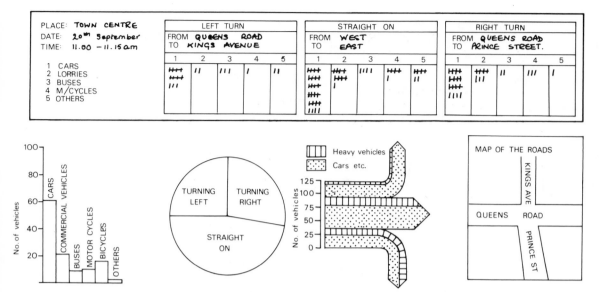

FIGURE 3.16 A traffic survey with the results expressed in a histogram, piegraph and flow graph

the town, provides opportunities to involve the class with the work of the local authority and to meet its officers.

The children's own experience of travel to and from school or from home can be expressed on maps and in the construction of time and distance charts (Fig. 3.17). Information for similar charts can be obtained from carefully organised questionnaires to find out, for example, the area served by a town centre, or shopping centre (Fig. 3.18), or to calculate the value of an amenity (Fig. 3.19). The illustration is a park but interesting and useful studies can be made for other amenities such as churches, bus stops, libraries and public telephones. Code letters or symbols can be used to add the distribution of amenities to a large-scale map and the findings linked to important issues such as the facilities available for old people or for those without cars. As suggested previously, qualitative judgements can be encouraged on the effect of traffic on the town and on the appearance of the street furniture, such as parking meters and traffic signs and on air pollution caused by traffic.

Town trails can be a most effective teaching technique. Similar to parkland and woodland trails, the earliest trails devised were 'I-Spy' guides but a considerable literature now exists on devising trails constructed to explore the urban environment as a whole or to select themes of, for example, architectural, historical or geographic interest. Hundreds of trails have been published by local authorities, amenity societies and teachers centres but the teacher will probably

TABLE 3.1

TRAFFIC CONGESTION

Passenger Car Units (P.C.U.) per vehicle

½ PCU	Cycle or Motorcycle
1 PCU	Car or Van
2 PCU	Bus or Lorry
3 PCU	Very heavy vehicle

Limit each hour	
375 PCU	2 lane road
688 PCU	3 lane road
1,512 PCU	Dual carriageway

OVERCROWDED

Amenities : Time and direction

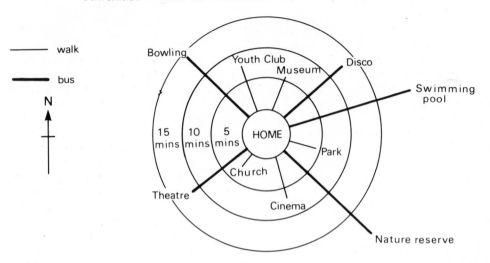

FIGURE 3.17

wish to devise a trail suited to particular needs, incorporating geographical and other skills as necessary. Some of the best trails pick out one or two main themes. These may be homes, places of work, dereliction, words or many of the themes already considered in this section. Careful guidance is necessary along a town trail as the children are likely to be working in groups without a teacher immediately to hand. There are many

opportunities on town trails to work with cameras and tape recorders. Instructions will include not only a map but carefully worded directions and questions, possibly with partially completed sentences and drawings to be filled in. Good vantage points should be sought and opening times carefully checked. Safety must be considered, including checks that such work is permitted by the school and local authority.

PARK USER COUNT				
PLACE : PARK GATE RECORDER				
DATE : 19ᵗʰ MAY John Smith				
	TIME 10.15–10.30			
Under 5 yrs	ﬀﬀﬀ I			
5–15 yrs	III			
Young Adults	ﬀﬀﬀ			
Middle Age	ﬀﬀﬀ IIII			
Elderly	ﬀﬀﬀ ﬀﬀﬀ ﬀﬀﬀ III			

PARK USER CENSUS

Male or female ?

Are you walking straight through the park ?

How often do you use the park?

In which part of town do you live?

How did you get here ?

How long did it take?

What do you dislike about the park ?

FIGURE 3.18

Scale
2 cm = 5 minutes
walk

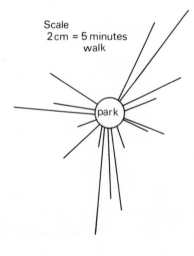

FIGURE 3.19
The area served by the park

3.2   Fieldwork in rural areas

Tom Dalton

Few rural areas of Britain are beyond the direct influence of urban centres. One should therefore view the human geography of rural areas within the context of a highly urbanised society. Towns act as magnets to rural residents who journey there for work, services and entertainment while town residents travel into the countryside in search of leisure and recreation. Regional decisions create population movement on a more permanent basis as New Towns and commuter villages have been established away from the large conurbations.

A base for concepts and skills development

A rural study provides for both town and country pupils a widening geographical experience. Like work in towns, fieldwork in rural areas will help to equip pupils with an array of skills such as the use of maps, accurate observation and recording and interpretation of data. Similarly skills can be developed in the use of such 'secondary' data as historical records and census returns so that the pupil appreciates the temporal as well as the spatial dimensions of the rural scene. First-hand experience can help to establish many primary concepts for pupils likely to be characterised by many aspects of the 'concrete' stage of development in Piaget's terms. The immediate experience of such phenomena as farms, villages and rivers facilitates the pupils' ability to understand complex relationships later. The gathering of factual information should be seen as a means of understanding key concepts relating to the rural environment. In a study of road transport for example, the Schools Council History, Geography and Social Science Project suggests that

PLATE 4.   *A group of juniors with worksheets and clipboards*

key concepts relating to conflict/consensus might be introduced at an early age: what are the conflicting interests and values relating to road development?, or the key concept of similarity/difference: are our road transport problems similar to those in the past—or different? By focusing on a series of concepts, the rural study therefore enables a range of skills to be deployed in practical activities.

Other organising concepts may demonstrate the processes of decision-making. Within the middle school it is desirable to encourage pupils to understand how decisions within the community are made. Returning to the topic of transport would we think it appropriate among many other questions, to ask 'Who has the power to make decisions about roads?' There are many community issues relating to bus-services, play space, leisure amenities and control of development which can be incorporated into a rural environmental studies programme.

A progression of concepts and skills

In rural study a progression of concepts, ideas and skills should be evident. In *New Thinking in School Geography* (DES, 1972), it is suggested that the pupils' learning is assisted by defining a sequence which moves from a foundation of elements and simple relationships and classifications in the primary school to systems, general

---

1. What is the relief of the farm?
2. How does the soil vary in type, texture and depth from one part of the farm to another?
3. Does the clay with flints present any special problem?
4. What is unusual about the structure of the farmhouse?
5. How large is the farm?
6. How large are the orchards?
7. How much pasture is there?
8. How much arable land is there?
9. List the crops and acreage - C for cash, F for fodder.
10. How many sheep are there?
11. When are most sold?
12. At which market are they sold?
13. Have the types of sheep any special advantage?
14. How many cattle are there?
15. What machinery is there on the farm?
16. How many people are employed on the farm?
17. Are any extra hands taken on?
18. What is the best position for the orchards on the farm?
19. What fruits are grown?
20. How old is a tree before it becomes fruitful?
21. For how long does the average tree remain fruitful?
22. Is irrigation practised?
23. What is the ideal weather for a bumper harvest?
24. Can the orchard be protected against frost?
25. How is the fruit stored?
26. Is the fruit moved by the farmer's own transport?
27. To which markets is it moved?
28. How does the farmer combat such fruit-growing problems as disease?
29. What advantages has this farm for fruit growing?
30. Sum up the pattern of land-use on the farm.
31. How are the hops planted, cut and grown?
32. Do they demand special conditions of relief or soil?
33. Sketch the stringing system and the plan of an oast house.
34. Say briefly how the hops are dried and prepared.

FIGURE 3.20   An example of a farm study questionnaire: Heart's Delight Farm, near Kingston, Canterbury
(From Archer, J. and Dalton, T. *Fieldwork in Geography*, 2nd ed. London: Batsford, 1970, pp. 104-5)

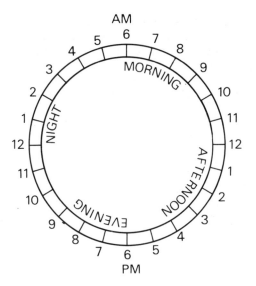

FIGURE 3.21   The farmer's day

concepts and theories in the upper secondary school. Let us illustrate a progression of work on the topic of *farming*.

Farm Studies

For younger pupils a farm visit will be a 'discovery' type of exercise in which the *distinguishing and classification* of kinds of animals, crops and machinery can lead on to a great deal of creative 'interdisciplinary' work. The jobs of the people who work on the farm will be significant. The shepherd, the dairy herdsman, the tractor driver will be people the children will want to question. In the upper stages of the primary school the processes of classification and systematising become more important. As the land use of a particular farm is studied it can be compared with other farms and the idea will be developed that farms may be classified into types such as arable, stock or mixed. The children will still be gathering information about the farm but will begin to ask questions about why one differs from another. Why is the land use different in the valley floor to that on the steep hillslope? Why are certain crops/activities more accessible to the farm-buildings than others? Such questions lead on to an establishment of relationships and the understanding of geographical ideas. There is an ordering of knowledge into recurring patterns and relationships.

A teachers' preparatory procedure for a farm study with upper juniors might be as follows:

1. Reconnoitre the area to identify range, type of farms, access for coach etc., using 1:25 000 maps, geology maps.
2. Interview the farmer. The local National Farmers' Union Branch is often a useful contact for farmers willing to collaborate.
3. Devise a questionnaire (Fig. 3.20) together with plans of the farm—buildings, the fields in the unit and circular charts to illustrate the use of time on a daily or yearly basis (Figs. 3.21 - 3.24). Incorporate children's own questions.
4. Decide on organisation and recording apparatus for the visit. How far will the interview with the farmer be structured? Will the children make notes at the time? Will they *all* do this? Will portable tape-recorders be used? Will there be an initial class activity with the farmer and then particular groups undertake certain tasks, e.g. soil collection, further interviews with members of the farm staff, sketching (see Fig. 3.25), undertaking a transect walk across the farm etc?

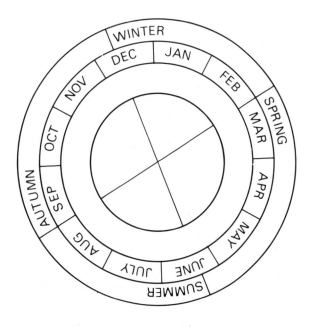

FIGURE 3.22   The farmer's year

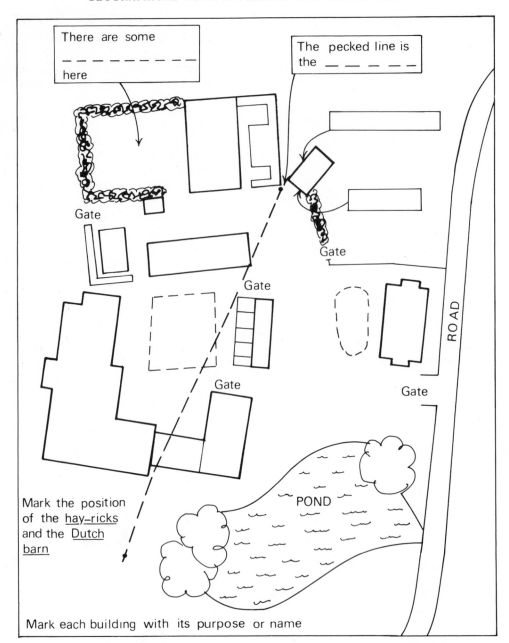

There are some _ _ _ _ _ _ here

The pecked line is the _ _ _ _ _ _

Gate

Gate

Gate

Gate

Gate

Gate

ROAD

POND

Mark the position of the <u>hay–ricks</u> and the <u>Dutch barn</u>

Mark each building with its purpose or name

FIGURE 3.23 The buildings of a farm on the Isle of Wight

5. Discuss with the pupils the plan for the visit. It is useful to make reference material available, e.g. books, pictures on types of crops or machinery.

Following the visit other kinds of activities can be introduced such as games playing. One farming game for example illustrates how 'unseen' variables such as the weather, and political decisions about subsidies not only affect the profitability of the farm in the current year but

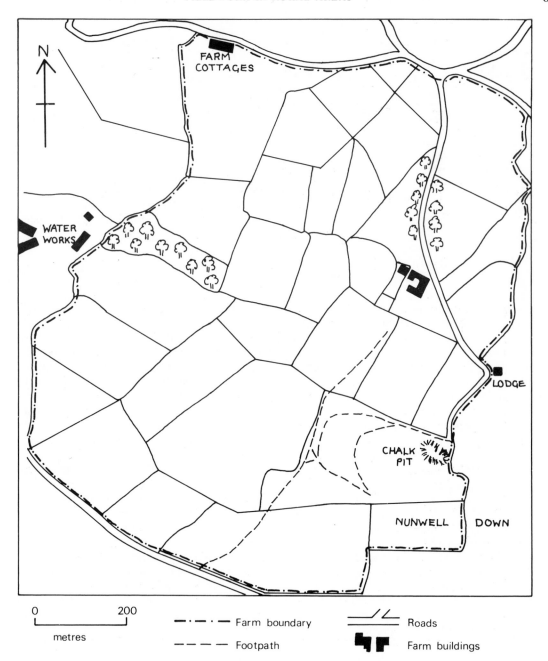

FIGURE 3.24   *Map of the fields of an Isle of Wight farm (on which pupils can insert land use)*

FIGURE 3.25   Sketch of Timberden Valley, Kent, for completion by 11-year-old pupils

lead to different decisions about land use in the following year. Such pupil activity avoids superficial conclusions about the variation of land use based on visual evidence alone. The pupil's understanding of the impact of distance, varying altitude and geology can be tested out by getting them to make decisions as role-playing farmers. This introduces problem-solving and facilitates the transfer of understanding to new situations. Examples of this type of exercise are to be found in *'Food and Farming'* (*People and Places,* 1) by Tony Crisp (1974), where ideas on slopes and farming are applied to Andean farms (p.39) and where the effect of soils is considered (p.47). Similarly Cole and Beynon (1969) in *New Ways in Geography* have designed exercises concerned with distance and spatial arrangement.

A study of a rural parish with 11-13-year-old pupils could include group surveys of a number of farms. A picture of land use could also be built up by allocating sections of the 1:25 000 Ordnance Survey maps mounted on card to the groups and finally putting together the mosaic of the parish. 'Secondary' support materials can also be introduced comprising recent parish acreage returns presenting types of land use in simple graphical form.

Residential Land Use

In a rural area there are many opportunities for surveying the varying styles and locations of residences. Developing from picture drawing of houses and model making with infants, simple plans for recording can be introduced from 7 years onwards. The recording on these plans may relate to type of houses (flats, detached etc.), type of building materials or age. It may of course be part of a wider survey, including services and industry. It may be related to the 'natural' growth of an old village centre or to the mushroom growth of a new housing estate on the outskirts of an existing centre. An example of a building survey in a Kent village (10-12-year-olds) is given in Figures 3.26 and 3.27.

A useful method of introducing varying types of buildings to the pupils is the trail or structured walk. This is the equivalent of the nature trail aiming to give the pupil an understanding of the changing built environment. The worksheet for the pupil will include simple maps, questions about particular buildings, drawings to undertake completely or line drawings to annotate. For older pupils a photocopy of an historical map of the village is a suitable base on which to record recent developments.

The mobility of rural residents is a modern phenomenon. A survey of the period of residence of those who work in agriculture, those who work in the village providing a service for those in the village or other villages and of those who work elsewhere can provide an illuminating corrective to the idea of a predominantly farming community. Interesting data could be gathered on what residents perceive as the advantages or disadvantages of living in this community. Historical accounts of village life in the 19th century can be

VILLAGE BUILDING SURVEY — Chilham, Kent

On the outline map we shall classify buildings according to use and age. The age groupings will help us to see the original site and nucleus of the village. It will also show us at a glance the later areas of development. The actual shape of the village will be of interest to us - it may give a pattern which was one of defence - houses were often built close to the church which itself could be a stronghold - does Chilham look this type?

Key to use

Houses	H
Shops	S
Cafes and Restaurants	R
Farms	F
Workshops	W
Churches	C
Social Centre	Sc
Any other building	M

Dating a House
TIMBER & PLASTER HOUSES
Overhanging upperfloors 15th, 16th or early 17th century.
Pointed gable fronts
Uprights close together 15th Century Medieval

Few uprights, diagonal braces 16th or early 17th century Tudor
BRICK HOUSES (Usually red)
Elaborate doorways, panelled doors, fanlight over door, fashioned 17th, 18th, 19th century
MODERN HOUSES
Larger windows, plain design, 20th century

Other activities:
a) Do sketches of these different types of houses and the church
b) Discover how far away the nearest urban centre for work and entertainment is. What is the means of transport? How long does it take?

FIGURE 3.26   A building survey in a Kent village

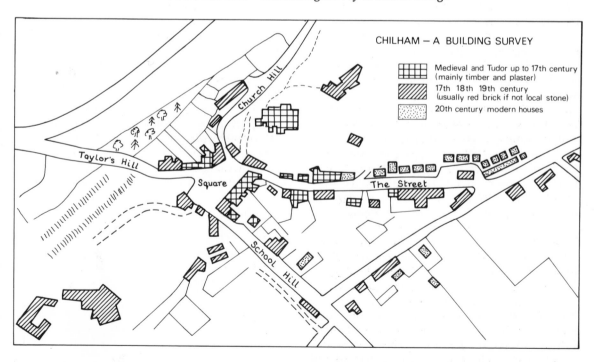

FIGURE 3.27

PLATE 5. The Square, Chilham, Kent

compared with life today. Some elderly residents may be willing to be tape-recorded on the changing village.

Environmental Quality

This could be examined in terms of quality of life in a community. What happens when rural dwellers have to choose another residence? What are the alternatives available to them when houses in the village are bought by 'outsiders?' How far have the people concerned got any control over events? What values guide the planners? What values do the people concerned use in deciding where it is best to live? This could lead to pupils of 10+ looking at the facilities available in their own neighbourhood—play, shopping, work (and school), recreation and housing—and seeing how far these meet the needs of various groups in the community—children, teenagers, housewives, fathers, old people. Points could be allocated according to availability/distance of these amentities. Material such as New Town Development films would illustrate the comparative advantages or disadvantages of other centres. A survey of the views of local inhabitants would indicate what they perceived as the qualities of their home area.

Ways of analysing how children perceive their own neighbourhood were investigated as part of a survey of young children's views of Small Heath, Birmingham. One method relating to environmental quality involved the compilation of a series of adjectival pairs arising from the children's own comments about Small Heath e.g. safe for children, dangerous for children. These two descriptions judged as opposite in meaning formed the extreme poles of a 5 point scale. Thus a '1' would be recorded if he viewed the environment as 'safe' and a '5' if it was considered 'dangerous' with 2, 3 or 4 if it was judged as somewhere between the extremes. A rating of '3'

Village	A	B	C	D
Play Group (1)				
Play Park (2)				
Football Pitch (3)				
Hall for Scouts/ Brownies etc. (4)				

FIGURE 3.28 *Provision of recreational amenities*

would represent a midway position. This semantic differential technique was applied in the following 15 cases.

1. Friendly - Unfriendly
2. Safe for children - Dangerous for children
3. Well kept - Badly kept
4. Interesting - Boring
5. Violent - Peaceful
6. Dirty - Clean
7. Like to live there - Would not like to live there
8. Polluted - Free from pollution
9. Littered - Tidy
10. Noisy - Quiet
11. People nice to know - People are not nice to know
12. Makes me feel happy - Makes me feel sad
13. Good schools - Bad schools
14. Old - New
15. Good - Bad

(From Spencer, D. and Lloyd, J. *A Child's Eye View of Small Heath, Birmingham,* Birmingham: Centre for Urban and Regional Studies, 1974, p.63).

The first case judged Small Heath as it is. The children then repeated the exercise indicating how, ideally, they would like to see Small Heath in the future. This exercise could be adapted in very different kinds of school environments. Children will want to express their views in very different ways—in stories, poems, picture form.

The role of planning is likely to become an important discussion point—how could the amenities be developed, how could the environment for them and for other groups be improved? Plans and models might be made and consultations with local authority planners arranged.

Children are very aware of *recreational amenities* in rural areas. The location of places to play or centres of entertainment such as cinemas can be located and mapped, recording the children's views on accessibility and extent of provision. Rural areas despite the amount of 'open space' are sometimes seriously deprived of appropriate recreational areas. If a rural school draws in children from several villages the extent of provision could be compared and a matrix constructed to show this (Fig. 3.28). Points could be given for each and a league table built up or single graphs (Fig. 3.29) could be mounted adjacent to each village on a 1:25 000 or 1:50 000 map.

Transport

Surveys could be made of the use of local roads in the rural area. What is the proportion of cycles, motor-cycles, cars, lorries, buses, etc.? What is the flow of traffic at different times of the day? Is there special pressure on the area at weekends, holiday times—where are the parking facilities? If it is a tourist area a sample survey of how people have travelled and the areas from which they have travelled could be conducted.

One may start with a local issue and work outwards towards a more general consideration of roads. For example, the irregular/insufficient provision of bus services in some rural areas is a very contentious issue. The number of buses per day along certain routes into the nearby urban centre could be recorded and drawn on a tracing overlay of a 1:50 000 or 1:25 000 O.S. map. The thickness of the line would indicate the number per day. The pupils could decide on the basis of discussion and interview with local inhabitants which villages are deprived. The intrusion of new motorway development is a common experience in rural areas. The planning materials, local

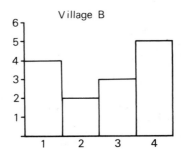

FIGURE 3.29 Graphs showing provision of recreational amenities

newspaper coverage, public enquiries, views of pressure groups and other interested parties provide pupil resources. There may be two or three alternative routes at the planning stage. Junior and middle school pupils are capable of discussing these, making models, taking photographs and getting the views of interested and opposing parties leading to simulation and role play exercises.

Rural Service Centres

The provision of services—libraries, medical, fire, police, etc., but especially shopping—provide a wide range of variation in rural areas. There will be the single village shop, the larger village centre and the new hypermarket set away from existing village settlements. The interdependence of town and country is well illust-

rated by the kinds of shopping village residents do locally and the kinds for which they must travel into the nearby town. Recording the ways local shoppers travel, their origin and frequency of visit can be done by single questionnaire and perhaps subsequently compared by exchange of information with a nearby settlement. Alternatively for older pupils the importance of competing neighbouring towns can be worked out. A list of shopping goods is arrived at—furniture, shoes, clothing etc. If the interviewee in the village replies that only one urban centre is used a full point is awarded to that centre but if two centres are used each gets ½ point or if three are regularly used each gets ⅓ point. By adding up each town's score at the end of the list the extent of the village's dependence on particular centres can be worked out and discussed.

4. Resources for learning: using primary and secondary sources

4.1 Games and Simulations

Rex Walford

CHILDREN ARE NO STRANGERS . . . .

Children of primary and middle school age are no strangers to the idea of games and simulations—even if they may not explicitly recognise the activity in the classroom as the cousin of what they do in the playground. There is little doubt that from their very earliest time in school (and in many cases preceding that, at home) they imaginatively enter the world of other people by pretending to *be* other people. Hardly a reception class is without its 'Wendy' house in which the duties of householders are simulated for both learning and enjoyment; the 'classroom shop' is a regular feature of many infant classrooms where numerous (and numerate) transactions take place, as children alternate between playing shopkeepers and customers.

And in other areas, also, the simple simulation of some experience is a natural consequence of a teacher's desire to make a situation 'real', and to supplement exposition and individual inquiry with some kind of activity which appeals to both cognitive and affective domains and which makes suitable group work. For instance, at the conclusion of a unit of work on a particular country in one primary school that I visited, the teacher had acquired a film which she wished to show the children. Instead of sitting them down to view the film in the orthodox 'cinema' tradition, by judicious and imaginative use of chairs and tables, she turned the classroom into a motor-coach. The film was projected from the 'back of the coach' so that it appeared to the 'passengers' (the children) that it was the scenery being seen through the front window. The sound-track of the film was turned down, and commentary was supplied by some of the class who acted as 'couriers'—having already studied particular parts of the country (and the film) in advance. This was an activity entirely in the spirit of simulation, and one which, according to the class teacher herself, enhanced both class participation and geographical understanding beyond what might have occurred in more traditional approaches.

A good deal has been written about simulation as an activity in secondary school classrooms, but it would be unwise to extrapolate the same principles into work with younger children without some preliminary considerations.

SIMULATONS: VARIETIES AND OBJECTIVES

It may be unprofitable to become involved in an arcane discussion about what simulation actually 'is', since there is no doubt that the edges of the methodology are blurred and that definitions in themselves become the focus for a quite separate and self-generating set of arguments. Suffice it to say that the act of simulation usually stems from the injunction to 'put yourself in the place of . . . .' and that varieties of the technique have developed from such a starting point. Within some classrooms a structured set of rules may be introduced so that children 'play a game' as they simulate; in other classrooms, the teacher may be developing a free-form improvised discussion with pupils contributing from the role viewpoint which they have been given (or have chosen to take). Again, some simulation become primarily an activity in which pupils work at problems through pencil and paper; in other cases, they may be quite actively involved in moving about the room, or even the whole school environment as they play out a particular situation.

What binds such diverse activities together is intention; the intention to replicate some other situation in order to better understand it, or to reveal its conflicts and facets. Consequently, it often also represents a simplification of that situation, and a compression of it in time and space. For example, if children are to represent different groups of people in different countries, they may go so far as to go into different rooms, but they clearly will not separate out into an exact parallel of the physical spatial separation; similarly, if the activity is to replicate, say, a set of meetings between villagers and their local government, the meetings will not take the actual time that they would in real life. This collecting of the essence of a situation is usually referred to as 'modelling' by those who make simulations, but it should be clearly realised that the term encompasses *more* than the purely physical hardware modelling which is a regular ingredient of primary and middle school work. But in using the term, the link between say, the physical modelling of a farm, and the human modelling of a farmer's problems is properly made.

Within the primary and middle school, simulation often looks like drama—with which it has many affinities. Simulation is *not* 'pure drama' however, partly because of differences in intention and partly because to simulate, one does not always have to enter into the other world as fully. It is possible to seek to simulate a decision-making problem, for instance, and concentrate on the evidence, the data, and the conflict of the decision without necessarily adopting the lifestyle; thus, within simulation activities there is often the curious and rather useful attribute of being able to consider dispassionately the whole situation whilst arguing from a particular point of view. With younger children, however, the wholeheartedness of participation does not always induce such a potentially useful 'schizophrenia'; indeed, it is the very absence of self-consciousness of many children in the 5-13 age group which gives them easier access to the understanding of simulation's purpose than some of their older counterparts. But in post-simulation discussion, the 'other point of view' can usually enhance the wholeheartedness of the original stance.

The affinity between simulation (used as a teaching tool to develop knowledge and understanding of particular events or environments) and techniques used in educational drama for their own sake is sometimes striking; there is no doubt that these two happily overlap on many occasions and that teachers may be teaching something *about,* say, coal-mining by a colliery simulation, whilst at the same time developing self-expression, imagination and control *through* drama approaches. The work of such educationalists as Dorothy Heathcote and Brian Way has much in common with those who come to use methods of improvisation and role-play for other purposes. There should be no particular concern to draw boundaries, let alone battle-lines in this area; those teachers whose training has given them 'drama' proficiencies may well turn the insights of such courses towards the improvement and the greater effectiveness of simulation approaches in history, religious studies, geography or that multitude of activities within 5-13 classrooms which it is either impossible or unprofitable to label by subject.

There are several general educational aims and objectives which are furthered by almost all simulation activity, irrespective of topic. These include:

1. the development of participation in group activity;
2. the establishment of social skills in talking, negotiating, persuading and working with other pupils;
3. the development of literacy and numeracy through the incidental work required (and often achieved successfully because of great motivation to do so);
4. the practice and development of decision-making in a rational and considered manner;
5. the combining of thinking and feeling about

situations and problems (the linking of the 'cognitive' and 'affective' domains of the child).

SIMULATIONS AND GEOGRAPHY

More distinctively, however, simulation approaches are useful to *geographers* because of their ability to illuminate and transmit understanding of parts of the subject at various levels. Those advantages most usually claimed include:
1. the development of empathy with people of other places and cultures;
2. the understanding of working processes and systems;
3. the realisation of the interdisciplinary nature of most 'real-life' situations.

In the last decade, the great growth of simulation activity in all forms of education—spreading initially from war-gaming and business studies at the adult level—has stimulated much research into the validity of claims about these objectives. Though this is not the appropriate place to consider at length the findings of such research, it can be said that simulations have proved themselves in most cases at least as effective in teaching information as alternative methods, and (again, in most cases) better motivators. The technique could scarcely have survived its early honeymoon period were it not also for the fact that many teachers have continued to use the technique following their own personal evaluations of its use within their programme of work.

It is difficult, however, to apply orthodox educational evaluative tools to ·the 'understandings' which the technique often seeks to promote, and this is frequently a cause for frustration; if a group takes part in a farming game, for instance, it may be relatively easy to test their understanding of crop yields or weather frequencies—but these are only the nuts and bolts of the game. If the teacher is aiming to have the children become aware of the problems facing Third World farmers, it is difficult to easily scale the 'awareness' or the 'problem-solving ability' induced, except by another farming game! Indeed, the problem is often compounded because group experiences may be interpreted and received differently by individuals, and the prospective evaluator knows that there may not be 'right answers' to which he can conveniently ask 'right questions'.

SOME EXAMPLES

Most users of simulations are those who themselves have experienced the power of the technique through involvement as a participant in the activity; and writers on the topic can do small justice to the essence and the charm of the technique. It may therefore be most useful to describe briefly some different kinds of simulation which are appropriate for the 5-13 age group and which have been put to practical use by teachers.

A 'Hardware' Simulation: *Operation Columbus* (with 9-year-olds)

The teacher was trying to find a way to give the class an experience of what it was like to *be* an early explorer—rather than have them merely read about it. So, with the prior agreement of the Head, one morning at break she devised a 'mock universe' in the school hall (see Fig. 4.1) made up of tables and chairs. She then told the children that they were going to explore the mock 'world' to see if they could bring back the treasures from the Spice Islands, but that it would be a long and hazardous journey.

The 'hazards' of exploration were introduced by blindfolding the potential explorers and then letting them loose at the hall doors to 'feel' their way cautiously around the chairs and tables. Of course, some children explored carefully, others boldly; they were told they must take only five minutes before they came out of the hall, otherwise they would be deemed to be dead or shipwrecked. A transistor radio fixed near the door acted as a 'compass bearing' for them and gave them a clue as to which direction they were facing.

An added factor in the unexplored world was that of 'natives' (other children) standing within the continents that were set up. These natives were told that they could not speak to the explorers, but could aid or hinder them as they wished (i.e. they could be friendly or hostile) in pointing them towards or away from the 'Spice Islands' (which were, in fact, a plate of chocolate drops in the centre of a table).

Some explorers circled the same islands aimlessly and fruitlessly; others sought more systematic approaches and although lucky enough to find the island, failed to discover the spices themselves. Throughout the exploration, the *actual*

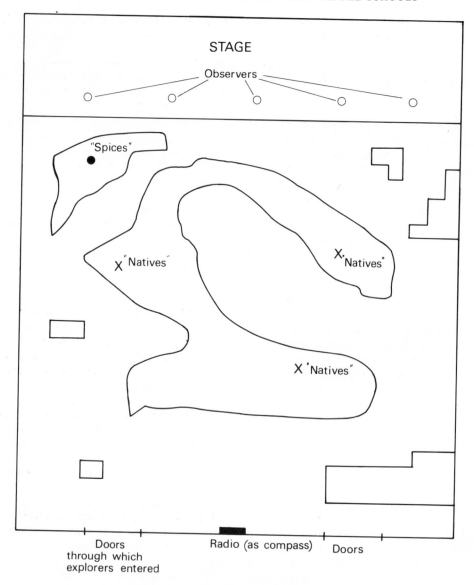

FIGURE 4.1 Operation Columbus

routes of the blindfolded explorers were carefully charted by another group of children standing on the stage of the Hall—these routes were used for discussion afterwards; the explorers themselves, however, had to draw maps as best they could remember 'the world' when they came out of the Hall. Thus there were many exaggerations and imperfections from their memory; these were passed on to a second generation of explorers who examined them before being blindfolded and allowed into 'the world' to carry on

the explorations. Three generations of explorers went into the Hall in all.

Following the explorations (an activity of much excitement and seriousness at the same time), the class returned to their classroom and recounted their experiences, looked at the maps of the observers and compared their own journeyings with reality (e.g. Henry Hudson's belief that the Hudson Bay was a new ocean, etc.). The teacher reflected on the simulation and revised it for further use. On a subsequent occasion the school field was used, since there were less obvious 'boundaries' to the world than in the Hall: this had the effect of inducing more cautious exploration and of 'losing' some unfortunate explorers altogether, as they wandered away from the 'continents' into limbo . . . .!

A Pencil and Paper Operational Game:
Third World Farming (with 10-11-year-olds)
The teacher was developing a unit of work concerning life in Africa. The class had already looked at some pictures and a filmstrip about a West African village, and also considered some simple pamphlets produced by a charitable organisation. But the teacher sought to give the children an insight into the problems of making a living in such circumstances, so she introduced a version of a 'farming game'. The class were set up into small groups and told that they were neighbouring villages (the groups were threes and fours). They were then given a list of crops that they could grow (see Table 4.1) and told that these would grow differently according to the climate. Some time was spent explaining the reasons for differences in cash yield. The class were then told that they needed to make a certain amount of money each year to buy other food, and clothing for their basic needs.

The groups discussed their views, and decided on a planting policy, each group working under the assumption that they had five fields to plant and that these could not be sub-divided. When they had noted down their plantings, the teacher announced the weather for the year (drawn from a disc) and also a chance factor occurrence which affected some of the crops (e.g. a disease striking cassava and reducing its yield, or 'locust swarms decimate all maize fields and make the crops unsaleable'). Having survived the chance factor, the villages added up their cash yield from the year and announced if they had managed to make a basic living or not. Those who had not then 'borrowed' money from the teacher, who chalked up the 'debts' on the blackboard—this, she explained was how Third World countries became debtors of developed countries like Britain and America.

The groups tried again . . . .

After four rounds one group had done so badly that they were deemed to be 'near starvation'. The teacher asked other groups if they could spare any money to help them; this was met with

TABLE 4.1 Crop yields for Third World Farming Game (given to children)

These are the crops you can grow:	In a wet year the yield is:	In an average year the yield is:	In a dry year the yield is:
Maize ('mealies')	4	8	7
Millet ('Guinea corn')	5	7	6
Peas	4	5	6
Beans	4	4	5
Cassava (tapioca)	9	7	5

You must plant five fields each year. At least one must be maize or millet; at least one must be peas or beans. You need to make 30 units each year.

negative response since all the other groups were in difficulty. The teacher then assigned the 'starvation' group as refugees to the other groups and raised the amount of money that each of those groups had to make each year. This caused much consternation and argument and the teacher judged it the moment to stop the game and become involved in a discussion of the rights and wrongs of the matter and of the realities behind the simulation.

A Role-Play (based on a local issue) with 12-year-olds
A middle-school class were involved in a project about their own neighbourhood. One of the key issues current in the district was whether or not a new by-pass should be built around the shopping centre; in discussion before the project the class expressed their own views and were divided. The teacher decided that he would develop this into a simulation and evolved a list of people interested in the problem; the Chairman of the Shopkeepers' Association, the local police-sergeant in charge of traffic, a lady whose house would be knocked down if a particular by-pass route was chosen, a reporter from the local paper, and so on.

He then told the class that there was going to be an 'Inquiry' into the proposal for the by-pass in two weeks time, and that the Inquiry would be held in their classroom. He asked them which 'roles' they would like to take on, and assigned roles where no preference was expressed. Those who showed doubt or dismay in doing this were either made 'members' of a group of whom only one need speak (e.g. shopkeepers), or given some administrative role in the Inquiry. Each person role-playing was given a postcard with:

1. some background information about the role to be assumed;
2. some questions to help structure thinking about the problem;
3. some suggested sources and references to consult.

The pupils then had ten days to consult material available in the classroom (e.g. wall maps of the district with possible routes for the by-pass marked on them), and to go and visit anyone in the town who might be of help. The teacher arranged for other source material to be available in the school library, *if* asked for by the children.

Then one morning the 'Public Inquiry' about the new road was held; another teacher came in to play the role of the Government Inspector. The pupils were solemnly called to 'give evidence and state their views'; they were then asked questions by the Inspector, and sometimes by other children. Some disputes of fact broke out and were settled by recourse to library information; at other times impassioned feelings about the preservation of old buildings and of people's own homes were made very apparent. At the end of the Inquiry the Inspector deliberated and then offered a decision; it so happened that the decision almost exactly replicated that which was ultimately made at a similar Inquiry held in the town some six months later, when the participants were arguing realistically!

SOURCES OF SIMULATIONS

Sources of simple simulations may be found in the books listed in the appropriate section of Appendix 4. In addition, many simulations are to be found embedded in other materials, or produced in series (e.g. ILEA Simulation Kits, Longman Resource Unit Kits, etc.)

Elaborate simulation activities are often organised, either in schools or on their 'home ground' by local theatre-in-education teams, who have the opportunity to develop ideas in an extensive style. These are often absorbing and powerful, besides being original. But some of the best simulations are undoubtedly those designed simply by teachers for their own classes: a reliance on 'outside material' may be useful as a start, but not as a recurring policy.

The British society which encompasses the information and expertise about this technique holds an annual conference of simulations and talks about simulation. It is the Society for Academic Gaming and Simulation in Training and Education (SAGSET) and its Secretarial Office is listed in Appendix 2. An annual subscription brings not only membership, but a regular journal about simulation at all levels of education.

4.2   Pictures and slides

Gordon Harris

A well chosen set of illustrations or slides will often provide a valuable supplement to a given text or theme being studied by a group of children as they can provide a focal point for discussion and further development. As far as slides and filmstrips are concerned the problem at the present time is not one of shortage but rather of surplus. In deciding what choice to make it is preferable to select the theme to be studied and then to collect relevant illustrations rather than the reverse. If all planning and preparation of work-cards etc. is done well in advance it is not an impossible task.

There are two main sources of illustrations: there are those that are professionally produced and those that can be produced by the school. Many firms produce high quality slides which are to be preferred to filmstrips as they allow for greater selectivity and are easier to handle. In making a selection it is better to select the clear and uncluttered slides that do not try to cover too much detail. There is a tendency for some slides to be rather 'arty' which may be good art but tends to obscure their teaching value as far as geography is concerned. For most children in the 5-13 age group slides which cover one or two important points are a better buy. As with all other materials there is a need to see that the slides are up to date and present a true picture of current knowledge.

Magazines, coloured advertisements and newspapers are other useful sources of pictures. Many firms will also provide teaching materials and illustrations if approached. Wallcharts produced by a number of firms are generally concerned with particular themes. They need to be chosen with some care as they are often designed for a specific age group and because of production costs involved in up-dating them may be a little out of date. It would be a wise precaution, as with all visual aids, to order materials on approval.

School-produced illustrations, especially for locally based themes, are probably the most valuable as they are more likely to involve the children and teacher directly in their production. Colour slides and black-and-white photographs may easily be taken using a simple camera by even the most inexpert. In one infant school, for example, six-year-olds successfully took black-and-white photographs to illustrate a project they were involved in (Lawdale Infants School, Bethnal Green, London). Colour prints are a little more difficult and costly, but certainly not beyond the capabilities of most children. Teachers should also be able to take photographs to illustrate their teaching. Far greater interest will be shown in illustrations taken by and involving the teacher and the class. Children's own drawings and paintings are another valuable source which will involve children more closely in their work. Each drawing or painting should be titled and have a short and relevant text.

Many schools have a central collection of pictures and slides located in the school library or some other easily accessible point within the school; this is to be highly recommended. A simple method of classifying the pictures linked to that used in classifying the books needs to be used.

Even the best illustrations will lose their impact if badly displayed. They should be carefully trimmed and mounted on card or backing paper and clearly titled. There are several books giving ideas on displaying pictures and materials. Pictures should not be left on display for too long; after a time they will become an accepted part of the background and lose their point.

There is a certain amount of basic equipment that is needed if the best is to be made of a school's slide collection. As it is not always desirable to show slides to a whole class—especially if they are involved in group work—a number of cheap pocket viewers should be available for the children to view the slides individually. A simple child-proof projector is a useful addition so that children may run their own slide show, with the possible addition of a cassette recorder to allow them to tape their own commentary. Screens may be made from hardboard painted white and ideally should be part of the basic equipment of each classroom.

The following suggestions for the practical use of illustrations may be of use to teachers when planning lessons and schemes of work. They are only intended as suggestions, for each teaching and learning situation is unique and therefore there cannot be a single, common approach to a theme or lesson.

Workcards

Photographs, magazine illustrations etc. may be mounted on cards with directions and questions relating to them. For example:

Look at . . . . .
Find the . . . . .
How many . . . . .?
What do you think . . . . .?

Workcards may also be linked to a set of slides. Their great advantage is that they allow children to work at their own speed individually or to work within a group co-operatively.

Matching Illustrations

Packs of selected illustrations may be used that may be grouped together because of their particular relationships. For example:

A farmer and a tractor
A miner and a coal mine
A train, railway lines, a porter and signals
A river, a bridge, a barge and a dock

This exercise will be of value to young children but can be made more difficult for older children. For example:

A Stevenson's Screen and a wet and dry thermometer

A piece of chalk and a piece of flint

A map, a plane table, a compass, and a bench mark

A corrie, a glacier, moraine, and a U-shaped valley

In each case the reasons for the grouping should be given orally or written down so that children make it clear that they have understood the relationship of each member to the others in the same group or set.

Local Photographs

These are useful if the scheme of work involves local studies. The preparation should be similar to that for workcards. Questions and directions could be prefixed as follows:

What is this . . . . . ?

How can you get to . . . . . ?

Why is this building . . . . . ?

Look at the people in the street. What are they . . . . . ?

What do you know about this . . . . ?

Illustrations and Maps

Local illustrations may also be used to match actual locations on a map. This is a useful exercise as it gives practice in matching photographs with their symbolic cartographic representation. In choosing examples care should be taken to see that the illustrations are clear and contain sufficient evidence of their location. For example:

A bridge over a river

Crossroads

Part of a valley

A church

A level-crossing

Old and New Illustrations

Sets of 'then' and 'now' illustrations may be compared to form the basis for a discussion concerned with developments and changes over the years. Suitable topics might include:

Farming techniques

Transport (land, sea and air)

The docks

Holiday resorts

Shops

(Some local libraries have loan collections of old photographs).

Overlays

Photographs may be used with overlays to illustrate particular features; for example:

A scarp

Area of arable land

Buildings of a particular age

Road network

Areas of erosion

Photographs and Sketches

Photographs may be used as the basis for a sketch or a sketch map which may simplify or concentrate upon particular points of interest. For example:

Flood plain

Land use

Shopping areas

Illustrations as Clues

A small pack of illustrations could be used as clues to the location of a city, country or local site. The pack could be made more sophisticated with the inclusion of written clues, names of streets, bus tickets, annual events etc.

e.g. A pack to include Tower Bridge, The Mint, H.M.S. Belfast, part of the Tower of London, etc.

A set of questions could also be included relating to the area, for example:

Put a name to the illustrations.

How would you get to this area?

Name the tourist attractions of the area.

Have you been to the area?

What did you like in the area?

What are the different ways you can get to the area? (River, road, train.)

Tape/Slide Presentations

When children have completed some fieldwork, they could present some of their findings in the form of a tape/slide report. Ideally the children will have taken the photographs themselves and as many as possible will be involved in making the tape. A children's production under the guidance of the teacher will be of more value than a purely teacher-designed and operated report.

Exhibitions

A good way of completing a project is to stage an exhibition including some of the following:

The original scheme of work

Children's written work

Mapwork
Diagrams
Illustrations of children working in the field
    and in the classroom on the project

Photographs of places visited
Individual photographs to go with children's
    written work etc., etc.

4.3   Radio and Television

Brian Wright

The following may give something of a flavour of
the range and types of geographical resources
provided by school broadcasting:

The trouble with walking in towns is that we
spend so much of our time dodging the traffic
and hurrying to get to our destination, that we
don't have time to look around and see how the
town is put together. Our eyes tend to get lazy
and don't bother to tell our minds about all the
things they see, there's just too much going on
anyway. In this programme I'm going to suggest how we can use a town trail to help us
make more of your town. And town trails are
just simple guides—routes around any town
which you can make and use to get to know
your town better.

That was how a radiovision programme from
Exploration Earth (Radio, 10-12s) began.

The Teachers' Notes for the series *Near and
Far* (Television, 9-11s) contains the following
extract about life in an Alpine village:

Livigno was, until recently, a relatively inaccessible village, particularly in winter when
the winding narrow roads into Italy ('into'
being very much the way the people of Livigno
regard their relationship with the rest of Italy)
were liable to be blocked by avalanches and
heavy snow falls. The long winters were a
relatively quiet and inactive period for the
population. The opening in 1970 of a new road
tunnel providing access from Switzerland has
changed all this.

The radio series *Man* for 10-12-year-olds aims
to help children towards a fuller understanding of
man and the societies in which he lives. For

example, in a programme called 'A camp in the
forest' the listeners were introduced to the life of
the Baka Pygmies.

Resource Unit: Geography (Television, 11-13s)
covers popular geographical themes like the
effects of glaciation or the location of the iron and
steel industry or life in an under-developed
country. Each programme is self-contained so
that teachers can record the programmes and
place them in their own schemes of classwork.

Geography broadcasts for primary and middle
schools set out to use the strengths of radio and
television to:

1. encourage children to be active and interested;
2. make pupils aware of their own environment
   and the wider world;
3. create empathy not only with the person who
   lives far away but also with the one just around
   the corner;
4. help develop simple geographical skills like
   map reading or observation and recording or
   finding, conveying and analysing information.

Radio and television programmes for the
primary school, though firmly founded on good
geographical practice, are made very much with
the non-specialists in mind. They are there to
help and enrich, not overwhelm and mystify. For
example, in an age when geography has a more
and more specialist vocabulary the language of
radio and television at this younger age range
remains both everyday and imaginative.

What is it about radio and television that user-
teachers most value? Many say that it is the
reality and immediacy of broadcasts. A description of an Atlantic storm direct from a weather
ship can claim in a sense to be more first hand
than your rain gauge which tells you how much
rain has fallen since noon yesterday. The sound

of a tropical downpour is perhaps more meaningful than any written or spoken description. And meeting James Abongo who is 16 and shares the family compound with 19 other relations adds a whole new dimension of understanding about life in a less-developed country. There is too another sense in which broadcasts are especially real; as one school television producer put it:

Even when exploring popular territory, television has a natural tendency to come up with the unexpected—surprises, inconsistencies and all. This is partly because filming is guided very much by the way things really are, irrespective of whether they fit a preconceived model.

The reality conveyed by broadcasts allows the pupil to compare and contrast the world outside the classroom with his own world. The events and situations in broadcasts often have a particularly direct and personal appeal to pupils so that their involvement is heightened, their imagination engaged and their experience extended and enriched.

Teachers also value broadcasts because they provide information not otherwise readily available and in a form which cannot be matched in the classroom. The information will be up to date and the illustrations vivid. Television, for example, is increasingly making use of animated designs to explain things like how a volcano erupts or a glacier moves. Non-specialist teachers look to broadcasts to provide them with a framework in which to work. They can, in the best sense, depend on television and radio. The programmes provide a balanced diet and a logical structure, and take account of the latest developments in the subjects and teaching methods. Of course, they still require good preparation and follow-up by the teachers. Only the classroom teacher knows the abilities of his or her children and is uniquely able to exploit the broadcast material.

A very big reason for using broadcasts is that children like them. They find them lively, interesting and stimulating. Thus while there is no reason why a teacher who wishes to study moorlands or deserts or the River Amazon should wait for the BBC to start him or her off, it is surprising how often a broadcast—in radio and television—does give just that initial impetus. Or is it surprising—because a broadcast is (or should be) an expert production based on up-to-date information and geared to the level and interest of the watching or listening class.

In the 5-9 age range most 'geography' programmes are included in miscellany series like *Watch, Merry-go-Round and Springboard.* Currently (1980), for example, in *Watch* (Television 6-8s) there are some programmes on Africa. *Merry-go-Round* (Television, 8 and 9) has a unit on simple map work. *Springboard* (Radio, 7-9s) has programmes on rivers and on Ireland, Scotland and Wales. In the 10-11 age range a series called *Mindstretchers* had five-minute programmes which encouraged children to consider problems based on, say, an environmental dilemma or a weather observation.

In the 9-11 age range the programmes tend to be labelled as geography because the evidence which the BBC receives from teachers indicates that, even if teachers are approaching geography through the medium of integrated studies or topic work, they prefer series to be subject labelled. At present the main series in the age range are *Exploration Earth,* and *Near and Far.* At 11-13, whether children are in middle schools or secondary schools, they require broadcast resources of a distinctly specialist geographical nature and *Resource Unit: Geography* is designed for mediation by specialist subject teachers.

Exploration Earth (Radio 10-12s) aims to interest children in their environment, to be active in exploring it and to lead them to understand the environments of people elsewhere in the world. Further, the programmes try to provide a structure which will help teachers to organise their classroom work in a way which will give the children a sense of variety and logical development. *Exploration Earth* usually contains some radiovision programmes. Radiovision, consists of a filmstrip which is bought from the BBC and the broadcast, which is tape recorded off-air, and the two are run concurrently. *Near and Far* (Television 9-11s) aims to widen children's knowledge and understanding of their environment and to help them to compare it with environments of people in more distant places. The series endeavours to introduce a number of simple geographical ideas and to encourage the development of skills. As mentioned earlier, *Resource Unit: Geography* covers popular geographical themes taught in both years of the audience age range. The BBCs *Annual Programme for Schools* shows which topics these series are currently covering or what new series may have been established since this article was written. Teachers in Scotland, Wales and Northern Ireland will need no reminding that the BBC in their national regions provides programmes of local geographical interest.

Broadcasts are not a magic cure-all. But nor are they just a kind of audio-visual waffle. They *are* providers of real-life flavour, vivid illustrations, up-to-date information and they *do* present in a lively, stimulating and catalytic way things not available elsewhere.

4.4 Books

Gordon Harris

While first-hand learning situations for children are likely to be more vivid and best remembered it is obviously not possible—unless the child's education in geography is to be severely parochial—for all learning to be of this nature, even if it is desirable. Few children are able to absorb and understand all they see or hear for the first time. Books, properly used, allow children to learn at their own speed and for themselves; they provide a valuable source of 'follow-up' material that may be linked with periods of discussion and other audio-visual aids (see section 4.2).

The use of books in the classroom is an important way of reducing the amount of 'chalk and talk' as well as giving a good indication of how to write and the difference between spoken and written language. The books should be related to the interests of the children and to those stimulated by the teacher, but it should be remembered that '. . . .the prime purpose of books in the school is not to provide the impetus for work—although on occasions they do this—but to supplement the personal experiences of the children with further information' (Purton, 1970). Books are not, and should never be used as, a substitute for teachers and good teaching but as a useful and important supplement. 'Whether interests originate with the children or are stimulated by the school, the teacher must not abdicate in favour of books but give continuous guidance and support' (DES, 1967). This implies that teachers must be well read: ' . . . activities and investigations by children demand that the teacher must read: unless the teacher naturally enjoys and uses books and reference sources, it is unlikely the children will' (Ministry of Education, 1967). Books, too, should be readily available, as children's interests, especially those of the younger ones, are immediate. Availability will also mean that the children get into the habit of referring to books and they should ' . . . . be encouraged to handle books and browse, look at pictures and talk about what they have seen' (Ministry of Education, 1967).

The Department of Education and Science has stressed officially the importance they give to the use of books and their part in the education of children. 'A room equipped with books . . . is a storehouse of geographical experiences which may be left to carry their own messages or used by the teacher as he might use a series of broadcast lessons, to stimulate questions, discussion and further enquiry ' (DES, 1972, p.16). The use of books in this way gives purpose to reading which is not always apparent in many of the reading books and reading schemes in schools. The geography books in the classroom should be part of the overall reading scheme of the whole school. They should be selected to match the reading ability and age of the children who will use them. A useful addition to the ordinary text and reference books would be a selection of story books from other lands. Many publishers now include these in their catalogues and they can be an important source of background material and give additional interest to work in progress.

When children are asked to refer to books they should be given direct references: e.g. 'Look at page 9 of *Roads*. Find out all you can about Stane

Street. Where is it? Why was it built? How was it built?' etc. Teachers, especially of younger children, should use the books with the children. They should read from the book and show the pictures to the class and discuss what they have read and can see in the pictures. This co-operative effort by the teachers and the pupils will lead to a greater understanding of the book's contents and will encourage children to use books as a form of reference.

Workcards are a useful way of directing children's attention to books. Workcards may direct children to particular books, refer to particular sections of a book, pose questions to be answered in the children's own words from the text of the book or base their questions on particular illustrations in a particular book. Having collected the information and ideas the next step might well be for the children to write their own book. In this way they will be able to have practice in the writing of factual as well as the more usual imaginative material.

The choice of books is important: they should be attractive and have 'child appeal'. They should be suitable for the reading ages and chronological ages of the children concerned and should be well illustrated and printed. Where possible they should be written by an author with first-hand experience of the area with which the book is concerned and of the age group for whom the book is intended. Illustrations are especially important when considering younger children. This does not mean that the quality of the text should be ignored. It should be clear and straightforward with the correct terminology used instead of misleading euphemisms. The books themselves should not be more than a few years old as geographical information can become out of date very quickly. Publication dates need to be checked and if books have been revised the extent of the revision needs to be ascertained. If no publication dates are given it might be sensible to ignore the book or check with the publisher before purchasing.

Catalogues should be freely available for the staff so that they are aware of the latest publications. Some schools have a book purchasing committee which is to be recommended as it does enable teachers to select for the whole school rather than just considering the needs of a particular class in isolation.

There is probably little value in having a set of more than half a dozen texts for the class or school. It is generally agreed that it is better to have a large number of small sets which will have a greater variety of interest and presentation and ideas which may be linked to a well thought out scheme of work. The Gittins Report of 1967 complained that '. . . there are still too many text books and too few books of information in the school' (Ministry of Education, 1967). In a great many schools this situation has now been remedied. A collection of reference books in the school library would be an added bonus.

There are certain basic skills that children need to learn if they are to get the most out of books. It should be remembered when considering these that from the infants' school through the junior school to the middle school and secondary level and beyond the learning processes are—or should be—part of a continuous development. The groundwork of this process is done in the primary schools and it is important that teachers in primary schools should be aware of what is needed both for the age range with which they are concerned and for the post-primary stage. The following points need to be considered when children are being shown how to use books.

1. Priority must be given to reading with understanding; just because a child can parrot his way through a text, little or nothing of value will be achieved if it is not accompanied with an understanding of what is being read.
2. Children should be encouraged to put what they have read into their own spoken or written words: there is a need to be able to paraphrase and summarise. It is a pointless exercise for children to copy directly from the text into their own books.
3. Children should be encouraged to be critical in their reading. Too much teaching revolves around the sanctity of the written word.
4. Children should be shown how to make use of chapter headings and indexes so that eventually they may be more selective in their reading.
5. Children should understand the way books have been classified in the school. It is important that the method used should have some relationship with that used in the public libraries if children are expected to carry their reading habits beyond the confines of the school.

There is some doubt about the value of making

a selection of recommended books for use in schools as such a selection becomes quickly dated and can not take into account the interests and capabilities of particular children and teachers, nor the bias of current and proposed work within a school. It would seem to be a more worthwhile proposition to recommend books that are worth looking at (see Appendix 4), not necessarily with a view to purchasing but because they are examples of a particular type of book and are useful as a starting point when they are compared and contrasted with other books of a similar type. It is for this reason that schools are strongly recommended to obtain copies of books on approval before making a final selection, for with their present cost it is better to see what the market has to offer before a final choice is made. Some authorities keep a wide selection of school books for inspection by teachers—as in the Inner London Education Authority—and in some areas teachers' centres have a range of the more popular books.

4.5 The Use of Museums

John Baines

There are few teachers today who would take a group of children to a museum just for an outing; the cost of transport and the time-consuming organisation require more justification than just a 'nice day out'. There is no doubt that a well-organised visit to a museum can greatly enrich a child's experience and, by introducing a touch of realism, greatly add to his or her understanding of a topic being studied in school.

It is the purpose of this section of the handbook, to identify ways in which a museum can be of value to school children and teachers and to suggest guidelines as to how such a visit should be planned.

Bringing lessons to life
As can be seen from other chapters in this handbook, by necessity much of the subject matter of the geography lesson is beyond the experience of the children being taught. But teachers are no longer content to pass off a list of facts about a foreign country as geography. They give much more emphasis to 'getting-the-feel' of the place with facts and figures backing up the impressions. This task of making the subject-matter 'real' is an exacting task for the teacher's ingenuity. How for example does a teacher put over the feeling of life in an African village, the atmosphere of a Trinidad Carnival, or cattle ranching in Australia? The thoughtful use of slides, films, tapes and other visual aids can go a long way to injecting a touch of realism, but the school's and the teacher's resources are usually very limited.

Today, however, there are a variety of museums which with their specialised resources can bring this realism one step nearer. Staff in museums are keen for children to use their resources and get the maximum benefit from them. Some lend materials out to schools and some have teachers on the staff preparing special programmes for children and teaching them in specially equipped classrooms. Once a teacher starts to enquire about the facilities and services provided by individual museums, a whole new dimension to teaching is opened.

THE VALUE OF THE MUSEUM

Each museum has its own particular range of exhibits and ways of presenting them to children—information about which is only a telephone call away. In general the value of a museum lies in its ability to specialise and build up extensive resources so that a visit can be very rewarding. Special facilities may include the following.
1. The central feature of any museum is the exhibitions. Here the treasures of the museum are displayed to best effect. To increase the impact of these exhibitions, there are not only objects to look at. Increasingly, working models, slide and tape presentations, sound effects, life-size models, etc. are found. Some special exhibitions go further; at the Geological Museum they even simulate an

earthquake. Museums are justly proud of their exhibitions which will form part of any visit.

2. There may be talks, demonstrations, etc. by experts on a particular topic, using films, models, artefacts and other resources not generally available to teachers in schools. Increasingly in museums, these experts are also teachers, able to adjust their 'lessons' to the needs of the individual groups.

3. Handling or using the real thing from another place or time be it a railway engine or fragile musical instrument, is one of the most valuable of the museum experiences. Children, and many adults too, want to touch the exhibits because for them it seems to heighten the experience of 'realism' which is the purpose of the visit. Instead of jealously guarding all the exhibits in glass cases, many museums now have a collection of artefacts especially for people to touch and handle.

4. Some museums organise special programmes for school children where they can actually join in a re-enactment of some event from a distant country. At the Commonwealth Institute in London, children are invited to attend a Trinidad Carnival, a Commonwealth Food Fair and the like.

5. Advisory services and publications are often available from museums. It is worthwhile to let the children buy a small souvenir, even if it is only a postcard, as it provides a link between the visit, the home and the classroom when it is shown to friends and family. The museum may have a library or loan service.

Where to go

There is a very large range of museums and clearly not all of them are of relevance to geographers. Local museums often concentrate on the local area, but with so many schools having some kind of combined studies, some of the geographical skills and concepts can be introduced while studying subject matter of a non-geographical nature. However, with an increasing number of industrial, folk, transport, and other museums, there is usually something within reasonable striking distance that can add that extra touch of realism to a geography lesson. Those living close to London have a much larger choice with several museums offering exciting programmes relevant to geography, including the

Natural History Museum, the Geological Museum and the Commonwealth Institute.

Any teacher wanting to start museum visits should have access to *Museums and Galleries* published by ABC Historic Publications (see Appendix 2), which lists all the museums and their facilities in Great Britain.

How to Use the Museum

The teacher can approach a museum trip from two directions. First the teacher can examine the syllabus to identify the topics where a museum would seem able to help and then set about finding the location of a suitable museum, the facilities it offers, etc. The other way is to find out what museums are within reasonable travelling distance, examine what they have to offer and then adapt the syllabus to make use of what is available.

Personal contact

Whichever approach is adopted, a personal visit to the museums and preferably a talk with an education officer there is most desirable. Only in that way can the teacher find out what the museum has to offer to particular age groups. Bear in mind that the museum staff are likely to welcome you with open arms, for without you, they are out of a job. Not so the other way round! Once this preparatory work is done, the task of organising the visit follows.

THE ORGANISATION OF THE TRIP

Once the groundwork has been done, it is easy to build ideas of a grand tour which requires very little extra organisation and will impress parents as good value for money. But the golden rule is never to be over ambitious; don't go to excesses, don't take too many children, don't go too far away, don't try to cram too much into one day, don't come home too late, etc. For some children, the journey itself is a new experience, and a host of impressions are going to be made on the child's mind apart from the actual visit to the museum. The whole trip is an educational experience, don't over-crowd it.

The organisation falls into two areas:

1. the content of the visit; the work they will be doing, what they will be looking at, and the like;

2. the organisation of the trip itself including transport, cost, etc.

Content

The purpose of a visit should be to bring the classroom work alive. The children should be visiting the museum as part of a programme of work. As a result it is absolutely essential that the teacher should contact the education staff of the museum so that each knows what the other is doing. Even if the teacher does not want to use the museum teachers or education facilities, it is still advisable to contact the museum and explain what you want to do. Such contact avoids the necessity of disappointment and makes it easier for the museum staff to make sure the visit goes smoothly.

Before making the visit with the children, it is always beneficial to go alone to look at the exhibitions, to identify which ones are relevant and find out what they contain. It is a good idea to produce a worksheet for the children so that they have some definite work to do while looking at the exhibitions. Without a worksheet children tend to flit from one exhibit to another without really taking them in. They will not be able to digest all the information if the scope of the visit is too large, so it is best to concentrate only on those exhibits that are relevant to the topic being studied, and then if there is time at the end, they could be allowed to have a more general look round. Some museums produce their own worksheets which are available to the children and if this is the case it may not be necessary to produce one in school. If the museum staff are arranging a programme for you, then they will produce any worksheets, or other material which is necessary and you will only be asked to supervise them.

Back in school, the teacher will want to follow up the visit to make sure there are no loose ends. A display of the work done is one idea, but teachers will have their own ideas. However, it is important to follow up the visit and show how it all fits into the scheme of work being done at that time.

Administration

The administrative organisation of the visit is very fiddly and time consuming but it is very necessary if the visit is to be successful and have as few headaches for the teacher as possible.

Each school tends to have its own way of organising visits, but there are some points in common. The following may seem over-fussy, but learning from mistakes is not usually a pleasant experience.

1. Raise the matter with the head-teacher well in advance.
2. Inform colleagues of the visit and who will be going.
3. Arrange for adequate supervision of the children during the visit, check with the museum the desired staff to children ratio. If they are eating a packed lunch, check if a room is available.
4. Arrange for transport; coach is usually the best as it transports children all in one group from door to door. Check on parking facilities at the museum. Coaches generally have seating capacities of 12 (minibus), 29, 41, 45 and 53 seats, and if you can fill all the seats the unit cost will be lower. It is possible to book double-decker buses for larger groups.
5. Send a letter to parents with full details of the visit and a tear-off slip to be returned with any payment due. From experience, it is always best to over-charge *slightly*, to allow for a last-minute cancellation in the group. Any surplus can always be returned, or if it is a small amount donated to the school fund. Under-charging may mean paying extra from your own pocket.
6. Confirm arrangements with the coach company the day prior to the visit.
7. Remind children of the visit, what to wear, what to bring etc., the day before. A stencilled sheet can save a lot of bother.
8. At the museum leave the children in the coach under the supervision of a colleague while you go to the reception desk to collect instructions. Tell pupils how they are expected to behave, details of the programme, where to go if lost, and time of departure.
9. Once in the museum, maintain constant supervision.
10. When the visit is over, count the number of children in the coach. (It is surprising how many times museum staff have to accompany a young child back to his or her school!) If you return after school has finished, make sure that each child can get home safely.

Museums have a lot to offer teachers and school

children, and their staff are very willing to arrange visits, but it is worthwhile to repeat the feelings of some curators about some school visits.

Frequently the children are too rowdy or too tired, too unprepared or too over-directed, to summon up even the faintest flicker of enthusiasm for what is before them.

It is hoped that these few notes will help schools have successful and meaningful visits to museums, experiences that the children will enjoy and not forget.

A CASE STUDY: THE COMMONWEALTH INSTITUTE

The Commonwealth Institute in Kensington High Street is a centre for learning about the Commonwealth, its member countries and peoples. In its splendid building on the edge of Holland Park are permanent exhibitions from all the Commonwealth countries, a cinema/theatre, an Art Gallery, a Library and Resource Centre and well equipped conference and teaching rooms. The Education Department is responsible for a great variety of educational activities, and on its staff are four full-time teachers who give lessons, organise events and go out to schools.

The following describes what happened when a teacher of ten-year-olds brought her children for a programme at the Institute.

A School Visit

Miss C . . . teaches in a school about 20 miles from London, and as part of a project on the Caribbean she decided to bring her class to the Commonwealth Institute. At the beginning of the term she rang the Schools Reception Centre to arrange the visit. She was told that later in the term there was a week of special programmes on music and dance in the Caribbean, when nationals from the area would be in the Institute to give lessons. She returned the booking form that had been sent her, booking a lesson at 11.30 and space for eating packed lunches in the Schools Dining Room at 12.40. After lunch the children would visit the Exhibitions of the Caribbean countries using the worksheet prepared by the teachers at the Commonwealth Institute.

Miss C. decided to visit the Institute before the children and came one Saturday morning. She went to the Library and Resource Centre where she borrowed some slides, posters and books on the Caribbean for use in the project. (If she had not been able to visit, the library staff, on request, would have selected some material and sent it by post.)

Two weeks before the visit, the children began the project, finding out the names of the different islands and where they were, studying the history and geography of the area, and learning why so many people from the Caribbean had come to live in Britain.

When they arrived at the Institute, Miss C. reported to the Schools Reception Centre, and then told the children in the coach what they had to do. They filed into the cloakroom to hang up their coats and leave their packed lunches. They were then taken to the Activities Room where they were to have their lesson. As they walked into the room a Trinidadian was playing a tune on a steel pan. Roger Ali, a teacher from Trinidad on the staff of the Institute, introduced the class to Doris Harper-Wills, a choreographer, dancer and writer from Guyana, and Victor Phillip, a steelband player and tuner from Trinidad. Through dance and costumes the children are taught the history of the peoples in the Caribbean. The children were not expected just to sit and watch; with a few giggles soon both boys and girls were putting on some costumes and joining in. Later Victor talked about Steelband music, explaining how it developed, how the pans are made and tuned and why some are longer than others. Then came request time, when children asked for some familiar tunes, and there were even some modest attempts by the children themselves to play the pans.

Some artefacts from the Caribbean including hats, clothes, sugar cane, steel pans and other musical instruments were laid out on a table for them to handle and ask about. The 45 minutes passed very quickly and at the end it was difficult to persuade the children to leave, but the programmes are fully booked and it was the turn of another class.*

* This is only one of many programmes arranged at the Institute. For full details of programmes and Educational Services write to: The Schools Reception Centre, Commonwealth Institute, Kensington High Street, London W8 6NQ.

PLATE 6.   A Caribbean programme at the Commonwealth Institute

At the end of the lesson the children went back to the cloakroom to collect their packed lunches which they ate in the Schools Dining Room where they could also buy sweets and soft drinks. The children then had one hour to go to the Caribbean exhibitions to answer the questions on the worksheet under the supervision of their teachers and buy a souvenir from the Shop.

Back at school, Miss C. decided to make a classroom display of the Caribbean. The children drew a map of the Caribbean, naming all the countries and how many people lived there. Symbols were drawn and stuck onto the map to show what was produced in the countries, and labels from goods produced in the Caribbean stuck around the edge. One group tried their hands at making carnival costumes from Trinidad. To a record of Trinidadian steelband music borrowed from the Library and Resource Centre, the children paraded their costumes in front of the others.

The visit to the Commonwealth Institute had brought a touch of realism to the lessons on the Caribbean in a way that would be very difficult for a school to organise itself. This was only one programme in one museum.

4.6   Hardware Models

David Rowbotham

Making models can be a very useful way of concentrating ideas, beginning or summarising a new topic of interest, particularly with young and less academically minded children. Models can be a novel way of recording and presenting information. On the other hand it can all too easily become a time-filler activity with no real purpose or structure. Criticism has been levelled against children who spend too long assembling boxes and other 'junk' pieces together with no real purpose and sense of learning save that of being creative, and with the possible result that basic skills become neglected.

Properly introduced, models do help children to appreciate the reality they are studying, giving greater precision to their learning and providing a

PLATE 7.   *Contour layer model*

sense of achievement if the product is finished well. They provide a chance for other skills to be demonstrated while the various geographical concepts of scale, form, function and distribution can be demonstrated and reinforced depending on the type and purpose of the model.

The point of making the model needs to be carefully decided beforehand and all relevant materials collected together. There must be a careful choice of work geared to the particular pupils, the time available and materials that can be gathered. To be geographically relevant continuous teacher guidance and stimulus is necessary rather than allowing free-play with the materials. Properly done it should provide an enjoyable, worthwhile activity for all abilities and ages from the imaginative models of infants to more complicated models at the top of the age range (13+).

If modelling is going to be undertaken regularly, a store of a wide range of useful materials is handy, but storage space can become a problem, particularly when one has to keep before and after products. It is very easy to end up with a huge 'junk-box'. It is perhaps better to limit material storage to a small basic stock of boxes of various sizes; detergent packets and cereal packets, washing-up-liquid bottles, supermarket polystyrene meat trays and other plastic containers which can be augmented when necessary.

The main types of model it is possible to make are centred on buildings and objects in a town or street setting, or alternatively landscapes with emphasis on the shape of the land surface. Individual objects such as buildings and street furniture can be made by single children or small groups and put onto a base or background produced by the class, leading to a class model.

The first practical considerations in making a model are the possible size and the materials available. A suitable base table, board or tray needs to be found before construction is started and relevant materials collected and allocated to the class.

LANDSCAPE MODELS

A very quick model can be produced in damp sand, clay or plasticine to illustrate simple hill and valley relationships if no great accuracy or permanence is required. Boxes and screwed up paper can be used to pack under a surface that is moulded and made stiff by a layer of cloth soaked in plaster or filler or strips of papier mâché. Again only generalised hill shapes are really possible by such a method. Chicken wire can be

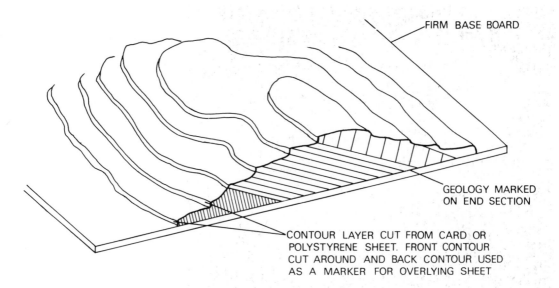

FIRM BASE BOARD

GEOLOGY MARKED
ON END SECTION

CONTOUR LAYER CUT FROM CARD OR
POLYSTYRENE SHEET. FRONT CONTOUR
CUT AROUND AND BACK CONTOUR USED
AS A MARKER FOR OVERLYING SHEET

FIGURE 4.2   Model hill made from contour layers prior to the terraces being smoothed over with filler

pinned down to a board and bent to the desired surface shape. It needs little other support. The surface is then treated in a similar way to the above.

The surface can be painted when dry to give a greater idea of realism. For quick overnight drying it is best to build up a solid crust surface over the packing materials, rather than using thick mounds of sodden paper or boxes. Pasted paper strips laid over the newspaper or boxes are enough to hold it together and to dry to a crust surface. Where more detail is required, some method linked to using countour lines from an Ordnance Survey map is better for providing the accuracy and obvious links with bringing a two-dimensional map into three-dimensional reality. Considerable skill and teacher guidance are needed, but the result should be very worthwhile. For a local area the 1:25 000 or 1:10 000 maps are probably the best.

In the first method contours need to be traced from the map. These could be left at the original scale but if space allows are better enlarged (2 or 3 times) by grid squares. In areas of moderate relief the enlarging may be done free-hand, or tracings taken and enlarged by the use of an overhead projector to the scale required. In this latter case the contour tracing could be directly projected onto the main material of the model

which could be plywood, card or perhaps most conveniently a polystyrene ceiling tile or sheet. Care needs to be taken with the thickness of material chosen and the ultimate vertical exaggeration of the model, particularly in areas of high relief with 6mm polystyrene sheets. Two contours are traced onto each sheet of material. The outside one is cut around, the inside one is a marker to lay the next sheet against. The layers are then stuck in order onto the baseboard (see Fig. 4.2). The terraced effect that this method produces can be smoothed over with plaster, filler or papier mâché. The surface can then be painted as in the previous models. By lightly greasing the surface of the model a plaster cast reverse could be made so that copies of the original in plaster, or perhaps plastic, could be taken. Such a job may best be handled by older and more able children. Repeated plaster or plastic duplicates could then be made if necessary.

During the construction of this type of model the concept of contour lines is obviously brought out and the flat map is literally brought to life. A similarly accurate model could be made by firstly taking repeated cross sections of all or part of the map. Contour lines are plotted onto graph paper to give a cross section along a chosen line. Several parallel sections are taken close together. These

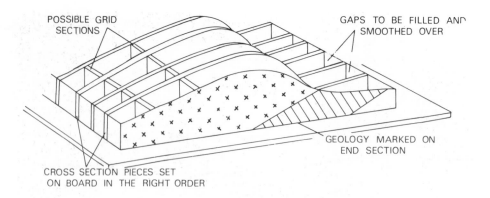

FIGURE 4.3 Landscape model made from cut-out cross-sections prior to the filling and final surface being added

are drawn onto thick card or polystyrene sheets, cut out and set up on the base board in the correct order and distance apart as on the original map (see Fig. 4.3). Prior enlargement could be achieved as before by means of free-hand drawing by grid squares or overhead projector tracing. The more closely spaced the section lines are drawn the more accurate the finished model can be. Once set up on a base the gaps between the sections can be packed with screwed paper and the whole covered with plaster or filler to give the surface crust which can be moulded while still wet to blend in with the cross sections. A grid system of cross sections could be made and set up to give increased accuracy.

Unless some initial enlargement of the base has

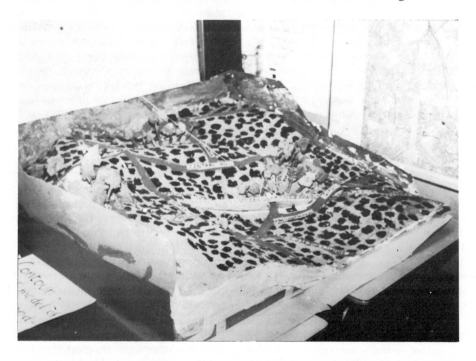

PLATE 8. Contour layer model with surface placed on

PLATE 9.   Model of a squatter home

been made, surface detail is difficult to add to the above models to any degree. Roads, railways, field boundaries and main built-up areas can be marked and the way they are influenced by the relief readily demonstrated. However, individual buildings will be extremely small. A variety of surface textures can be tried where these might add to the value of the model. Some of these can be obtained commercially from model suppliers but sand, foam rubber and polystyrene are cheaper alternatives.

Both the contour and cross-section models have the advantage that the sides can be left to end in a section and the underlying geology can then be marked on to show the relationship between rock type and surface features (see Figs. 4.2 and 4.3). The cross-section model lends itself to being built up as several block sections with the geology marked on each section side. The whole is then just pushed together for the final model allowing the block sides to be inspected by pupils.

With these models the emphasis is on providing a three-dimensional representation of the main landscape forms of hill and valley rather than on surface features such as buildings and vegetation.

BUILDING/TOWNSCAPE MODELS

These are obviously most relevant to the urban child. Individual buildings can be made by groups or by single pupils and placed on a large-scale ground plan or linked by pointer lines to a wall map. It is probably easier to employ large numbers of children on such a model project. Detail can be added according to the age and ability of the class concerned. Buildings on these models are made out of boxes of various sizes. High-rise blocks of flats, slab blocks or even rows of terraced houses can be made from whole or part boxes, depending on the scale needed. Single houses and other types of building are better made in sections from card or parts of boxes. Again the detail put into such buildings will depend on the time available and the ability of the children involved.

It could be that actual building methods become part of the project and thus prefabricated sections of buildings could be made to put together on the site of the final model. Tall buildings could be arranged around a balsa or wire skeleton frame (see Fig. 4.4). Ordinary soap or cereal boxes are best covered in a thin plain paper surface detail before erection. Polystyrene meat trays can be cut to give roof and/or window detail. The slightly moulded surface gives the tile effect of the roof, or the glass panes of a window.

If desired, for a small village or individual street, some basic street furniture could be added to make the model even more realistic. Pillar boxes, bus shelters and lamps can be made out of pieces of card or match boxes. If the model is

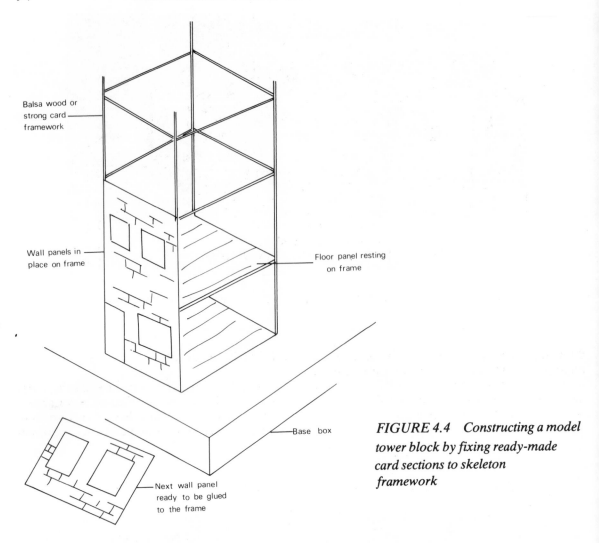

Balsa wood or
strong card
framework

Wall panels in
place on frame

Floor panel resting
on frame

Base box

Next wall panel
ready to be glued
to the frame

*FIGURE 4.4   Constructing a model
tower block by fixing ready-made
card sections to skeleton
framework*

built on a base-board of suitable thickness a section showing the underground services, such as water, sewage, gas and electricity, could be drawn to give further visual aid to the idea of a street as a line of communication. On a table the underground pipes can be slung underneath.

Such models can be attempted by almost any children in the age range as a follow-up to a study of a local street with location of shops and services. Simple vehicles could be made to make the model more life-like. Boxes and card or plastic discs are useful for this.

To attempt a whole town or collection of several rows of streets may be rather ambitious and time consuming. A model frieze can be attempted. Background streets can be made as card front cut-outs and placed on a backing frieze. Only the front road of most relevance then needs to be modelled properly. If this is done in a large box or cupboard with the model facing the open side, a diorama effect can be produced. Models of farms or areas of towns such as docks, markets or stations can be made in this way with the maximum detail put into the immediate foreground with painted scenery flats cut and set out behind (see Fig. 4.6). This is effectively done in museums and the Commonwealth Institute displays, but can be adapted to the classroom situation.

To combine a landscape and urbanscape model into one is going to demand a scale even larger than 1:2500 and 1:1250 Ordnance Survey plans if

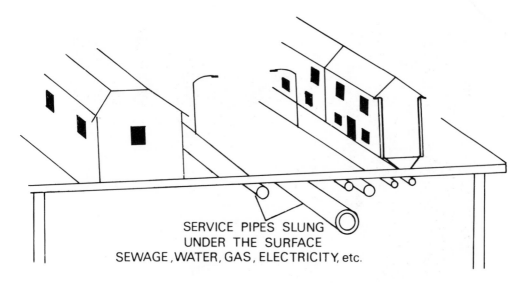

SERVICE PIPES SLUNG
UNDER THE SURFACE
SEWAGE, WATER, GAS, ELECTRICITY, etc.

FIGURE 4.5   Model of street on a table with underground services shown

the buildings are going to be of suitable size. To attempt something on such a scale over even a local school neighbourhood would be rather ambitious for an average school in this group and would almost become a model village project on its own.

WORKING MODELS

An added feature of some models to bring them closer to reality can be the effect of making them work in a small way. Sutton has produced a book *Models in Action* (see Appendix 4), in which

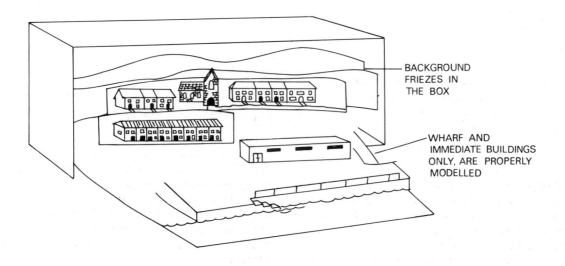

BACKGROUND
FRIEZES IN
THE BOX

WHARF AND
IMMEDIATE BUILDINGS
ONLY, ARE PROPERLY
MODELLED

FIGURE 4.6   Diorama model of a harbour town

PLATE 10.   Model of an oil platform

ideas for several working models are mentioned. A working geyser, and a harbour with rising and falling tides are suggested. Other ideas can be explored if patience and time are available.

The models in this context ought to be thought of as an aid to understanding geographical methods of recording information and analysing data obtained in the field or from other sources such as pictures and photos. Creative initiative and manual dexterity are obviously brought into play but should not be thought of as the main reasons for attempting these ideas. Ideas for working experimental physical models such as a stream and a wave tank can be found in the Geographical Association's Teaching Geography Occasional Paper *Hardware Models in Geography Teaching* (Anderson, 1969).

4.7   The Use of Case Studies

David Mills

The use of case studies is to be recommended as a very effective way of introducing reality into geographical work. The value of the case study is that it is able to extend the pupil's experience of the world while avoiding dull abstractions and generalisations which often occur when studies are made of large areas or broad topics. The use of case studies is particularly valuable with junior and middle-school pupils as the size of the unit studied is usually one which they can readily comprehend.

One of the major advances in the use of these detailed studies took place when Long and Roberson published their article 'Sample Studies: the development of a method' (1956), and this was further developed in their book on *Teaching Geography* (1966). In this book they state that

A sample study is a detailed study of a unit, chosen particularly to show human response to environment, and chosen so as to be typical of the major region concerned. In the classroom, the word 'study' is meant to be taken in an active sense. Geographical details should be presented in a variety of ways so that children may make for themselves conclusions concerning man and the world he lives in.

Sample studies, as the phrase states, are studies based on samples which have been randomly chosen to illustrate a theme. The term 'case study' is now being used more often to avoid the linking with statistically tested samples.

The main advantages of using these detailed studies is that:

1. they ensure reality by studying real farms, valleys, factories, etc.;
2. they provide studies in depth which encourage children to gain a balanced understanding of factors which affect such things as crop rotation, functions of a village, siting of a factory;
3. they enable pupils to identify themselves more closely with situations and people as the studies themselves show reality;
4. they enable the development to take place from the particular to the general.

There is a wealth of material available though most of it is written at the level of children aged eleven and over. A list of useful sources is given in Appendix 4.

A good case study will include a variety of material such as maps, pictures, written text and statistics. It is the task of the teacher to decide how the material is used but clearly the pupils should engage in mapwork, study the pictures, comprehend the text, analyse the statistics and produce some written work. At the top end of the eleven to thirteen band the pupils can be led towards generalisations from the particular topic they have studied.

The material for case studies is usually available in single form unless there are class sets. If it is only available as a single copy then the teacher will need to duplicate some of the material and this will also enable him to produce worksheets written appropriately for his class. A typical example of a case study is given in Book 2 from *Study Geography* (Rushby *et al* 1967-9), which is a study of a coffee estate in Brazil. The maps given include two general maps showing the position of the estate within Brazil; a detailed map showing the estate, the buildings, including part of the coffee producing plant, the picking of the crop; diagrams giving the work carried out on the estate during the year and the day; a climatic graph; a text and many questions. The teaching material is thus very varied and can be adapted as appropriate by the teacher.

The advantages of the method are clear. It is possible to fit the use of case studies into almost any kind of syllabus, and they can be used with almost any level of age and ability. However, it is necessary to state that, as with almost all teaching methods, the case study approach must not be overused, for otherwise the pupils will obtain a large amount of unsystematised snippets of the world.

5. Maps and Mapping

5.1   Introduction

Colin Conner

In an article in the *Times Educational Supplement* in 1965, Balchin and Coleman argued that graphicacy should be the fourth Ace in the pack; that is, that there was an additional important factor in a child's education beyond being able to read, to speak fluently, and to have some understanding of numbers. In an increasingly complex world it is becoming essential that children are able to understand and appreciate material presented in the form of graphs, diagrams, photographs and maps. Since such means of recording are of significant importance to the geographer, particularly where maps are concerned, one might expect the problems experienced by children to have been diagnosed, and learning approaches devised to overcome such problems.

The difficulties involved have long been recognised at a research level, but as Satterly (1964) points out, it is too often assumed that there is nothing to teach where maps are involved, maps are merely an adjunct to class lessons 'something to wave a hand at'. Satterly's research into map drawing and map interpretation concluded that there are children aged 15 and 16 who are unclear about maps, and that their work exhibits errors characteristic of earlier ages. This conclusion is in direct contradiction to the work of Piaget (1956) and Prior (1959), who concluded that the concept of a map begins to emerge with the onset of Formal Operations at about the age of 11 or 12. Satterly believes that doubt must be cast upon the value of mapwork in the primary and early secondary school. The locational value of using maps with young children,

however, has much support, particularly through David's (1940) research with 6-9-year-olds, which found that since the difficulty for this age group lay in the ability to visualise in plan form, she felt that the first maps ought to be a compromise between picture and plan. David also emphasised the fact that direction and relative position are understood before scale, and that any course in mapwork should take account of this fact. The interest of young children in maps and mapwork has long been advocated by Storm, and this belief is to some extent substantiated by the work of Blaut and Stea (1974) in America, who showed that 3-year-olds are capable of recognising aspects of their own environment when it is displayed through aerial photographs. Long's research as long ago as 1953 into the learning of geography through pictures has emphasised the younger child's inability to be selective in observing the geography in a picture, yet this should not prevent the use of pictures and photographs, nor reduce their value to geographical work with younger children. Although expense is of major importance, Blaut and Stea's work seems to suggest that in order to help children develop an understanding of the language of maps, aerial photographs are essential. Their research showed that very young children are capable of recognising features of their own environment on photographs, and that they were able to move to a form of symbolisation by first making models, and then a diagrammatic representation of these photographs. The value of using photographs with young children is further supported by Bayliss and Renwick

98

(1966), who believe that simple concepts could be profitably introduced with young children, but they emphasise starting with photographs of the children's own locality. They concluded however that with the younger children in their sample (7-year-olds) the use of photographs inside school did not necessarily lead to better perceptive abilities out of doors.

5.2   Using Maps and Aerial Photographs

Simon Catling

It might almost be described as a tenet of geography that what the geographer cannot map is not worth his study. It is, of course, like all generalisations, not entirely true. But it is true that the map is a vital tool of the geographer; and as aerial photography has developed it has also become the case that oblique and vertical aerial photographs are increasingly used in geographical study. Maps and photographs can be of large and small scale, and can show the structure of a village or the Earth from Space.

Before describing a variety of ideas about how maps and photographs can be introduced to, and understood and used by young children, it is most important to realise why children should develop map and photographic skills. A brief statement along these lines will be followed by an outline of the types of maps and photographs relevant here. Then, the important elements of the map and photograph will be noted. This will lead to a statement on approaches to teaching, followed by a final section outlining ideas that can be usefully employed.

WHY TEACH MAP AND PHOTOGRAPHIC SKILLS?

It has already been stated that the map is a very valuable tool in the geographer's kit, but geography is not the only user of maps. Essentially, maps may be described as serving four functions:

1. A map is a locational document. *You can find places on a map,* whether on an atlas map, a street map or a map in an advertisement showing where a particular shop is.
2. A map can be a *route-displaying* document. It can be a great asset when wanting to get from A to B. Using an A-Z street map, or the AA road atlas, or an Underground map are illustrations.
3. A map can also show you *what a place or an area looks like,* its structure, shape and features. The use of an Ordnance Survey tourist map, or 1:2500 or 1:1250 maps to comprehend the look of the landscape is something which takes time, practice and patience to learn. This may be of value when choosing places to visit, landscapes to see, or when analysing areas of a country.
4. A map is also a very useful way of *storing and displaying* information. There is a wealth of information depicted in the Ordnance Survey maps, facts about places, what they look like, how they develop, what is there, and so on. Maps can be used to show the distribution of things, like towns in the British Isles or where different diseases are more prevalent, and can show relationships, as in maps depicting the network of major streets in a town, the catchment region of a school or the towns and villages within the sphere of a centrally placed city. In other words, they serve very well for displaying information *not* obvious on the ground.

A vertical aerial photograph serves the first function well; it can also serve the second, third and fourth though by declining degrees. Whereas a map is a 'discriminating' document, the photograph is merely a 'now-print' of the situation at the time it was taken, though maps are subject to change too.

The adult—and many children—in today's society is likely to move about a great deal, whether as part of his work or for pleasure. He needs to be able to find his way round and to be able to work out something of places as and when he needs to use a map. There are many different sorts of commercially-produced maps: AA road maps; street maps; city map guides; Ordnance Survey maps and atlas maps. Almost every newsagent stocks one or more of these map types. Therefore, simply on utilitarian grounds, if merely for locational and route-finding reasons, map skills need developing in children, so that they come to use these maps correctly as adults. But if people are going to be able to understand information presented in map form, such as the weather map or the mapped distribution of shops, it is also necessary to introduce children to the map as a storage and resource document. Further, for pleasure purposes, with the production of more tourist maps by the Ordnance Survey it will be of value to people if they develop some idea of how to read the mapped landscape (Catling, 1980).

The vast majority of children will never be geographers. Therefore, using maps solely as a geographical tool is a secondary purpose of teaching mapping skills. However, some children will become interested, even if only for a short while, and so it is sensible and rational to develop children's map comprehension through geographical and environmentally-related work in school. Map ability—making and reading maps—is a skill, it is a medium of communication, and as such the skill is best developed through using maps as means to ends, hence in geographical and environmental studies. Maps have a purpose; they are not an end in themselves.

MAPS AND PHOTOGRAPHS AT A LARGE SCALE

Maps

There are a great many different types of larger-scale maps available. The interest here is in the more commonly used map types. The sorts of maps to be included are those which cover, at most, about the area of a county.

The most common maps that children will have come into contact with, if at all, will be route-finding maps, such as local street guides, for example, the A-Z *Geographia* street maps, and motorists' maps such as those produced by commercial publishers with the AA or RAC. These are, essentially, route maps, though some detail of major buildings or certain types of buildings, such as post offices or AA call boxes will be included. The more sophisticated, such as

the AA *New Book of the Road* include information culled from the Ordnance Survey. These maps vary in scale, content, sophistication and value to the user, but can usefully serve different purposes. For instance, local street maps form a good basis for noting which streets can be followed when going to school, or to visit a place, or for local walks. Smaller-scale road maps can be used to find routes travelled across London or on school field trips to distant places, or to look at to see how one would get from London to Edinburgh.

The second most likely type of map that children will have had contact with is the Ordnance Survey map selection. The Ordnance Survey produce a wide range of maps varying in scale from 1:1250 through to the most common 1:50 000 and to smaller scale maps, such as the 1:250 000. These maps have gone through several editions for all areas, and it is possible to obtain maps of a region as it was 100 years ago or older (the first 1" : 1 mile maps were produced in 1816). However, it is quite likely that the current large-scale map of any area is out of date, possibly by as much as 20 years. This, though, should be no deterrent to using Ordnance Survey maps, particularly of the 1:1250 and 1:2500 scales, with primary and middle-school-age children. These two maps show the size of buildings adequately enough for their use in local survey work. (In fact, it can be greatly stimulating to the children to recognise that the map is wrong, and that they can up-date it.)

The Ordnance Survey also produces historical maps, such as that of Roman Britain, which can be of value in other than geographical studies. But obtaining copies of previous editions of the 1:2500 and 1:10 000, possibly through the local authority or library, provides invaluable information about the growth of an area, and about how it has changed.

A third variety of commercial maps are those produced by such companies as London Transport or British Rail, showing bus and train routes. Waterway maps, pub maps and so forth can also be obtained. These are *thematic*—concentrating overtly on one aspect of the environment that they wish to promote. These maps can be just as informative and useful as the previously mentioned street and topographical maps. It can be fun plotting bus routes to get from one point to another. They can also show how maps make the environment convenient and easy to understand, such as the topological London Transport Underground Map and the British Rail Inter-City Overground Map. It can be very stimulating discussing why this has been done and comparing the map with topographical maps showing the actual routes on the landscape.

Aerial Photographs

There is much less to be said about aerial photographs, for a photograph is merely, in this context, a visual record of a place or landscape captured as it looked at the time, winter or summer, rush-hour or off-peak.

There are two types of aerial photograph. One is the oblique photograph; the other is the vertical aerial photograph. The former presents a picture from a high-up, *side-on* position, the higher up the photograph is taken the better the shape of the area appears. This is a valuable transition from the ground-level photograph to the vertical view, and is worth using in conjunction with photographs of streets, buildings, etc., in the area, as well as with the vertical aerial photograph. The latter is the directly overhead view, but one must be wary of the fact that there is only one point which is in fact viewed from a purely vertical position. The nearer the edge of the photograph, the more side-on and distorted the view becomes. However, for the purpose of map teaching with young children it is a surrogate map, an iconic map-form.

Whereas most maps can be bought locally, photographs are not readily on sale. There are few suppliers and orders need to go direct to them.

THE ELEMENTS OF THE MAP AND PHOTOGRAPH

Before proceeding to present teaching ideas there remains one vital aspect of map and vertical aerial photograph studies to be covered. It is important to be aware of the nature of maps and vertical aerial photographs, their structure and elements. In three ways the map and the vertical aerial photograph are alike, but in several other ways the map is a more complex document. A number of things need to be understood about maps, if children are to comprehend them properly.

Perspective

The first element of both the map and the vertical aerial photograph is the perspective that presents features in plan form. It can be said that they are both views from directly overhead which display the shape and spatial arrangement of things we see on the ground. There is no 'dead ground' on either; they enable us to see what is hidden from view at ground level.

Position and Orientation

The map and vertical aerial photograph show how features are spatially related to one another. Both show where features are located, and from them directions (relative and absolute) can be given. Grid reference systems have been developed to aid accurate location giving and finding on maps. A map is of little value if the user does not appreciate the need to read off position and direction carefully, and to orientate the map to the landscape when in the field.

Scale

A commercial map is usually drawn to scale, based on the Ordnance Survey maps. Strictly a photograph is not to scale, because distance is distorted towards the edge of the vertical aerial photograph, but for our purposes, and for the scale of photographs likely to be used, they can be described as internally correct in terms of distance. This is one aspect of the concept of scale. The other is that both are scaled down representations of reality. The correctly orientated, plan-view of the landscape is depicted on a smaller than 'life-size' sheet of paper. This would seem to be an adequate definition of both map and vertical aerial photograph, but it is not entirely true of the map. It is at this point that it becomes possible to discriminate between the two. As the scale of a photograph becomes smaller it becomes less and less easy to pick out the detail, though it is all there. The map, though, shows the information in a different form.

Map Content

Whereas the photograph is a non-discriminatory record the map is selective as to the inclusion and exclusion of phenomena. The photograph simply records what is at a place at that time, while the map displays what the maker wishes to show. Hence, there are so many different maps. The scale of a map is vital here. At 1:50 000 scale, it is impossible to show the shape of every building, but this can be done at the 1:1250 or 1:2500 scales. The purpose of the map is the second factor that affects its content. A street map will not concentrate on housing types, or vice versa. Different details are emphasised.

Symbols

A second difference between the map and vertical aerial photograph is that whereas the photograph shows the actual view from above, the map often uses symbols to show what is recorded. Different things are shown differently. Not all features are necessarily shown in plan-form, as on the 1:50 000 Ordnance Survey map, where windmills are drawn in elevation. A key is therefore necessary for interpreting a map's symbols.

Additional Information

A third difference lies in the way that a map of an area can be used to give information about places. Vertical aerial photographs are not literary documents. Maps generally are. Streets are named. Towns, suburbs, villages, fields, rivers, farms, and so on, are named. Even historical sites are specially marked on some maps. Shop type, land use and so forth can also be displayed. A map, therefore, goes further than an aerial photograph in the information it can provide for the user.

APPROACHES TO TEACHING

A map may be described as a scaled, orientated abstraction of the reality of which the vertical aerial photograph is the picture, the view the child can rarely personally have, the view of the landscape from above. It is foolhardy to think that children will understand this without the influence of teaching, even though research has shown that even young infants can display map-like notions through playing with toy roads, buildings and vehicles. It is important, therefore, to develop children's understanding of maps, and the use of vertical aerial photographs can aid this, in a carefully structured way.

It is possible to discern a structured approach to developing map understanding. The following is an outline of this approach, but it must be stressed that each strand is not absolutely

dependent on previous stages; indeed, they may help by being carefully used in conjunction. Revisiting and reinforcement is sound practice here.

Developing Locational Awareness

A basic idea is to develop in young children a ready knowledge of directional words, like left, right, back, forward, up, down, and so on, through practical activities, by asking children to point in certain directions, so that it becomes natural to them to use these descriptions. Getting children to say which way they would turn to face a certain thing in, say, the classroom, without turning, helps to instill this. Later getting children to see direction from another's view helps.

Developing orientation awareness can also take a graphic form with very young children. The child can draw his desk in the centre of his paper and then draw arrows from where he is sitting in the direction of objects in the room called out by the teacher. He could then attempt to name them on his 'signpost map' (see Fig. 5.1). With older children this can take a more advanced form, the direction of external places being requested, as in figure 5.2.

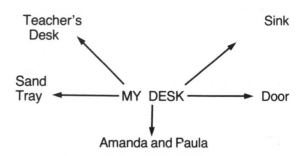

FIGURE 5.1   'Signpost map' (classroom)

With junior-age children it is possible to develop an understanding of the cardinal directions of the compass, and as children mature they can come to understand that places and objects have a fixed position. By using sun shadows at midday the children can fix the north direction in the playground. This can also be done by using a compass or by aligning a large-scale map of the

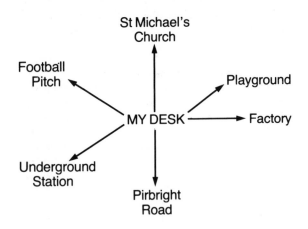

FIGURE 5.2 'Signpost map' (external places)

locality. A prepared and marked map of the classroom or a compass (though beware of the influence of iron objects) could be used inside the classroom. Once the idea of north, etc. has been introduced, objects and places can be located in this way. The direction of objects in the classroom, school or playground can be identified. This can be done for the neighbourhood too (e.g. in which direction is the church from the school, according to the compass?). This can be extended to include references from other points (e.g. in which compass direction is the church from the station?), by using maps.

The final level of this development is in terms of grid reference systems. The initial grid system that is best used is that utilising both letters and numbers, usually letters across the top and numbers down the side. Only the square reference is given (see Fig. 5.3). Using this method children can learn how to locate places on a map when given a reference, or how to tell others where places are. This system is commonly used on commercial maps, e.g. A-Z maps, road maps, Underground maps. However, this method is not used by the Ordnance Survey in their maps. They use a purely numerical system for giving references (see Fig. 5.4), the reference across the top (eastings) being given first, followed by the reference down the side (northings). This has the advantage that each square can be subdivided into square hundredths (tenths across the top, by tenths down the side), so that a more exact six-figure reference can be given for a point within a square. Only as children come to use small-scale Ordnance Survey maps (1:50 000 and 1:25 000) need they be introduced to this latter system, at the upper end of the junior/middle school range (11+), generally.

Map-Making Activities, 1: Real Situations
A variety of ideas are outlined here, involving both free-hand and measured map-making activities. With young children, very imprecise and untidy maps are more likely, while older children's maps can often be expected to be reasonably accurate, and to be as neat as their other work.

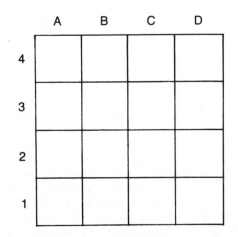

FIGURE 5.3 Simple grid reference system

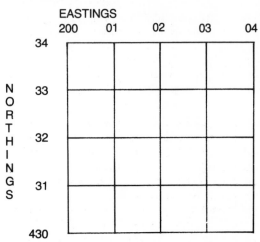

FIGURE 5.4 Numerical grid reference system

Freehand maps

Probably the first activity that the young child can do—or the inexperienced mapmaker—is to make a 'literal map', that is, draw round the base of an object, which is then removed, revealing its base shape and size, its ground form (see Fig. 5.5.).

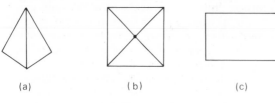

(a)   (b)   (c)

FIGURE 5.5

This can be done with a variety of objects. It is a good way of introducing both the idea of shape on a map as representing the ground space occupied, and of showing the child that when he looks from above it is the 'plan-form' that is mapped. That a plan-shape should be accurate in shape and proportion is introduced too. This, though, is drawing the outline of an object its true size.

To go a step further is to scale down the size of the object. This idea can be simply introduced by choosing a larger object, for example, a desk, and providing a smaller piece of paper for it to be 'mapped' onto. Objects on the desk might be included too, and named, introducing an additional map element, in this case nominal information about the objects portrayed (see Fig. 5.6). This can be undertaken with infant-age children, there being no need to present scale in definitive, absolute terms. Necessity introduces the idea. An advantage of mapping the desk initially is that it can also be viewed from above

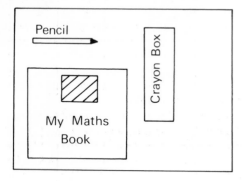

FIGURE 5.6

by the child. He is in a 'bird's eye' position. He could even stand on his chair to get a more 'distant' view.

At the next level of size and difficulty, in practical and visual terms, comes mapping a room, whether the classroom, hall, bedroom or lounge. It is very difficult to give children a view from above so they need to begin to be able to imagine themselves as if looking down from the ceiling when they draw their plan. At first several difficulties will occur, if done from scratch (see next section about partially completed plans). Children will find it difficult to draw the room the correct shape, and proportionally correct for wall lengths. Also they find it difficult to locate objects correctly and to get size right, for example groups or rows of desks (they tend to move to one side of the room or group in the middle—see Fig. 5.7). In this situation, it is always best, where the child may be dissatisfied with his work particularly, to allow children to do their maps in rough then draw them neatly afterwards. This gives room for amendment.

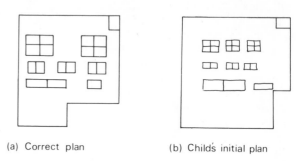

(a) Correct plan   (b) Child's initial plan

FIGURE 5.7

They should also be able to move around the room in order to draw their maps, looking, then returning to their places to work. At this stage a more abstract idea of plan-form is developing, from first-hand. Children often like to add colour to their maps. This represents an opportunity to introduce the idea of a key, identifying the codes used, unlocking meanings. This can be explained to the children. Scale automatically comes into the activity, as do orientation and direction, and the question of content. A look at the children's maps, if allowed free choice, will introduce a debate about why certain things have been included by some, but not by others. This can develop into a discussion about what to include or not, and why, on a class-produced map. (See below, re scale.)

Whereas the mapping undertaken in the activities above can be described as done in a small space, there are large space areas that can be mapped freehand, both in the environment and from memory. One type of larger space would be the school playground, often a fair-sized area, but open and visible. Once again the child can wander around and imagine a view from above. The difference between this space and that of the classroom is that it is usually a large, open, 'uninhabited' space—objects are around the side, not in the centre.

Another outside environment, which is also open, and can be viewed all at once by the child, is a street outside the school or home. This presents a different shape to the child for him to visualise and map, a corridor shape (indeed, corridors could be mapped, preliminarily, inside the school). It also provides the opportunity to develop to the next level of mapping activity, for a major element coming in at this point is how to map the buildings that line the street, how they can be presented. Children often do this, to begin with, by presenting an elevation view, which is not necessarily wrong for it is a representation of the feature that is included in the map (a pictorial symbol) (see Fig. 5.8.). It is also often the case that children draw detached house shapes, though they know perfectly well that the street in question has terraced houses on each side. Such drawing can be regarded, to a certain extent, therefore, as symbolic rather than 'realistic' or founded on ignorance. Talking to children about their maps, especially of large areas, is very important.

The next level of mapping takes the child away from the immediate situation to one in which his memory and imagination are called much more into play. This is the situation in which he is asked to draw a map of the school, either the building or a floor of it, or the grounds and the building. The difficulty here is that the child is no longer able to see all of the area to be mapped at the same time; he has to pass into and out of view of different parts of the whole in order to visit it all. As such, he therefore has to carry in his head a mental picture (sometimes called a cognitive map) of where he has been, and eventually of the whole area, in order to be able to draw it with any chance of reasonable accuracy. His map, then, depends to a large extent on his experience of the particular floor of the school, or of the shape of the grounds and building. This is not an easy activity for children to undertake, but it is an exciting one. Class discussion, perhaps leading into scaling and modelling, is a good follow-up here.

A similar activity used in this context, on a larger scale, is to ask children to draw a map of, or simply to draw, their route to school from home (Catling, 1978). (This can be varied to the route to the shops, to the local park and so forth.) When restricted to a single piece of paper (not necessary to adhere to—let the children stick two or three together if they wish to—after all they are not yet doing it to a set scale) this helps to develop further the idea of scale. Discussion can lead to developing each of the map elements referred to above—what is included, how is it symbolised, what additional information is added, is it correctly orientated and relatively scaled, and is it in plan form? Comparison with a local road or street map or with the 1:2500 map of the area to check accuracy would be valuable. The children can check the route as they walk to and from school, improving their map as they do, adding some information, removing other, correcting this direction, that shape, where the junction is, how many roads crossed, which buildings are where, and so on.

To take this further with young children is not always easy, because it depends to a large extent on their experience of and familiarity with the local environment. However, an extension of the above mapping activity is to ask the children to draw a freehand map, from memory, of the locality, the neighbourhood of the school. This

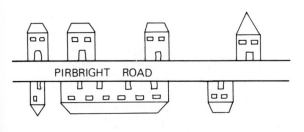

FIGURE 5.8

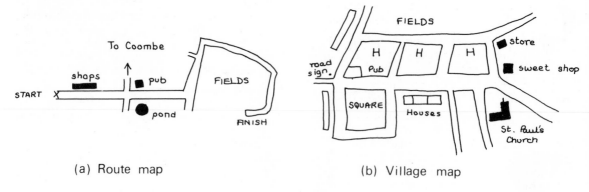

(a) Route map   (b) Village map

FIGURE 5.9

can be useful for showing up gaps in the children's local knowledge, besides being a useful mapping exercise that encourages them to concentrate on the skills involved as well as the layout of the street, buildings, park, and so on.

The final level, in terms of freehand map drawing, is to get the children to map an un-familiar environment, while on a school journey or a day's field trip, for example. This can be a useful way of discovering what interested them in the area, but it can also show how well they use their mapping ideas and skills, how quickly they familiarise themselves with the new 'layout', how they cope with building shapes they do not have time to examine, etc. Children's maps at this level tend to be more abstract in that *less* is often included (though content discrimination is not necessarily well thought out) and symbols are used to a greater extent, whether pictorial or coded. This activity can be undertaken in two ways, either the map started, and added to as the route is followed—in which case the children may well relate it to a route-map they should have anyway—or the map is drawn from memory back in the classroom, say, that evening or the next day. The situation can vary too, which will influence the map type; the children may map a route followed or an area they have explored. These tend to produce different map styles (see Fig. 5.9).

Scaled Maps

All the activities mentioned above have in-volved the children mapping an area, of greater or lesser extent, wholly visible or only visualised in the mind, undertaken either in the classroom or in the 'field'. These maps have all been drawn freehand, with distance, location, shape, scale and so on being relative, not absolutely measured. Map-drawing activities though, should not be limited to freehand mapping. It is important that the idea of accuracy in location, orientation, shape and scale be developed too. It is an activity that can continue side by side with the above, though it does to a certain extent rely on measuring and accurate drawing ability; equally, it can help to develop these too. A few alternative approaches are suggested in the following paragraphs.

The most obvious objects to draw to scale are those easily grouped and viewed by the child. A ruler or box can be drawn to half their actual size, a 1:2 scale being introduced. This is best done by using a 1 cm^2 or 2 cm^2 graph paper. This activity follows quite naturally on from the freehand drawing of such objects on smaller pieces of paper.

The next stage is obviously to draw a scaled plan of the desk on, say, 2 cm^2 graph paper. If objects are located on the desk, not only will they have to be drawn to scale, but correctly positioned too. One way to do this is to draw such objects to the same scale on separate pieces of paper and then to glue them on to the plan of the desk top, having measured from the edge of the desk where they are located (see Fig. 5.10). At a more complex level this idea can be used in the scaled mapping of the classroom. An outline can be drawn, and then the room contents to be included, measured, drawn and cut out—this could be a group or whole class activity—then coloured in or covered with sticky coloured paper before being glued to the classroom outline.

This method can be applied when drawing a

scale plan of the whole school, the grounds or a local street, though a smaller scale may well be required, e.g. 1 cm : 1m (i.e. 1:100). At a higher level the children can be required to *draw* all the features to be included *on* the map, so more care and thought are required. This is not easy and is best tackled at the latter end of the age range.

Second-hand Mapping

The penultimate element of mapping activity included here is that of tracing or sketching maps from second-hand sources, such as an aerial photograph. The aerial photograph is a picture-like map-form, and as such it resembles a map, but to be able to see it as such, children can be encouraged to draw from it and to notice what they have drawn. This, particularly, helps plan-form understanding. Discussion about content, symbols, etc., can also follow.

The most straightforward way to do this is to get the children to trace from the aerial photograph those things they wish to. They can then be asked to identify them, perhaps by colouring them and adding a key. Obviously large-scale vertical aerial photographs are needed here. These can be obtained blown up to almost any size, though 1:2500 or 1:1250 are the most valuable for tracing buildings. The first element noted will be the plan-form shape of the tracing. Also noted will be the lack of identification on the photograph. The familiar will be seen on the photograph, but once the tracing is removed it becomes necessary to add information if one is to remember the meanings

and identity of places, streets, etc. This can be undertaken while other activities are going on. By using photographs of the local area, the children's awareness is heightened.

Map for Others

The final point to be made here is to do with the purpose of the maps. It was noted earlier that mapping should best be integrated with other work, whether a local study or measuring in mathematics. One interesting addition is to get the children to draw the maps for someone else to use. This brings out elements like the necessity for a key, for common sense to prevail in content choice, and the need to state the purpose. Children often try harder to be accurate if they feel the map is going to be used.

Map-Making Activities, 2: Working with Prepared, Partially Completed Maps

Working with prepared, partially completed maps (see Fig. 5.11) helps children to develop their understanding of the idea of a map. This sort of activity involves a degree of understanding that should have begun to develop through early map-making. First, children need to have some idea of the plan-form of the map and of the symbolic code in order to comprehend what the teacher-drawn map displays. Second, the idea of scale comes into play, since it is already set by what has been drawn, even if only approximately. Thirdly, it is necessary to be able to sort out direction and orientate the map, particularly

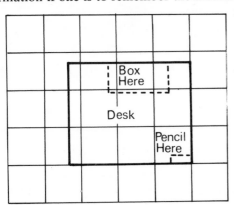

(a) Desk drawn to scale on graph paper

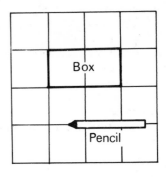

(b) Objects drawn to scale to cut out and glue on

FIGURE 5.10

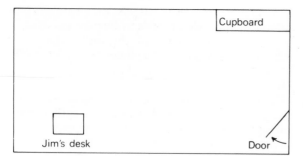

FIGURE 5.11
Exercise
Add the following to this map: all desks, the windows, the sink, bookshelves and the blackboards

if it is of a known environment, such as the classroom or a local street. Fourthly, children also need to be able to follow instructions, since these are usually more precise with this type of map activity.

An early activity may involve completing a map of the top of a desk. Children can be given the shape of the desk and chair (see Fig. 5.12), and asked to draw certain objects as if on the desk, seen from above. In this exercise the idea of plan-form is being stressed. Alternatives to this are to stress that the objects are drawn, comparably, to the correct scale or correctly orientated to where Jim is sitting. If the duplicated outline is to be of most value the desk shown should resemble the child's own and the objects those he uses daily. To carry this further, and to make it easier with younger children, it is often worthwhile asking the children to place the objects on the desk and to get them to draw them 'from reality'.

A follow-up to this approach is that already displayed in Figure 5.11, namely, getting the children to complete an outline and partly filled map of the classroom. It is useful to include in this sort of activity either the door, the blackboard, display boards or windows to be mapped,

because they are difficult items to map unless the child has grasped the plan-form/symbolism notions and is thoughtful in employing them. If they do not understand these ideas yet, these objects will often be displayed in elevation, even though desks may be in plan-form (see Fig. 5.13). A second major problem when working at this scale is that it is not easy for children to locate objects correctly or draw them to scale. Hence maps often end up looking rather inaccurate, as in Figure 5.13. With young children there are bound to be inaccuracies and problems in orientation, scale, symbols, plan-form and content. With the use of a variety of the ideas outlined both above and below these should grow fewer as children's experience and understanding develop.

At a smaller scale the same ideas can be encountered when completing partly-drawn maps of the school and its grounds. Whereas in the above examples the child will be mapping an environment he is in, it is possible in this context to use it as an opportunity to get him to think about what is in the school. Again, a partly-completed map, of the exterior walls of the school, for example (see Fig. 5.14), can be given

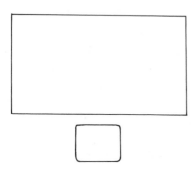

FIGURE 5.12
Exercise
Draw these to show that they are on your desk (remember you are looking from above): your maths book, pencil, ruler and rubber

FIGURE 5.13

to the child, and he can be asked to draw in the classrooms, corridors, staffroom, hall, toilets, head's office, secretary's room, etc. This can also be done as an active exercise, the head permitting, with the children in small groups walking round trying to get things right. The size, and enclosed nature of the building, makes this a more complex task.

The most complex situation in which this sort of activity can reasonably be used is in the local environment. Outline plans of streets can be used, with the children being asked to fill in missing items, e.g. streets, buildings and open spaces on the map at specific points on a walk in the area (see Fig. 5.15).

The final example given here also has bearing on the next section (as has the previous section), in that children can simply be given an outline of a place, for example, an island or group of streets, and be told to draw their own map using the outline as a starting point. This might be used not only for imaginative purposes, but as a means of

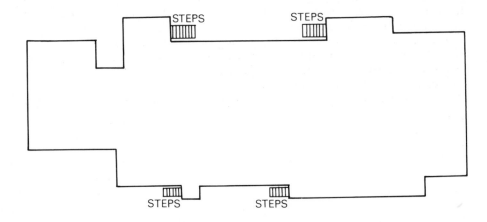

FIGURE 5.14   Plan of school buildings: ground floor

Exercise

Draw these places on the map: hall, corridors, classrooms, head's study, staffroom, secretary's office.

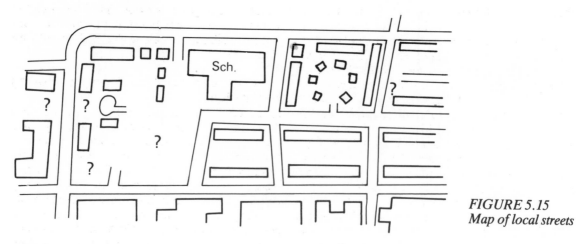

FIGURE 5.15
Map of local streets

Exercise

When we reach the areas that have been left out on the map, look round carefully. Then draw them onto your map. Remember to try and make them the right size.

assessing children's utilisation of the elements of map making.

The above are a few ideas which serve to illustrate the situations and scale in which they can be used. More stringent demands can be made of the children. The outlines might be drawn to scale, and the children requested to add specific items using the scale line, as, say, in Figure 5.11. Ideas used in other sections, both above and below, could be adapted to use here. Expectations of the children will obviously depend on their age, ability, manual dexterity, experience, and so forth.

Map-Making Activities, 3: Using Imagination

The idea of using one's imagination in map-making has already been introduced. It has a number of values, not least in that it releases the child from trying to get a real-world situation 'right'; he can design his own. It allows for assessing the child's understanding of the map-idea through the way he draws his map. It also allows for the possibility of working out one's own ideas; the idea of re-planning one's own environment can be encouraged.

One idea has already been expressed. It is that in which the child is given an outline map of a place or area and asked to develop it as he wishes, naming his place, putting in what he wishes, employing the symbols he wishes, and so forth.

This often allows children to include items that they may not normally put on large-scale maps, such as hilly areas, mountains, caves and suchlike. Some of their ideas may derive from seeing maps of imaginary places, such as Tolkien's map of Wilderland in *The Hobbit,* Milne's map of 100-Acre Wood and its environs in *Winnie-the-Pooh,* Adam's map of the Beklon Empire in *Shardik,* or, of course, Stephenson's map of *Treasure Island.* In many ways, maps of imaginary places, for children, are simply outlets for occupying space with their imagination. They can also tell a teacher a lot about what children think of, read, are interested in, and so on.

An alternative to free-running imagination is to restrain it in the context of a story. This can take two forms. On the one hand the child can be asked to write his own or a pre-titled story and then to draw a map of the place encountered in the story, or to draw a map of a place before or as he writes the story. This can have the effect of 'brightening up' the place element of the story and of controlling the sudden jumps from one thing to the next that children are prone to make in their imaginative writing. The second approach is to get children to draw a map of a place that has appeared in a story read to or by them. Again, they have complete freedom on the paper, no outline constraints, but the places mentioned in the story. In such cases one often finds that no two children's images of the same place are alike. Indeed, unless the author has drawn a map, there is no right answer as to exact place and orientation, perhaps even scale. The image generated by the story is all the child has to go on.

The most constrained creative context is to ask the children to plan their own environment. This can be done freely (e.g. futuristic worlds), but it is not always easy for children to think how they would like their classroom laid out or how they would alter their own locality. This sort of activity needs to be preceded by thought, discussion, perhaps writing, and possibly research. It can be taken a stage further in local study work, where local residents can be consulted and their ideas included in a class-produced map of what they feel their neighbourhood could/should be like. Once again, this may involve producing accurate, conventionally styled maps, in plan-form, to scale, correctly orientated, and so forth.

An alternative map-form is modelling. Children can be encouraged to make, in plasticine, paper, balsa wood or the like, a model village. By using papier-mâché a landscape of hills and dales can be constructed. Here, the children can use their imagination to lay out the village, street or whatever, perhaps to a pre-drawn plan. Alternatively, the site can evolve and a map of it can be drawn-up later, possibly full-size, based on a grid system and measured, or to smaller scale. This is a good way of introducing or backing up work both on grid reference location and orientation and on scale. Such work can be of a very simple nature—putting plasticine houses on a prepared village plan—or complex—a scaled model of the school

building and grounds. But, as a map-related activity, modelling is best founded in imaginary plans, leading to modelling the 'real world' with older children.

Working with Prepared Maps, 1: Adding Information

Prepared maps, in this context, include both those that a teacher might prepare, e.g. of a classroom or a street, for a specific purpose, *and* commercially available maps, such as those produced by the Ordnance Survey, or street plans, at varying scales, which can be updated by children. A number of different uses can be made of prepared outline maps. This section is concerned with those to which children can add information or use to produce their own maps which set out to communicate information to the map-reader.

One approach that can be undertaken with young children, but used equally well in larger environments with older children, is to require them to name on a map objects in the classroom. They can be named either on the map, or next to a set of numbers or letters (see Fig. 5.16). This activity requires the children to orientate the map and sort out its relationship to the internal structure of the room, to see the classroom in plan-form, and to understand the meaning of the shapes. It serves, therefore, as a useful activity in seeing how well children are able to 'read' their map.

Another activity that can involve children of all ages involves sorting the contents of a room into categories. Again, the classroom can serve as a useful introductory site, with desks being

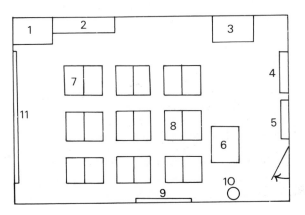

FIGURE 5.16
Exercise
Next to each number write the name of the object.

1.	6.
2.	7.
3.	8.
4.	9.
5.	10.

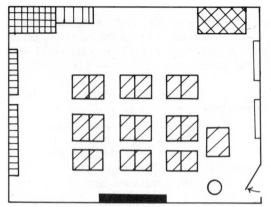

KEY (Choose a colour for each
          type of object)
      DESKS
      SINK
      DRAWING BOARD
      WASTE BIN
      CUPBOARD
      BLACKBOARD
      SHELVES
      WALL BOARDS

FIGURE 5.17

coloured, say, in red, cupboards in blue, sink in white, shelves in yellow, etc. (see Fig. 5.17). Here the idea of a *key* for the colour code is developed.

Outside the classroom, the same idea can be employed in building surveys, shop-type surveys and land-use surveys, where colours can denote different building types (e.g. factories, houses, shops) or land-use (e.g. industrial, residential, commercial, recreational). Here a prepared outline map can be taken into the 'field' by the children, a code for building type having already

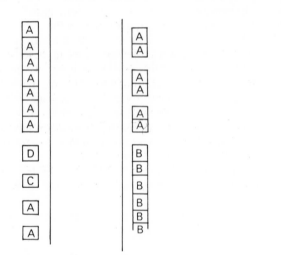

Key A — houses

     B — shops

     C — public house

     D — garage

(a) Outline map used in fieldwork

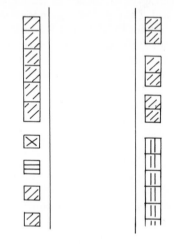

Key houses

     shops

     public house

     garage

(b) Finished survey on a second outline map

FIGURE 5.18

been decided for a local main-street survey. On this map the children would mark with letters or numbers the type of building, and on return to school would then colour code the items, sorting further if necessary, and on a fair-copy outline produce the finished map (see Fig. 5.18).

On a local street map, or a prepared street plan, other aspects of the locality can be marked, for example, the location of pillar boxes or of man-hole covers. The importance of the street in parking or traffic terms can also be mapped; such information might be gained by counting and being graphed. Different levels of 'use' can be discerned, and streets coloured according to the amount of use made of them (see Fig. 5.19).

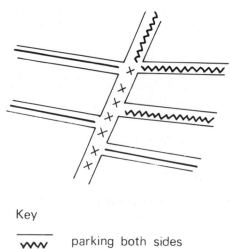

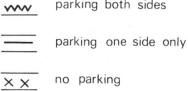

Key

〰〰〰 parking both sides

———— parking one side only

× × no parking

FIGURE 5.20

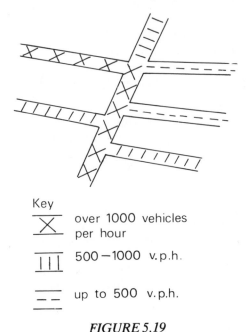

Key

✕ over 1000 vehicles per hour

⫘ 500 – 1000 v.p.h.

= = up to 500 v.p.h.

FIGURE 5.19

Other information which can be mapped includes parking restriction (see Fig. 5.20), one-way traffic systems, restrictions for different sorts of traffic (e.g. bus lanes, heavy lorries banned), bus routes, zebra crossings, traffic lights, and so on. There is a lot of 'street' information that can be readily mapped, and indeed, it provides an excellent opportunity for encouraging precision in the siting of objects often not included or out of date on the map, such as street furniture.

Maps can also be updated, by adding information. This can be done either as a result of local survey work, or by using recent vertical aerial photographs of the area. This, particularly, brings home to children a major limitation of the map, other than the problem of vertical representation, which is that maps are temporally finite; they are only maps of the place at the time the map was surveyed (probably already outdated at printing). Maps can be wrong, and it is important that children learn this limitation.

A further type of information that can be communicated by map is the lie of the land. Contour

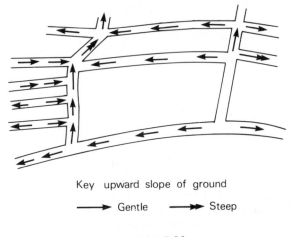

Key upward slope of ground

⟶ Gentle   ⟶ Steep

FIGURE 5.21

maps do indicate the height of land and in a general sense the lie of it. On large-scale maps they are often of little value. It is of more consequence to introduce children to the idea of high and low, rising and falling ground by using, for example, arrows indicating the upward slope of ground on street plans. This can help them to 'picture' the shape of the land (see Fig. 5.21).

Working with Prepared Maps, 2: Route-Finding

Map reading has been essential to many of the above activities. It can be further developed, before evolving to a more specific activity, by using the map as a guide to finding one's way about. This is best done, initially, using first-hand, and later with secondary sources. A few brief illustrations will serve to illustrate the value of this sort of activity.

A straightforward route-finding activity is to have the children take home a copy of a local street plan, following it either as they go home, or when they return to school next morning, marking the route they take on the map. (This can be a useful follow-up to the drawing of a map of the route to school.) The children can then see how the map depicts the streets they used, and it may well help them to develop their orientation, as well as encouraging them to look at the streets they use. A follow-up could be to mark all the routes on one map, perhaps at 1:2500 scale so that the routes followed and the houses of the children can be seen by all. This can show which are the most used streets (obviously those nearest to the school), which are used by many children (focal routes from different directions), and which are used near the homes of the children (the feeder routes).

An alternative, or follow-up to the above, is for children to take a map home for a week, and on it to mark, each time they use them, the streets they go down, and the destinations from home. Follow-up work similar to the above can be developed (see below).

As a class or group route-following activity, a walk can be undertaken. On their maps the children could mark the route that is followed. The teacher will need to check the accuracy of the children's recording, to inquire of them about directions, to help them use the compass to see which way to orientate the map, to encourage them to orientate the map without a compass but by reference to local features, and to enquire of

them which way to turn to go either in a particular compass direction or towards a particular destination. This can be undertaken by very young children around the school building or grounds, using a teacher-prepared map, in the local streets, and in unfamiliar environments, such as a country walk or field trip.

An alternative approach, as a field-trip activity for a day, for example, in an unfamiliar environment, is to put the onus for the route-finding on the children by utilising the method of the sport of orienteering. At this stage children will need to have an idea of grid references, orientation, map scale, symbolism, and some experience of route-following. The children could be divided into groups, each with a map, compass, etc., for the day's activity, which might be to find and leave helpful messages at five or six specific locations. A non-participating adult—not to be consulted, but to be relied upon to get the children back to base if well and truly lost!—*must* accompany each group. The map and compass should change hands at regular intervals, so that each child has the opportunity to be the decision maker about the route, in consultation with others if required (though never with the adult). It is a useful idea to keep a regular log of the activity of the group, made at each change of hands of the map, every half hour or so, since on this can be noted fortune and misfortune, map-reading errors and adventures. As a game it can be more exciting and interesting than as a straightforward walk from A to B.

Route-following activities at second hand can take a variety of turns! One is to prepare map workcards with locations marked on—local maps, Ordnance Survey maps, street plans, bus-route maps, etc.—the children being required to name the streets indicating the shortest route or a route from, say, B to A via C. This encourages children to consider alternative routes and to decide which to use.

Another class-based activity which can be used with young children is, again, a route-following activity that involves orientation understanding, symbol reading, and instruction following. Each child has a prepared map, and the teacher describes, verbally, a route which the children pencil in on the map as the teacher describes it. Directions need not be given only as 'turn left or right', but, if the compass points are marked, can include 'bear west at the crossroads', as well as directions not simply along streets but via objects symbolised on the map, e.g. 'go along Replington Road, turn right at the station and bear east at the church'. At times the teacher can stop and enquire where several of the children are. This can be most enlightening, for after a while, the same answer is not always forthcoming, and it can be entertaining finding out where the 'lost' children turned the wrong way, especially when they try to describe the way they went. This activity can be enjoyed by groups of children, using duplicated maps, where one of the group describes the route as the others attempt to follow it on the map.

Map Reading

The final group of activities to be described here may be termed map reading, though it takes two forms and involves two map products. Very often 'map reading' seems to be understood in terms of topographical or landscape interpretation. This is a very advanced skill, which depends a great deal on previous experience and constant activity in the field and classroom. Children of the 5-13 age range can achieve some competence in this skill, but it must be regarded here as the highest level of development, and, thus, children at this age will only be beginning to develop landscape interpretation skills. The other aspect of map reading is the understanding and evaluation of data from thematic maps particularly—what survey information can show, for instance—but also from local and Ordnance Survey maps. The two varieties of map product encountered here by children are, on the one hand, commercial maps, and on the other those produced in class from their own researches, often produced by one, two or a small group of children, but which must be understood by the others if information is to be communicated successfully. This involves not only good mapping, but correct reading and interpretation. The examples and ideas below illustrate these points. The interpretation of aerial photographs will also be noted.

One of the first activities that can be undertaken using a scaled map is measuring the distance of one place from another and interpreting it on the scale. Comparisons of, say, the distance of children's routes to school can be made; these can be compared to distance as the 'crow flies'. The distance of shopping centres from the community can be compared, and so on.

Thematic maps provide the opportunity to consider only one item, perhaps building types, or the distribution of pillar boxes, leading to the development of reasons why that feature occurs as and where it does. This may simply involve rationalising why pillar boxes are often placed at street junctions and outside post offices—a useful example with young children, for the analysis of spatial distribution of features on the earth's surface is a prime concern of the geographer. A different example may involve the use of more than just one piece of information. For instance, to explain the location of shops, awareness of housing and road communications is necessary. The explanation of neighbourhood shop types will probably involve a look at the shop types in the local shopping centre. A look at local industry will also involve a look at communications.

Where children have made a land-use survey of an area the analysis of the inter-play of the features shown—recreational to residential land, residential areas to industrial areas in old areas— can lead to more general conclusions about an area as a whole. Such information might be obtained from a careful examination of a 1:2500 or 1:10 000 Ordnance Survey map of the area combined with local knowledge. Such interpretations could lead to the examination of such ideas in the field. So, analysis and interpretation of a map in the classroom can introduce, as well as be involved in and conclude fieldwork, which will have an aim, whether information gathering or the testing of ideas.

An Ordnance Survey or street map can be used for the discovery of facts about an area. An aerial photograph—oblique or vertical—can also be used for this purpose. Such questions as: can you find a church, river, wood, park, tennis court, etc.? This is fairly straightforward information gathering.

There are certain things that it is difficult to ascertain from a map, and which an aerial photograph can help with. One is the height of buildings, particularly in an urban area. From a map it is not often possible to tell whether a building is low-rise or high-rise. A careful examination of a vertical aerial photograph can help here, because such a photograph is vertical only at one point, while elevation information becomes more pronounced, further away from the centre point of the photograph. Oblique photographs obviously provide a great deal more

ASPECTS OF MAP UNDERSTANDING	5 YEARS	7 YEARS
POSITION AND ORIENTATION	Pointing to place of features in classroom Developing locational/direction vocabulary (e.g. near to, left of) Developing knowledge of left-right relationships	Indicating direction of features in school Introduction to cardinal directions, and compass Aligning map by features in classroom Introduction to simple grids (e.g. A4, C3) Develop locational vocabulary
MAP SYMBOLS	Using own symbols in imaginary maps	Using own and class-agreed symbols in maps (develop understanding of why map symbols need to be understood) Develop understanding of need for KEY
MAP SCALE	(No reference in relation to maps) With shapes: relative size discussed (bigger, smaller) and shape (like, unlike)	Develop understanding of proportion and relative size Introduce scale readings: at very large scale (e.g. classroom)
MAP PERSPECTIVE	Using models, getting child to notice different views Drawing round 'life-size' objects: hand, toys, pencil, etc.	Introduce idea of map viewpoint: looking down from above: e.g. on desk, chair, etc. Looking at large-scale vertical aerial photographs Drawing the view from above (of desk, etc.)
MAP PURPOSE	(No reference needed)	Introduction to thinking why map has been drawn: location
MAP STYLE	Introduction to picture maps: imaginary places, classroom Introduction to oblique and vertical aerial photographs: large scale	Use teacher-prepared maps/plans of classroom, school, local roads Introduction to large scale O.S. maps: 1:1250, 1:2500 scale Introduction to street maps: games
MAP DRAWING	Drawing pictures/maps of imaginary places and from stories	Drawing maps of places in stories, from imagination, etc. Drawing map of route to school, plan of bedroom, etc. freehand
MAP READING	Talking about own maps, describing what they show Relating drawn shapes to objects Identifying features on vertical aerial photographs of home area	Following simple routes on maps Relating features to plan, e.g. in classroom, playground Finding information from map (e.g. can you go from A to B by road?) Finding information from vertical aerial photograph of own area
MAP INTERPRETATION	(Not at this level)	Introduction to giving explanations from map (i.e. cannot go that way because . . .) Introduction to using other sources with map (e.g. written information, pictures)

FIGURE 5.22   Outline of map skills

9 YEARS	11 YEARS	13 YEARS
Indicating direction in neighbourhood Developing knowledge of cardinal directions and use of compass, and north direction on map Aligning map of school and local streets by features and compass Introduction to 4-figure grid reference Develop vocabulary: accuracy	Indicating directions around globe Develop knowledge of cardinal directions and compass use Aligning map in neighbourhood, on field trips by features and compass Introduction to 6-figure grid references Develop vocabulary: precision	
Introduction to standard map symbols, 1:10 000 and 1:25 000 scale O.S. maps, and atlas maps Develop awareness of limitations of map	Using standardised symbols Widen knowledge: 1:50 000 O.S. map key Develop understanding of atlas map symbols	
Develop appreciation of proportion Develop scale reading: 1:1250, 1:2500 scale O.S. maps Introduction to scale drawing (e.g. classroom) Develop appreciation of need for scale bar on map	Develop scale reading and estimating Develop scale drawing Introduction to measuring area on map Introduction to comparison of map scales	
Develop understanding of map viewpoint: looking down from higher up Using large-scale vertical aerial photographs with relevant map Introduction to height on maps: slope	Increase understanding of map perspective reducing scale Develop understanding of height shown on maps, and slope (contours)	
Develop understanding of why map drawn: distribution Introduction to 'thematic' maps	Develop understanding of why map drawn: relationships Develop ability to choose correct map for specific purpose Introduce idea of relationship between purpose, scale, symbols and style	
Use of teacher-prepared maps/plans for study, and O.S. maps: 1:1250, 1:2500 Introduction to 1:10 000 and 1:25 000 O.S. scales Use of 'thematic' maps: bus, rail, etc. Introduction to atlas map for reference and use of globe	Use O.S. 1:10 000 and 1:25 000 for study Introduction to 1:50 000 O.S. maps for study Use of atlas maps and globe for study Use of 'thematic' maps for study	
Drawing maps from imagination, etc. Drawing maps of neighbourhood, school, etc. freehand Introduction to scale drawing of classroom, playground etc.	Designing places in map-form from imagination, or related to study Drawing scale plans of larger areas Drawing 'thematic' maps	
Stating and following routes on maps Choosing routes for journeys: shortest, correct, etc. Relating map of area to vertical aerial photograph Introduction to relating oblique aerial photograph to map	Describing and discerning routes on maps Develop ability to pick out chief characteristics of mapped area Develop ability to relate oblique aerial photograph to map	
Introduction to describing small areas shown by map Developing need to give reasons for distribution shown on map Develop ability to relate other information to map (e.g. graphs, aerial photographs), and maps to each other	Develop ability to describe the mapped area Develop ability to explain relationships shown on map, using additional sources (e.g. settlement patterns, drainage patterns)	

information and can be used to considerable effect in conjunction with maps and vertical aerial photographs. As with the map, the vertical aerial photograph is not a great help when information about the lie or shape of the ground is wanted, but oblique photographs are useful here.

An important interpretative value of using a recent vertical aerial photograph in conjunction with the same scale Ordnance Survey map, particularly at 1:2500 scale, is its usefulness in indicating where the map is out of date and the changes that have occurred. By comparing the photograph with the map, and by mapping from one to the other, children can see what needs bringing up to date, identify the changes, and perhaps even produce their own updated map, further corrected in the field.

Boths maps and vertical aerial photographs can be taken out to be used in the field, though the latter presents greater difficulty to children because of its lack of labels, e.g. street names, park names etc. But a walk along a street, comparing photographic or map features to the building frontage, provides a valuable opportunity to show the 'reality' of the map content, and to allow for the 'dead ground', unseen at street level, to be placed and identified in the map or photograph.

The essence of the map is its two-dimensional portrayal of the three-dimensional world. This makes it a very difficult type of document for young children to use to interpret landscape, and, indeed, to do so in the classroom after no field experience is simply purposeless teaching. Being able to 'imagine accurately' an area, even if familiar, from a map is an advanced skill, but children at the upper end of the age range are capable, with experience, of developing some of this skill. Constant use of maps in local studies helps to provide initial experience, but it is important, since subsequently as adults children are most likely to use 1:10 000, 1:25 000 or 1:50 000 maps, to introduce them to maps of these scales in the field. This can be done in the locality, but may better be done through field trips to less familiar or unfamiliar environments, particularly where high ground allows for a good vantage point. In this way features can be easily pointed out and compared with the map features. This is one way of introducing the child to contour reading—the idea that contour lines

represent height (see below). By using maps constantly, children can become familiar readers of maps and begin to be able to draw some conclusions about an area from a map. The extent of this will depend on other knowledge: place names, river development, types of relief features—and this depends on the studies the child has undertaken.

One important area in which experience is important is in the reading of contour lines. A useful introduction for the child is to use a 1:25 000 Ordnance Survey map in a hilly or upland area, where a steep slope is well shown by the contour lines on a map. Viewing the site from the bottom, marking the route and viewing it from the top, are useful ways of practically experiencing the fact that contour lines represent the height and indicate the slope of land. This can be well followed up in the classroom by modelling the area visited using a suitable contour interval to help create the slopes (see Chapter 4.6). It is important to discuss what is happening as this activity is undertaken.

Geological maps can be introduced to older children of this age range, but their interpretation depends to a large extent upon experience and knowledge of rock types and visits to obvious outcrop areas. Where a school is in a chalk or limestone area, for example, it can be useful to use the geology map to look at the idea of springline settlement, in conjunction with appropriate Ordnance Survey maps. In many cases though it will be only the occasional day field trip or school journey that allows for such an introduction.

CONCLUSION

The above has been a presentation of a range of activities, situations and ideas for map work, some in the context of wider studies, some as skill exercises in mapping. It was stressed early on that mapping as an end in itself is of little value. The map is a medium of communication, whether of a route, facts about a place or general statements about areas. In setting out a structured basis for developing map skills it is not intended that work in one area must be preceded by work in another. Sometimes one activity will serve two or three different purposes. Adding information to a map involves reading it, orientating it, and so forth.

It is important that children come across these

ideas throughout their school lives. We do not teach reading or arithmetic in only the infant years and never touch it again. Similarly, work with maps needs to be structured and begun early, concepts and skills being revisited continually as the child develops, presented in different ways at different levels of understanding and skill.

Finally, the chart in Figure 5.22 is intended to give some indication of when to introduce, and of the need to develop, the understandings and skills the child needs in order to be able to use maps. The division of the chart into two-year sections reflects the breaks of various school systems and is not intended to present a rigid structure of what should be taught when. The outline is intended to act as a guide to aid the teacher in developing map work in a geography/ environmental studies curriculum. Furthermore, the reference to an idea at a particular age does not preclude its use at a later age, or at an earlier age when appropriate. This chart should be treated as a flexible guide to be adapted to the circumstances of the school.

5.3 Environmental Perception and Maps

Simon Catling

Environmental perception studies involve more than looking at the neighbourhood to see what is there. The prime concern is *how* the environment is seen, what different people make of it, how they represent it, what they think of the places they inhabit and work in, of the routes they use, the shopping centres they visit, and so on.

How can children of 5 to 13 years possibly consider the question raised by any study of environmental perception? Obviously not overtly, but it is quite possible to utilise perception study methods with young children. Much work of this sort will chiefly involve the personal views of the children, but other children and adults can be enquired of too.

One traditional introduction to mapwork is to ask the child to draw a map of the route he follows to school. This also provides an excellent example of environmental perception. Two aspects of this approach can be drawn from such maps. Firstly, the aspects of the environment that the child includes on his map provide an insight into the important (to him) features of the route. A class activity would be to examine each map and to note the common feature types, for example, sweet shops, that the children include. Where children follow the same route their map contents can be compared to find out who includes which features. This leads to the second aspect which is to enquire of the children why they notice those things and why they put them on their maps. This can raise an interesting discussion, and not infrequently the children state that they do not know why. Such work can lead into a closer look at the route to school and more intricate mapping/drawing of it. This can be followed up—or, alternatively, introduced—by asking the children to write about or describe orally the route they take.

The above idea can be applied to wider and larger environments. Children can be asked to draw a map of their neighbourhood. This will help to identify those local features which are regarded as important. Children can be sent home to ask parents where they think the local neighbourhood is, by drawing a map. These maps can be compared by the children with their own. To take this a stage further the maps can be assessed against the five elements that have been identified as structuring the individual's image of urban places. These elements have been outlined as:

1. Paths—that is, lines of movement; e.g. streets, railways, rivers.
2. Edges—that is, boundaries between areas, borders; e.g. walls, rivers, roads.
3. Districts—that is, areas having a common identity; e.g. city centre, suburb, council estate.
4. Nodes—that is, central points which one travels to or from, focal spots; e.g. major crossroads, city centre, market square.
5. Landmarks—that is, easily identifiable sites; e.g. churches, tower blocks, public toilets, open space, historic sites.

Children at the upper end of this age range can

examine the maps of others to assess the elements that people use to structure their maps, though statements about what they find are likely to be more of a factual nature, e.g. 'all the maps had roads on them, but on some that was all'.

Another approach, especially useful in neighbourhood studies, is to ask respondents, while conducting a shoppers' survey, for example, to draw on a local street map the boundary of the neighbourhood. From this can be traced a composite map of all the boundaries, and the widest boundary and core of the neighbourhood identified. Reasons for the boundary shape, core and so on can be considered, especially where anomalies arise. Attempts can be made to think why the respondents drew their maps as they did, an approach which indicates the limitations of research—though does not invalidate it.

A further activity is the production of a 'trail'. If well structured, and based on detailed local study, the preparation of, for example, a town trail can open children's eyes to much that goes unnoticed in a neighbourhood. Once children start to notice things they seem to go on noticing, and then develop the habit of asking awkward questions about what they have seen. To work on a town trail within their own locality will not only set them observing and enquiring, but will also present them with the problem of deciding what to include, in what order, and so on. Developing a 'trail' guide involves them, inadvertently, in structuring other's perceptions!

A final illustration relates to the imaginative abilities of the child. Children can be asked to draw maps of imaginary places, whether islands or suburbs, futuristic or based on concrete knowledge. Such images can provide insight into the way children regard their environment, what they think should be there, what they would include, and so on. But it can show the shortcomings of their understanding, and as such is a useful guide to the teacher, for often emphasis is placed on certain aspects of the environment at the expense of others. Making a model village as a class activity can bring this home to the children fairly clearly, especially if it is given 'life'. What do the people who live in it do? Where do they shop? What sort of shops? What is their reaction to a local council's wish to develop the area? With the class role-playing the inhabitants of such a village, these questions can be considered. Alternatively, some commercial games can be utilised, such as Coca Cola's 'man in his environment'. Teachers could devise a local redevelopment situation, with the children playing residents, shopkeepers, councillors, etc., in order to give them some insight into the way people view and value the places they live in.

The foregoing activities illustrate ways in which children can be encouraged to see *how* people feel about their environments, how they use them, what they see them as, and what they include in or exclude from their neighbourhood. Some activities, such as that involving modelling a village with the class taking the villagers' places, can be enjoyed by 7 and 8-year-olds. Others, such as the analysis of the elements of individuals' images of places, are best used at the upper age range. It is, or course, possible to go further than this, with children drawing maps of their idea of places they have studied, perhaps their map of Britain, South America or wherever. So the perception approach can be not only an eye-opener to the children but an assessment procedure that teachers can use.

5.4 Atlases and Atlas Mapwork

Herbert A. Sandford, assisted by Gerald Young

The youngest of children delight in turning the pages of a colourful atlas. As soon as they can read they eagerly search for familiar names. This leads us too readily to assume that they also understand the maps, that they are able to relate them to the real world. We overlook the possibility that the child's fascination might stem from the maps not being quite understood, familar names in a mysterious context. Even bright teenagers do not notice all the symbols, misread and misunderstand them, and generally read the maps in an uncomprehending and literal manner.

It is a prime requirement for every child to acquire a reasonably accurate and complete mental image of the world's surface, the 'great world stage' of James Fairgrieve. This is the habitat of Man, where he is born, works and plays, and dies. The phenomena on this surface that are most significant to us are visible and make up the varied landscapes. We extend our activities onto the seas, and seascape with landscape may be called the episcape.

A total or holistic image of the episcape is not obtained from separate studies, however interesting and lively, of an Australian sheep station, North Sea oil, animals in danger, a Canadian lumberjack, an Indian village, the food we eat, and so forth. Of themselves, these valuable topics provide no clue to the overall pattern and their interrelationships remain obscure. They are for the child like starting a jigsaw puzzle, finding a few recognisable pieces but not knowing where to lay them down as part of the whole and as yet unknown picture. Only when an atlas is used can these disparate studies be seen in context and in relation to each other, so that a global pattern emerges. At some stage it becomes essential for the child to be able to find his or her way about an atlas with assurance and ease.

Wall maps at 'atlas-scale' and projected (or diascope) maps are no substitute for the individual use of an atlas by a pupil at his own pace, though they are useful adjuncts for some teaching purposes. Neither is a demonstration globe a substitute for an individual atlas, though it *must* be used sufficiently to avoid the misconceptions as to direction, distance and shape that result from the unavoidable distortions in flat maps of a round world.

The major requirement of an atlas is that it shows the main features of the world's landscapes. Political maps, maps coloured country by country and overprinted with a few towns and railways, are at first the most attractive to the younger child, but they contribute little to a mental construct of the landscape. Physical maps, maps coloured according to height, attempt to portray the *shape* of the land surface, but not its cover of forest, farm and desert. Some towns and railways are generally added. The altitude colours used are quite unrealistic and engender errors that may never be eradicated. Relief shadow is often added in order to give a better visual impression, but this does not dispel the illusion of much of the Sahara being fertile or Zimbabwe a desert.

General-purpose maps combine both the political and the physical. Such maps provide a more complete portrayal of the landscape. They are generally coloured by altitude with added political frontiers, but they may be coloured politically with overprinted relief shadow. Relief shadow without altitude colours is often incomprehensible to young children.

A new kind of map has been developed in recent years. These may be called landscape maps and they are coloured, not by country or height, but by the cover of the land surface. Some show only the 'natural' land cover and so are merely 'potential vegetation' maps, but generally they depict various forest, farm and desert environments. Typically they bear overprinted symbols for towns, frontiers, rivers, railways and so on, and also hill shadow. They then become very realistic, general-purpose, landscape maps and are often referred to as 'environmental maps'. They provide the best available representation of our world in a manner readily comprehended by young children. It is much to be regretted that although these environmental maps show the towns as competently as any other maps, full advantage has not been taken of the opportunity to show townscapes comprehensively, to portray realistically the extent of this, our most important environment. No doubt future editions will put this right.

For young children the general-purpose map is the most suitable and may be used in various ways. It may be used to locate a new place that comes up in the course of the pupil's learning. 'Location' is a meaningless word unless it involves site (e.g. for Paris, that it is sited on the River Seine) and position (e.g. for Madrid, that it is in the middle of Spain). Through constantly locating places there will gradually build up a remarkably complete global overview. Meaning will become attached to the symbols and many important concepts will be acquired effortlessly and unconsciously. Such work involves the use of an index and, when the children are old enough, the geographical co-ordinates of latitude and longitude. Although very difficult, these provide the only standard reference system and no person can consider himself educated if he cannot use it.

The use of atlases in schools to locate places, and consequently all atlas work in schools and by non-professional adults, is becoming frustrated by the increasing adoption of revised spellings for place-names. Already in some atlases our pupils search in vain for Cairo on the Nile as it is given as El Qâhira on the Nahr en Nil, while the pupil must *already know* where Peking and the Yangtse are to recognise them when mapped as Beijing and Changjiang. Yet foreign atlases spell London variously as Londres, Llundain, Lontoo, Londyn, Londen and so forth, and every language has many proper names in the vernacular: this is normal and appropriate. Nor are we being required to make a sacrifice in intelligibility for the sake of international conformity: Beijing is all but universally known as Pekin or Peking. It is not pronounced as Beijing in China itself and seldom written that way. If the revised spellings eventually become received into our everyday language, our teaching and our atlases should reflect this. Until then it is desirable to select an atlas that uses the accepted anglicised names.

The atlas can also be used for route finding and route planning: the voyages of Captain Cook, the flight paths of Concorde, a trip down the Rhine or 'where I went for my holidays'. This work will involve direction, distance and time, and hence the use of scales, with the older pupils. In the third place, the atlas can provide a general background of information about a particular area being studied, such as Lapland or the Pampas. This involves areas, distributions and the use of the globe. By these three means the map of the world is studied at points, along lines and over areas so as to build up a complete picture.

A fourth use of the atlas is to study patterns of distribution such as the 'millionaire' cities or the great mountains of the world. Most distributions, however, are better studied with the help of thematic maps that are more suited to the topic, whether this is of volcanoes or animals in danger. The general map is still necessary, however, in order to maintain the environmental context and make the work more meaningful.

It is important for us to remember that what *we* can read on the map without effort is for the *child* a feat of laborious interpretation. Constant use of the atlas as part of all relevant class teaching will enable a gradual development of the required concepts and skills so that learning capacity is never strained. It is also important for us to remember that skill in number (or language) is *not* an essential prerequisite for atlas mapwork. That America faces Britain, Scotland is nearer the Pole, Tibet much higher, New Zealand on the opposite side of the world and furthest from us, are all facts crucial to an understanding of Man on the Earth. They are readily comprehended from the atlas, but precise distances, directions and heights may be left to later, when the child is sufficiently numerate. Atlas mapwork is *not* to be regarded as a suitable medium for teaching number skills. It is too difficult of itself for children to be given the added burden of coping with new mathematical skills or practice in using them.

Atlases vary greatly in the extent to which they cater for the needs of interdisciplinary enquiry. An increasing number include thematic maps, pictures and diagrams that serve the needs of the scientific, social, historical and religious elements in these general studies. Such material on the world's peoples, wonders of the world, famous explorers, vanishing species and so forth should be used with general maps in order to maintain the total environmental context that is a large part of their explanation. A diligent search of these general maps and of the more traditional thematic maps will reveal that they have a considerable potential, often unrecognised, for use with social and environmental studies.

Further information on atlases can be found in the articles by Sandford (1972-80) and Sorrell (1978) listed in the References section. For a guide to the selection of an atlas for young children see Appendix 3.

6. Teaching about distant environments

David and Jill Wright

Geographers who are educationists seem to be uniquely concerned about the appropriate age and method of introducing young children to distant environments. Such a concern is right and proper, but as every parent and infant teacher knows, by the age of five children already have concepts of 'different' and 'distant'. Television's 'Playschool' *assumes* that the rest of the world exists—people from overseas lead or take part in programmes, and film snippets sometimes show aspects of life in other countries or the origin of some of our foodstuffs and other familiar but foreign items. Many stories for young children are set in foreign environments—indeed, almost all pre-schoolers have heard of 'Darkest Peru' even if they think it is reached from Paddington Station!

It is most important to remember that 'distant environments' to young children are not necessarily overseas and far away. The suburbs may well seem distant and foreign to the inner-city child, while much of the inner-city is another 'world' to suburban children, even the well-travelled ones. To both these groups rural areas with cows in green fields and combines in the corn will be almost as foreign as the African savanna or Arctic snows. Many of the methods indicated in this chapter for making the distant seem near and real are as necessary for London children learning about Cornwall or rural East Anglian children learning about Manchester as they are for British children learning about Germany or Jamaica.

WHY TEACH ABOUT DISTANT ENVIRONMENTS?

Modern education involves drawing out from children the concepts they have in embryo and bringing them to birth and maturity. As we have seen, an awareness that the rest of the world exists is already present in very young children. Even the staunchest advocates of child-centred learning point out that the teacher must move children on from what they are already interested in and give them new dimensions and experiences. So the 'embryo-concepts' about the rest of the world must be developed.

This is worthwhile because the rest of the world *is* relevant. Few items in everyday use in this country are entirely home-produced—even local potatoes come in plastic or paper sacks made from imported oil or pulp. In many schools a proportion of the pupils have relatives—maybe their own parents—who were born abroad or still live abroad. Package holidays in Spain are often cheaper than family holidays in Britain, so it is not uncommon to find children of any age who remember a holiday abroad, or are looking forward to one. And in this TV age, the rest of the world is constantly invading our living-rooms, through 'Blue Peter' special assignments, 'John Craven's Newsround', other factual programmes, and also through 'Westerns' and other fiction. So there are plenty of opportunities to latch onto a world that already seems relevant to the pupils.

Teaching about distant environments reduces ignorance, which is one factor in the development of prejudice—a point emphasised below. Increasing contact makes the world seem a small place now, and it may seem even smaller than we can imagine when the children we teach are adults. Problems that involve us and our children—conservation, pollution, resources, economic development—are global in their effect and ultimately global solutions are needed. And, from the point of view of geography and its concepts, only a study of distant environments reinforces the absolutely basic concept of scale. Simple geographical terms can only be understood when seen in the context of distant examples: the local stream needs to be compared with the distant river, the local pond with the distant lake and ocean. British hills—even for the children who live among them or visit them—need to be related to the Alps or Rockies or Himalayas.

All this might seem too obvious to be repeated in a publication like this, and yet it is amazing how rarely the rest of the world crosses the classroom threshold. Geographical experience, like charity, should begin at home, but if it stays there year after year for the children, then they leave middle school with very little knowledge and awareness of the world of which they are a part. The practical administrative problem seems to be that if there is no trained geographer with oversight of the geographical experience of the children in a school, then 'topics' and 'integrated studies' become planned—or unplanned—without anyone noticing that a group of children progressing through the school may escape any teaching about the world beyond their own doorstep.

Besides administrative problems, which can be overcome once the staff of a school are aware of them, some teachers believe that there are sound educational reasons why distant environments should not be studied by young children. This fallacy seems to have developed through a misunderstanding of Piaget's writings. Piaget emphasises that most children below the age of 12 need concrete rather than abstract material to study, and some teachers have assumed that 'concrete' necessarily means 'local'. But a distant iceberg can become 'concrete' in Piaget's use of the word, if related to ice-cubes in a cold drink. Even the problems of permafrost—an 'advanced' concept not normally touched before the sixth form—become 'concrete' if a harsh winter has lifted the asphalt in the playground: *some* discussion of what effect prolonged freezing might have on waterpipes and foundations is possible with young children in this context, because the teacher has started from 'concrete' reality.

These pleas for distant environments to feature in the curriculum will be familiar to most teachers as being among the reasons why geography is an important field of education. The idea that the curriculum should include a study of distant environments as a matter of principle for all teachers has also received powerful support from two sources. Firstly, the UK Government has signed the Unesco declaration (1974), on 'Education for International Understanding'. This states: 'There should be an *international* dimension and a *global* perspective in education at *all* levels and in all its forms.' The phrase 'all levels' clearly includes first and middle schools. Among the objectives of education this document gives prominence to 'the promotion of understanding, tolerance and friendship among all nations, racial and religious groups', and 'awareness of the increasing global interdependence between peoples and nations'. By signing the declaration, Her Majesty's Government has also agreed to provide 'financial, administrative, moral and material support' for education for international understanding. Hence, in our decentralised education system, each school should be formulating a policy for introducing a coherent global perspective into its curriculum—which must include a study of distant environments.

A Unesco declaration may seem too remote to be significant, but the same can hardly be said of resolutions by teachers' unions. The NUT is affiliated to the World Conference of Teaching Professions, and their 1976 conference resolutions were on very similar lines. They speak of 'the concern of *all* teachers' (i.e including primary school teachers) 'and their professional organisations to achieve through the educational process a world that is more humane, equitable, more balanced socially and economically, and a society which eliminates narrow materialism.' If this sounds too idealistic, John Carnie's research (summarised in Carnie, 1972) suggests that it is between the ages of 5 and 13 that attitudes are formed, that tolerance can be fostered in these years, and that the later years of schooling have much less effect on changing pupils' attitudes to other nationalities.

The problem is to work out practical means of achieving such ideals. The 1976 World Conference of Teaching Professions resolution makes some specific recommendations.

1. Teachers should encourage *open discussion*, which allows students to develop a respect for all human beings.

2. Teachers should champion the cause of *social justice* for all students in their classes. (We suggest in this context that from the age of five, children have strong views on what is 'fair' and 'not fair': this can be widened to ask, for example, if it is 'fair' that tea-pluckers stay poor even if the price of tea doubles.)
3. Teachers should educate all youth to practise co-operation along with competition.
4. Teachers should make appropriate use of mass media and seize all other opportunities to publicise the concept of a global community.
5. Teachers should eliminate prejudice and bias from their teaching.

The conclusion from these summaries of the Unesco and WCOTP resolutions is clear; ways must be found of teaching effectively about the rest of the world. These conferences were not concerned with 'Geography' as such, but they *were* concerned about 'Geo', the world. The resolutions imply that any teaching about the world does affect attitudes and values, so geographers above all teachers should be concerned about the quality of teaching about distant environments.

POSSIBLE PITFALLS

One of the WCOTP resolutions called on teachers to eliminate prejudice and bias from their teaching. Various distortions have crept into the teaching of distant environments, often from the best of motives, and it may be helpful to spell out some of the possible pitfalls.

The teaching many children receive about distant environments is confined to those predictable and old-established members of the 'human zoo'—eskimos in igloos, pygmies in the jungle, aborigines in the outback, bedouin leading camel caravans, etc. This 'happy band' features in numerous books still advertised in publishers' catalogues. Indeed 'Pedro drives the llamas', 'Ali leads the camels' and others have been lifted from the printed page to become the themes of multi-media packs for any primary school with money to spare. Whatever the format, the approach is the same: a simple native living a simple life, explained by elementary reference to the environment. The emphasis is on the *differences;* on the strangeness of the life they

lead. These members of the 'human zoo' have often outlived the manner of life described, but eskimos aiding oil prospectors and living in shanties or wooden huts are not quite as romantic as the ones who live(d) in igloos! Yet we must teach about the world as it *is* and seek out the facts on the countries we teach. Even if the impact of up-to-date information and other approaches has transformed or abolished the human zoo from some geographical studies, it is going strong in other subject areas. Stories for little children may be the first to implant ideas— Dick Bruna's happy sailor sails north to chance upon a happy eskimo family who take him by dog-sledge to their cosy igloo where he spends a happy night beside a huge fire! (D. Bruna, *The sailor*, Methuen.) Older children may be given 'explanations' of historical events in terms of natural characteristics and a crude environmentalism long abandoned by geographers.

From the 'happy native' to the 'poor native': another area to be wary of is over-emphasis on poverty, and the over-simple and over-dogmatic explanations of the causes of poverty abroad. When experts still argue over the causes of economic underdevelopment, it is hardly desirable for pupils to equate poverty with laziness as *the* cause or 'harder work' as *the* solution. Similarly, 'too many babies' is not a helpful idea on its own. Nor should any one 'solution'—even the currently fashionable 'small-scale rural development'—be stressed above all others. Emphasis on poverty may evoke an emotional response, but it may be counter-productive in helping pupils to appreciate that other cultures are worthwhile and other people's ideas and ways of life are to be valued. Too much emphasis on poverty and problems can lead to pupils suggesting one big solution—an atom bomb. Study of problems *must* be balanced by the study of achievements—cultural ones, as well as economic ones.

Allied to this is the pitfall of excessive and misleading generalisation. We have argued that children learn more effectively from the 'concrete fact' but obviously this must be widened into a general concept. For example: 'Water is fetched in pots from a water hole three miles away'. (Concrete fact.) 'Getting water is a big problem in many places.' (General concept.) But this should *not* lead to 'Africa is short of water'. (Excessive generalisation.) There are thousands of pupils who know that 'Africans live in straw huts' and others who know that 'Africans live in modern skyscrapers'. Both groups are partly right, but both have suffered from misleading generalisations, which may be the basis of many prejudices.

A 'concrete' approach that is natural and commendable is to start a topic with 'product x comes from country y', with x being a product we consume or use in everyday life. But this approach is rather similar to an awful rhyme in our small daughter's *First book of animals:*

What does he do, this pig so neat?
He gives us pork and ham to eat !

This is not the pig's-eye view, to put it mildly— yet we do Sri Lankans an equal disservice if their *raison d'être* is presented merely as tea production for us. While a study may well *start* with product x from country y it should not finish there.

In connection with such studies it is appropriate to sound a note of warning about materials. Projects on products often use a lot of free material from big companies. Much of this is very commendable, but it is promotional literature and few companies wish to promote a critical view of their activities.

Another pitfall in studies of economic development is for schools to stress the 'big project' and to see the 'solution' to a problem as a multi-million pound scheme. The assumption that capital-intensive development is 'normal' and 'right' is a common way of thinking in Europe, but it is not necessarily true for the tropics. 'Intermediate technology' may not only be more appropriate for tropical developments, but it can be a helpful educational concept, for the big project is often *too* big for children to visualise or understand, while the small, village-level development (a new road or a new well or a new clinic) is much more concrete and comprehensible to them.

The emphasis on *economic* development that is likely to be a feature of any study of tropical environments must not be seen as a full statement of the purpose of life, even in the simple studies made by first school pupils. Economic development affects social life. Spiritual values are more important than material values for millions of people in the poor—and in the rich—worlds. A

new temple may be more important than a 'useful' road to an Indian village.

Finally, we must be aware of our pupils' preconceptions, which will effect their study of distant environments. Their concept of scale may be very rudimentary, so that the sheer size of a country such as India, length of journeys between main cities, the enormous distances that have to be taken into account in any development programme, will not be understood unless time is set aside to measure and compare distances, heights and journey times. Further, most pupils will assume that much of the accepted structure of modern British life exists in every country, for example, that the government looks after you if you are ill, or unemployed, or old. Only after such misconceptions have been discussed can they begin to see, for example, that a large family might make good sense to parents in a poverty-stricken area.

MAKING IT REAL

We have already suggested that the fact than an environment is distant does not mean that it is irrelevant—so there should be some point of contact between the pupils and the topic. This explains the popularity of the 'product' approach; children are familiar with bananas and chocolate and tea and aluminium saucepans, so a study of their production forms a link in a chain between the class in England and bananas or bauxite in the West Indies, cocoa in Ghana and tea in Sri Lanka. We have already noted the dangers arising when such studies form more than the introduction. There are plenty of other points of contact that may be made: through news items (a natural disaster, a royal visit or important sporting event), the holidays of the teacher or class member, a school visit, town twinning, etc. When such opportunities do not arise interest has to be aroused in less obvious ways.

Actual objects from a country attract attention and act as valuable and genuine 'specimens' in geographical work (comparable to rocks in geology or manuscripts in history). When very young children are asked to maintain an 'interest table', it is amazing how much they can accumulate! Can labels provide more than a patch of colour to a display about a country: they add a sense of reality to the study. Actual food-stuffs can be looked at—maybe eaten: everyday items, such as rice, or more exotic foods from shops run by immigrants. Some exotic plants —peanuts, grapefruits or even avocado pears— can be grown in the classroom from seeds. If the pupil responsible for watering them forgets, one may well have a concrete example of the problems of the dry season, or of the need for irrigation, or the disaster of the monsoon failing—truly, geography is everywhere!

As soon as pupils can read for themselves, it is excellent to encourage them to find out *where* things are made, and ask *why*. Difficult questions may come—why are there so many Polish shoes in the shops? Further discoveries about places and products, trade and prices, and inter-dependence are made here.

Coins and postage stamps can be sources of enormous interest and are often worthwhile geographically. Pupils guided to really study the pictures on individual stamps and on a series of stamps can learn a lot if asked 'Why was that picture chosen?' Many Third World and Com-munist countries show their major crops and industries on their regular stamps, and every major development project is celebrated with commemorative stamps. Tanzania has shown National Service (a form of community develop-ment); India shows tea-plucking, handicrafts and vehicle assembly—the examples are endless. To ask pupils to design a set of stamps for a country would be an excellent test of understanding! Maybe the next generation could persuade our Post Office to think more geographically and advertise our own 'distant environments'.

A little-tapped source of geographical work is the free and colourful catalogue of Third World craft goods from Oxfam-Bridge, and Tear Fund. The 1980 Bridge catalogue includes:

Item	Raw Material	Country of Origin
wine rack	cane	Philippines
hanging basket	cane and jute	Bangladesh
rug	wool	Kashmir
tray	vines	Philippines
doormat	coir	India
sandals	leather	India

. . . and many other items.

As well as being excellent source-material for aesthetic education, a number of concepts can be developed depending on the age of the children:
1. The variety of local raw materials used.
2. Most of the raw materials are renewable (animal and vegetable rather than mineral).
3. A small amount of money is needed to set up a workshop for such products, in contrast to factories.
4. A large number of jobs could be created by such projects.
5. People are asked to contribute skills and their work and their traditions are valued.
6. The 'differentness' of the items is the attrac-tion of them (why?).
7. In many cases, such items were once made by hand in Britain from local raw materials.

Most of the teaching techniques explained elsewhere in this book are apposite to work on distant environments. *Visual aids* are vital, since these environments cannot be viewed in reality. It is particularly important that pupils are guided in their viewing if they are not to jump to hasty and wrong conclusions. Geographical *games* can play a vital part in simplifying—but hopefully *not* oversimplifying—a situation and in developing *empathy* with people far away. *Case studies* focus on specific comprehensible examples. As long as these are representative rather than exceptional, and are set in context so that pupils realise that not *every* person in a country lives in exactly the same way, they are invaluable in making a distant environment real.

Then there are the human resources. Arrang-ing for visiting speakers is nearly as difficult as arranging a school visit away—and can be more frustrating because a distinguished guest may be incapable of holding the interest of children. Interviews are often better than talks because the teacher who knows the class retains more control. Inexperienced speakers, such as over-seas students from a local college, or immigrant parents, may respond well when interviewed tactfully. Interviews can be managed on tape as well—when the pupils speak their questions on to a tape which is sent to an 'expert' in this country or abroad, who replies by returning the tape.

Some schemes for teaching about distant environments

So far the importance of teaching about distant environments has been stressed, and some suggestions made of ideas that can bring children into contact with what is foreign. Next, ideas on themes for teaching about distant environments are given, whether the actual work is organised in the form of a project or a series of highly-structured lessons. Also appended are some examples that have been used by schools.

Obviously, details of organisation have to be left to the teacher who knows the class, but it is necessary to stress the importance for work about distant environments to be structured. Unstructured projects usually result in a lot of meaningless copying—maybe good practice in letter formation but definitely not a geographical experience! Unplanned project work within a school can result in pupils 'doing' one theme twice and omitting any excursions into overseas environments.

THE AREA APPROACH

Some topics focus specifically on one country, drawing a variety of themes together in a regional context. The examples here are of work with 5-year-olds on India and studies of Botswana made by 6-year-olds and 13-year-olds. If a little-known country can be studied by pupils at either end of the 5-13 age range, then one can assume it can be studied by 7-12-year-olds too! It may be worth emphasising that all three pieces of work are greatly enriched by not being confined to geography. India is more than a country that grows rice and has industries and cities: it is also a country with a unique history and culture. Of course, coverage of every aspect of a country is an impossible and useless aim—but a *balanced* view should be sought nevertheless.

Example 1. A project on India
The project was for 4 and 5-year-olds in a London school. I began to introduce it early in the term. The children came back from the holidays with plenty to say about their experiences at the seaside. The idea of introducing them to India came when one small lad said he had been abroad. Experiences of holidays in different

countries were discussed at length. So that we could pursue a more definite aspect of life, I showed the children a picture of an English home side by side with an Indian home. Homes in general were talked about, especially homes of rich people at first, then poor people . . .

To dress up and be ladies in saris was their greatest pleasure; while for boys we provided snake charmer's baskets, pipes, snakes (paper ones!—although we did have a visit from one that lived at London Zoo). I heard from parents that they they were learning about Bengal and Calcutta in a way they had not learnt in their geography lessons at school. The next step for a new awareness of Indian culture came when a Hindu teacher came and talked to the children. She showed them a sandalwood fan and a delicately carved paper knife. The jewellery and statues of Indian dancers were beautiful to look at. Many of the children made bangles and pots with plasticene.

The idea of making the children more aware of another country's problems came out very clearly when they saw some of the pictures of children that Mother Theresa is helping. Not only did they realise that India has a great deal to offer but that it has a great need for our interest and concern. Our next step will be to convey what it is like to live in a poor area and perhaps to try to understand what an Indian child of the Third World will experience this Christmas. I hope to continue along these lines to arouse sympathy, compassion and practical help during the coming weeks.

Sister Bridget
(Originally published in *Involved in mankind* - a visual record of an exhibition of work done by UK schools on a 'Third World' topic, held at the Commonwealth Institute, London, February 1976, published by the Voluntary Committee on Overseas Aid and Development (now Centre for World Development Education).)

Example 2. A project on Botswana with 6-year-olds, Old Oak Infants School, London W12
I decided to open the project by finding out how many children knew places other than East Acton. Few children had been away from East Acton and therefore introducing Botswana in Africa had to be carefully handled, since the

children would have little idea about the distances involved. I used a large map of the world to find London and pointed out (roughly) where East Acton is in relation to Botswana. The map not only fascinated the children, but was of great interest to them. Thus we used our map to find other places that might have been on the news or in the papers. This meant that the children had to look at the evening news and also talk to their parents about places they might hear about on the news. This aroused great interest in the parents and so I planned a visit to the Commonwealth Institute.

Many parents came along on this visit; even one working mother took the day off! I obtained a worksheet from the Commonwealth Institute for each parent and child. Everyone completed the worksheet section on Botswana. I had arranged with an auxiliary member of our staff to prepare some light refreshment for our parents on return from the Institute. This afforded an opportunity—during my lunch break—for a discussion with and among parents about Botswana and how I intended to proceed with the project. The parents were interested and I invited them to prepare some cooking at some time with the children.

The visit took place on a Friday morning so the children had all weekend to think about the project—or more naturally for 6-year-olds, forget about it! However, when the topic reopened on Monday morning all the children were very enthusiastic about what they had remembered. To reinforce our visit I used O.H.P. slides of the people of Botswana—these slides I had prepared myself. I also used workcards and large pictures about Botswana. The workcards were on loan from the Oxfam office and the pictures I had purchased at the Institute. I had mounted these and in print which I knew the children were capable of reading I had written captions for each mounted picture. Immediately, one could see each child motivated to read the print—thus their reading vocabulary increased because of the new vocabulary I had to use. I displayed several pictures each week of the project for the rest of the school. Some children were unable to read the print, but in any case the whole school soon became involved in the project.

For number work the children matched and sorted the wild and domestic animals of Botswana, studying their sizes, shapes, and in some cases, colour. We produced graphs of animals and diagrams of sets of animals. Addition was used a great deal as the children loved to count the animals used in each section of our work. The children made masks by finger-painting African patterns on to black paper. We made a collage of the diorama we saw at the Institute; some boys made models of the houses and tenements. We used beads to make patterned masks and patterned pictures, and having learnt to tie shoelaces, the children did tie-dyeing in two groups. As our project was coming to a close, we cooked some traditional recipes with the children, e.g. toffee apples, coconut ice and bread pudding.

Each piece of work was carefully recorded by the children. One boy even made himself a 'reading book' with his own pictures. The children learnt more about themselves through learning about people in Botswana. Each aspect of life in Botswana was carefully compared with the children's own home and way of life; for instance, under headings like family life, things we do, school life, music and so on.

On realising the quality of work the children had produced, I decided that we should display our work for the children's parents and the rest of the school. Our head teacher readily agreed and each child wrote an invitation to his/her parents and to the rest of the school. To include parents in our project we invited them to prepare two recipes from 'far away places'. They prepared (at school) Stuffed Parathas and Karridakia.

All the children's parents came to our 'exhibition'. They were taken round by their own children and each section of the work explained to them—if any explanation was required. The parents enjoyed trying the recipes and talking to the children. Our exhibition was a success—because the project was a success. It was also very helpful to have the loan of the film about Botswana from Oxfam, since this helped to show just how much the children were able to relate the project to the place and the people. I personally felt that the children were able to develop their abilities in every direction through the project.

Pamela M. Singh

(Originally published in *Involved in mankind*, see above.)

Example 3. A project on Botswana with second-year pupils, Dunraven School, London SW16 (i.e. 12-13-year-olds)

The course of integrated studies was carried out with the whole of the second year (about 180 pupils), and was intended as a pilot scheme on which to base a longer and more intensive course with other groups at a later date. Botswana was chosen as the central theme, a choice which, although limited to one country, synthesised the general problems of southern Africa. The aims of the course were (1) to encourage the children to carry out individual and group research; (2) to revise and develop basic skills; (3) to help build up a body of useful knowledge; (4) to stimulate appreciation of world problems; (5) to encourage thought about social values; (6) to show the inter-relationship of knowledge by breaking down the barriers between subjects.

Preparation

The early preparation took the form of discussion among staff and a team of eight was chosen. The team met regularly prior to launching the scheme, and for working lunches throughout. A programme was devised and agreed before the start. It was decided for the purpose of the course, which would operate on the afternoons of each Wednesday, Thursday and Friday over a period of seven weeks, that the whole of the second year would be de-streamed and re-grouped to include a full range of ability within each group. There were six groups of about 30 pupils, with a teacher permanently allocated to each. The pupils were given a choice to follow lines of interest within the framework of the scheme and were allowed to move from one group to another, when necessary, with staff agreement.

Each pupil was provided with: (1) a 25-page duplicated booklet of source material, including photos, prepared by the staff; (2) a set of Oxfam photos and an Oxfam booklet; (3) a sheet of suggestions for research and practical work; (4) a printed fact sheet from the Botswana High Commission; (5) a personal file. Each group was provided with a variety of other source material; a small library of books was available on loan; a Radio Botswana tape of songs and music was available. Art and craft materials were provided as required, and a variety of visual aids were displayed. Six classrooms on one floor, together with art, woodwork and domestic science rooms, were set aside throughout the period for use.

Summary of the course

The first event was a film 'Anatomy of apartheid', followed by 'Botswana'. This was reinforced next day by slides and a talk by the First Secretary of the High Commission. Subsequent films dealt with drought, tribal customs, pests and diseases, fauna, soil erosion. Speakers dealt with famine, aid, history, the Bushmen, education, home economy. Individual folders were compiled by each child, and many did practical work as well. Projects undertaken included a full-sized mud and thatch hut in the playground, pottery made from local clay and fired in a native-type kiln, dance-drama based on a legend for which masks were made. Pupils also made replicas of jewellery, an irrigation plan for the Kalahari, model mines, dolls, garden of native plants, large-scale relief maps, musical instruments, a large 'rock' covered with Bushmen-style paintings, a model cow and native dishes. Pen-pal relationships were also successfully started with children in Botswana. The course ended with a 'quiz programme' and exhibition open to visitors.

Assessment

. . . Research was carried out with more than the usual enthusiasm . . . Considerable initiative shown . . . A wide range of skills used and developed . . A lot of thought about problems of development . . . The allocation of time was adequate and well-timed . . . De-streaming was an advantage . . . Groups and staff altered so as to allow specialists to help (especially art and craft) . . . Children needed more guidance . . . Not enough intercommunication, though the quiz brought things together.

THE THEMATIC APPROACH

Many topics focus on a theme which can be 'internationalised'. For example, the favourite subject of 'water' does not need to stop when the river reaches the English Channel. It can include some study of life where there is too little water (e.g. the desert) and too much water (e.g. flooding in Bangladesh). A topic on 'power' can include ox-power in India, and ideas for using solar power in

Africa or trade-wind power in the West Indies. 'Transport' can include skidoos (rather than dog-sledges) in the Arctic, and lorries (as well as camels) in the desert. Indeed, it is difficult to think of a topic that cannot be widened to give something of a world view—but this makes planning all the more important so that pupils receive a 'balanced diet' of themes and regions; and of skills and concepts.

An example follows of a project with 8-9-year-olds on 'sharing' which could easily have been a parochial topic, but which in fact effectively incorporated a world view.

Example 4. 'Sharing': a film made at Sudbourne Junior School, Brixton

The significant characteristics of the Third World situation are not within the direct experiences of young primary school children (this class is aged 8-9); but it is possible to abstract principles of a moral or humanitarian nature from their ordinary day-to-day experience that provide a basis of application to the world beyond the classroom or the neighbourhood.

One such principle is that of sharing, which is of crucial importance in the society of the classroom, the school and the neighbourhood. To develop this principle turns the child's early egocentricity towards an awareness, first of his immediate social situation in the classroom and thence to the outside world (wherever the child perceives it). Sharing incorporates principles of respect for others, respect for common property and, in terms of skill and knowledge, consideration for the skills and limitations of others. The film therefore illustrates examples of sharing chosen by the children and employs their resources of interest and skill. It begins with sharing in the classroom and the school and thence, by animation techniques, to the world generally and the Third World in particular.

Included in the film are subtitles to enhance understanding of the material and to provide reading stimulus for a young audience, in conjunction with a voice-over soundtrack. All of the film was designed and directed by the children themselves after initial stimulation from the class teacher.

S. D. Howard
(Originally published in *Involved in mankind,* see above.)

Example 5. 'Survival'

'Survival' is a theme which harnesses pupils' imagination and creative capacities and can 'involve' them in distant environments. For example, the pupils could 'survive a "plane crash" in the jungle' (or desert, Arctic or Andes). Having survived the crash, can they survive in the environment in which they find themselves? They have no money and no government assistance: in other words, they are in much the same situation as many of the locals.

If enthusiasm and imagination are guided, the pupils will not only absorb a lot of the 'dry facts' about the physical environment, but their prejudices about the natives may well be transformed. While the crash victims wallow in uncertainty about survival, the locals have made intelligent adaptations and appear perceptive, responsible and ingenious—whatever their level of technology. The pupils might admit that they could appear ' . . . amazingly helpless . . untaught, unskilled, utterly incapable of fending for themselves; perhaps the last survivors of some peculiarly backward race.' These are the thoughts of the Aborigine boy in *Walkabout* (by J. V. Marshall, Penguin Books) after meeting two American children lost in the Australian desert. And pupils might admit that many features of distant environments that they regard as primitive—the shaduf, the shanty town, the thatched mud hut, for example—can be seen as remarkable achievements of self-help and adaptability.

Besides encouraging empathy with inhabitants of distant environments, the theme of survival develops the key concept of basic needs, along with the recognition that people's basic needs (food, water, shelter, clothing, fire, communications. . .) are the same throughout the world. Lots of creative activities can be included, but the emphasis is constantly on pupils' thinking and finding out for themselves, with clear objectives in mind.

An allied and equally exciting approach, which can anchor the work more closely to a case study, especially in a Third World environment, can run like this:

You are 6 (or 9 or 12—whatever the age of the class). If you lived in..........village in the country of..........you would have *no* ....
(pupils can suggest the items, such as electricity, piped water, packaged food, council

houses, and many physical limitations). Is this your fault?.......... (Obviously not!) How would you cope with washing/cooking/house-building, etc? What skills would you have at your age that English children do not have? (A vast collection.......even tiny children perform all sorts of really useful and necessary tasks in many societies.) So.........who is most useful? More grown up? More capable of surviving?

Both approaches soon lead on to the theme of *Intermediate technology* which is now recognised as important in Third World development. For teachers, information and visual aids are no longer in short supply, since the Intermediate Technology Development Group have produced slide sets with informative notes, and other material, in conjunction with the Centre for World Development Education (see Appendix 2). Even if all sets are too costly for primary and middle schools, teachers' centres should be able to stock them.

This is a good teaching topic for a number of reasons:
1. It is visual and 'concrete'.
2. Logical reasoning is involved. (How does it work?)
3. It is comprehensible; the relative simplicity of the machines, etc., make them easier to grasp than highly technical items such as blast furnaces, which are already in the curriculum for many pupils over the age of 10.
4. Creative thinking is encouraged (face a problem—invent a means of overcoming it). Anyone who has seen E. de Bono's book, *The Dog-exercising Machine,* will know how imaginative and creative young minds can be.
5. Choice—and hence reasoning—is basic to the study. (What level of technology, what cost, etc., is appropriate in a given case?)
6. It can be a very practical topic, even for pupils with no experience in technical studies. Shadufs and polythene water catchments can be designed and tested, even if the school field cannot be ploughed by oxen!

A THEME IN AN AREA

Example 6. The Political Geography of Africa with Mixed Ability 11-13-year-olds
Resources
A set of fairly modern atlases and a set of pre-1960 atlases.

Objective
To discover continuity and change in pre- and post-independent Africa.

Pupil Activity
Pupils work in pairs comparing an old atlas map of Africa with a new one. They will discover colonies that split up on independence (e.g. French Equatorial Africa) and colonies that merged (e.g. Somalia). But the dominant impression should be of the continuity of the boundaries of the 1880s, and the artificiality of the straight lines.

From this 'discovery' start, one can discuss what differences the past has made, e.g. main language, main trade links, legal systems, driving on the left or right of the road, railway networks, etc.

Follow-up
Any of these themes can be studied in more depth. A small area can be studied to develop the idea of the past impinging on the present. Gambia/Senegal is a good example. (Resource: 'Journey down the River Gambia', a slide set with notes from CWDE (see Appendix 2).)

EXAMPLE 7: TEACHING ABOUT THE WEST INDIES (10-13-year-olds)

The 'old-style' regional geography is clearly inappropriate and undesirable with this age-group. For example, it is much less satisfactory to start with the physical geography than to start with the people. Also, concepts are more important than facts, and facts tended to dominate the 'old' regional geography.

Nevertheless, a focus on an area can still be helpful, especially if it is in an integrated or inter-disciplinary framework. If pupils only study one theme from an area, a very distorted picture tends to emerge. For example, many pupils have studied 'Poverty in India'; hence they may see India as merely a problem area and remain unaware of India's great cultural heritage, and her achievements in agriculture and industry.

A focus on the West Indies could include the topics listed below. Many of the concepts are of wide application, but a focus on one part of the world is a more 'concrete' approach than a general discussion on the 'Third World'. The

West Indies is selected for discussion because it is important for pupils to know about this source-area of part of the UK population, and because it has been a neglected area of study in the past.

The suggestions deliberately concentrate on relevant and up-to-date issues which most 10-13-year-olds are capable of thinking about and studying, yet which have not figured in this form in traditional geography syllabuses. All of them will be more meaningful if comparison is made with the local situation.

Tourism

(This topic produces 'positive' attitudes to the area).

The reasons the area is attractive for tourists can be worked out from travel brochures; with the teacher's help the topic can be classified:
1. Physical factors: Coral islands—white sandy beaches. Volcanic islands—forests and mountains.
2. Climatic factors: 'Summer all year'. Why? Ideal for swimming, sailing etc.
3. Language: Look at the postage stamps to find out the language of the different islands.
4. Cultural factors: Historic towns; calypsos; steel bands etc.
5. Locational factors: How close to USA? How far from UK?

The case *against* tourism also needs discussing; this is more difficult, but pupils should be encouraged to think of the 'snags'.
Pupil activities could include:
Design a tourist poster.
Write a letter describing your holiday.
Plan a visit using an air timetable.

Farming

What West Indian products can you find in the shops? (There is a remarkable variety, even in non-multicultural areas: lime juice, treacle, rum, orange juice, bananas; and in some areas cane sugar, mangoes, soursoups etc.)

Pupils could consider such issues as:
1. Is it fair that we subsidise sugar-*beet* growing in the UK?
2. What advantages do West Indian farmers have over UK farmers?
3. What disadvantages do West Indian farmers have compared with UK farmers?
4. Why do you think many young West Indians do not want to be farmers?

Natural Resources

For this topic postage stamps can tell a lot.
Salt from the Turks and Caicos Islands (tiny islands but well known to pupils for their cheap and colourful stamps).
Bauxite from Jamaica.
Asphalt from Trinidad (on the school playground?).
Timber from Dominica.
etc.
Do the islanders benefit from the 'robber-economy'?
Who buys these products? Why?

Industry

Two important themes:
1. How to stop farm products from 'going bad': canning? processing? freezing?
2. The use of cheap labour: on several islands people earn less *per day* than Americans do *per hour,* so Americans have placed 'offshore industries' on some islands, e.g. computer assembly in Barbados, TV assembly on St Kitts, baseball stitching on Haiti. This will intrigue pupils. Is it fair? Is it 'development'? Or is it exploitation?

Migration

The themes of migration from country to town (why?), poorer (often smaller) islands to richer (often larger) islands, and from the West Indies to the UK and USA can be usefully linked. What were/are the 'push' factors (unemployment etc.) and the 'pull' factors? (e.g. London Transport advertising for bus conductors in Barbados in the 1950s).

CONCLUSION

The conclusion is clear: teaching about distant environments should be an essential element in the curriculum of all schools. The Unesco and WCOTP resolutions emphasise this point, children's interests and television viewing lend support to it, and the need for a 'world view' is more and more apparent every year. The chapter has emphasised the problems of implementing such a policy, because so much of what has passed for 'education about distant environments' has been counter-productive in the past. We have indicated some positive approaches, but there is a great need for more dissemination of successful teaching methods. If the Government ever acts upon its commitment to provide 'financial, administrative, material and moral support' to 'Education for International Understanding', we hope that they will give priority to in-service workshops and to the publication of examples of successful work in this area.

We would argue that a world view is an essential part of the curriculum, and that every school should formulate a policy to implement this. Just as the Bullock Committee advocates that each school should have a language policy, with a teacher appointed to implement it, we feel that a 'world view policy' is needed to an equal extent. This is not the same as arguing for geography as a subject to be re-instated in all schools, but it would make sense for a geographer to guide that policy.

7. Organising children's activities

7.1 Geography with 5–7-year-olds

Melanie Harvey

'Geography' rarely appears on the timetables of infant and first schools. There is the danger, therefore, that geographical concepts, skills and study methods suitable for young children may not be incorporated in their curriculum. An attempt is made in this section to show how typical infant topics such as 'The Home' and 'Transport' can be treated geographically; and to suggest how ideas often thought unsuitable for such young children can be considered. What is required at this stage is not so much the teaching of geography in a formal sense as a predisposition to think geographically on the part of the teacher.

Young children find much to excite and interest them. They are constantly asking questions in an attempt to explain their world. Much of what the child sees around him gives rise to enquiries of a geographical nature. The teacher's ability to think geographically may enable her to answer in a way that can develop the child's geographical understanding.

Geographical work at the infant stage will be very different from that in later stages. Every teacher has two important considerations: the needs and interests of the children; and the academic integrity of the subject matter. To a teacher of young children the first concern is their all-round development rather than the subject matter. Geographical studies may be seen as means to an end, rather than ends in themselves.

Young children learn differently from older pupils. At this stage it is a case of 'structuring the environment and helping the child to make his own discoveries rather than the presentation of direct verbal learning'. Secondary sources play only a minor role in the child's learning. The infant child is still learning to express himself. His writing is more likely to be the application of a physical skill, than the expression of what he has learnt. In addition one is aiming for an understanding of ideas. All this means that assessing learning is difficult. It takes time to discover an individual's level of understanding. For a whole class the problem is greatly multiplied.

However, difficulty in assessing understanding is no reason to omit geographical work from the curriculum at this stage for it has much to offer.

1. Individuals are constantly trying to make sense of their world in the light of their present understanding. The world of the young child is generally very small, bounded by his home, the homes of friends and relatives living close by, the school and the local shops. The attempts to make sense of his world can be seen as a desire to order his environment. Everything is a matter of curiosity and comment. His investigations result from this innate curiosity. One may conclude from this that environmental studies should form a fundamental part of the infant school curriculum, including aspects of geography, sociology, history, English, moral and social education.

2. It can help in the development of many skills.
   (a) Children working in the environment can **learn about scientific methods through their** own first-hand experience. They may develop their abilities to observe, select, describe, measure, interview, assess, record; to present their findings in a

variety of ways; and to evaluate the outcome of their work.

(b) Mechanical aids such as tape-recorders, projectors and viewers may be introduced to assist their studies. More unusual and sophisticated instruments such as a sound-level meter may also add to their interest and understanding.

(c) Environmental work can provide opportunities for children to apply and practise skills they have already learnt. A topic such as 'Transport' can enable the child to practise access skills when seeking information.

4. Language development may be assisted by their attempts to describe and explain phenomena and through their discussion of personal reactions.

5. Children's books, both the traditional stories and some modern ones may well have caused the child to develop a false view of society. Viewpoints may have been further influenced by popular, often American, television series. Neither of these accurately reflect the child's real world. Working in the environment may help develop a more realistic understanding of the world and counteract these false impressions.

6. Geography is often said to describe places. It can however extend beyond this and encourage a more personal response to those places. It would seem important that at this stage children learn not simply to find fault and to criticise but to do something about the faults they have isolated. In addition they can be shown how to use the environment for themselves and for their own pleasure.

7. At the infant and first school stage, children tend to accept what they are told; they are very open and trusting. This means that 'value-laden' topics, such as birth, life and death, and the multicultural community in which they live can be discussed without inhibition. If they can be encouraged to seek both similarities and reasons for differences, this may contribute to the development of positive and friendly attitudes towards all people including those from other cultures.

Two areas of concern for the teacher of young children are considered below—vocabulary and mapping. These are essential parts of a child's education, but they may sometimes be omitted.

Both are aspects which cannot be completely covered at this stage. They can, however, be considered as part of a spiral curriculum, in which skills and concepts are learnt in an elementary form at first. Subsequently they will be developed and refined to a more advanced stage.

VOCABULARY

Studies have been made of children's knowledge of terms such as alp, mountain, river, city, delta and estuary. However, there is a geographical vocabulary which comes before these more technical terms. These are words relating to position and location: up, down, over, under, on top, beside, next to, behind etc. Many children, not necessarily those for whom English is their second language, do not have this basic vocabulary and thus are unable to complete Piaget's three mountain test because of their inability *to express* relative locations. These words can be taught through games: 'Go and stand *behind* John'; 'Climb *on top* of the table'; 'Go *outside* the room'; through such books as Dr Seuss' *Bears in the Night, Inside, Outside, Upside down*, Breakthrough's *The Bird, the Cat and the Tree;* through Language Development Aid cards; through nursery rhymes such as Humpty Dumpty, Jack and Jill, The Grand Old Duke of York; or perhaps best of all through P.E.—what better way is there to teach a child what upside down means?

This vocabulary relates to geography, P.E., mathematics as well as general usage. Incidentally, many of these are key words. This approach provides a meaningful context in which they can be understood in both their oral and written forms.

MAPWORK

It is commonly thought that mapwork begins in the secondary school, or the top half of the junior school. It need not. Children shown a globe for the first time responded with 'It's on the telly', 'The News'. Although they could not comprehend the scale it did mean something to them. The exploitation of their personal experience provides a sound basis for learning, and the link between home (television) and school is always reassuring.

Mapwork can begin with a model of the classroom. The furniture can then be added and placed in its correct position. After discussion about the idea of position, particularly one feature in relation to others, and talking about how a fly on the ceiling could see the room, ask the children to draw a plan of the classroom. The children might profit from reading books such as *Playing with Plans* (Michael Storm, Longmans) and *Maps for Mandy and Mark* (Jenny Taylor and Terry Ingleby, Longmans).

The ability to draw maps will vary and will not necessarily be linked with an ability to produce high quality work: that is, a child's ability to draw 'nice' pictures may not be connected with his ability to represent geographical data. A 'poor drawer' may show more understanding by including more features in their correct position. It is often helpful to show the children an accurate plan of the area they have represented. Mapwork is not too difficult for young children but its development appears to pass through definite stages. The stage reached will depend upon the child's previous experience of maps.

Mapping the school is often more satisfactory than mapping the home because all the children and the teacher have knowledge of the school in common, discussion about the work can be more detailed and it is easier for the teacher to assess the work. The journey to school enlarges the scale and can be compared to the Nuffield Maths work in 'Environmental Geometry'.

It is possible to inspire highly detailed work and great care by posing the problem: 'How will Father Christmas know which is your stocking? Draw him a plan to go with your letter.' Interesting features are likely to emerge, such as bunk beds and how to represent them, and the size of 'my bed' compared with 'my sister's'!

Finally, three more detailed sets of suggestions for topic work are made. Each is geared to one of the three years of an infant school. The suggestions for 'Transport' are suited to a reception class, 'Homes' to a middle infant year, and 'Pollution' to the top infant year.

TRANSPORT (Reception class)
This topic includes a considerable amount of mathematical work

Classroom Activities	**Comments**
Naming types of transport	
Sorting models into sets	e.g. Fletcher Book 1—partitioning sets
Artwork—Drawing types of transport; also partitioning sets, pictorially	
More detailed work on types of transport, e.g. Those which carry people—people as passengers Those which carry goods Those doing specific jobs—refuse lorries, school buses, lorries for cleaning street lights etc. Types of transport needing special terminals, e.g. trains and aeroplanes	
Survey of traffic, over a set period, in one direction	Suggest rather than all traffic, buses, or taxis etc. Perhaps introduce idea of tallying
Record findings on a graph	

Repeat surveys, for both directions, at different
   times of the day, for a similar period of time

Record findings

Deductions   Encourage the children to make their own
evalution. Hints and leads rather than direct
presentation of facts. Ask for reasons for
differences and similarities and encourage the
children to evaluate their work, in terms of
results and the presentation of the results

Who has/has not a car?   Perhaps sets rather than another graph

Survey of teachers having cars; those who come
   to school by car   The interview/survey will involve the whole
school. Again the findings could be recorded
in sets (Fig. 7.1)

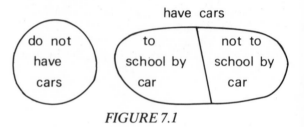

FIGURE 7.1

People whose work is connected with transport   An extension of the topic

HOMES (6-year-olds)
Suggestions with creative work as an important element

Classroom Activities   **Comments**
Asking the children to draw a picture of their   This may well be a picture of a detached house in
   home   a garden, with a central door and four windows
(Fig. 7.2)

FIGURE 7.2

A symbol of home—similar to Chinese writing.
This is interesting as a record

Writing about 'My Home'

Reading and discussing a book about homes around the world and in history, e.g. Macdonald Starters *Homes*

Discuss reasons for houses being different, e.g. climate, and changes in building style and technology

Discussion, artwork and writing about the kind of house/home you would like to have, and asking why they do not/cannot

Bring the children to see that housing depends on climate, money and space—particularly relevant to city dwellers

Types of houses in this country—house, semi-detached house, terraced house, flat, maisonette, caravan
Graph of the type of homes the children have

Stress different needs, depending on size of family, type of work etc., to avoid any hint of competition

Houses of different ages, different features and building materials

Encouraging the children to look more closely at what they have 'seen' many times

Specific visit to look at the places in which the majority of the children live

Point out actual features, e.g. windows are not right in the corners; storeys in the flats; colours of the front doors; numbers in twos, odds and evens; car parking—does it cause a problem; play space etc.

Again drawing their own homes, and writing about them

Is there any difference between this drawing and the previous one? Is it more realistic?

Discussion of any changes in the children's drawings

Encouraging the children to assess and evaluate their work

Group artwork—a model or a large picture of 'Our Street', 'Our Estate'

Group work can lead to some very interesting and fruitful discussion between the children. In this case it might be about scale, position, and the need for accuracy

Creative writing—Poetry
Where I Live—things I like
things I dislike
what could be done to make it better?
what can I do to make it better?

Children responding creatively and emotionally to their surroundings

POLLUTION (7-year-olds)

Classroom Activities	Comments
What is pollution? Ask the children to define it	The answers may well be very full. Rubbish is seen to equal pollution. Having put forward the word, the children will find all sorts of references to it; e.g. television, newspapers etc.
What pollution is there in school? What can you do about it?	Rather than encourage 'holier than thou' attitudes, give the children something positive
Artwork—Poster campaign; Keep the School tidy If possible, actual tidying, gardening and weeding	
Pollution around us. Rubbish—on the street, in the park	Making the children aware of their responsibility for sweet papers, drink cans etc.
Air pollution—car fumes etc. Smoking—smell the smoke in hair, clothes Effect on the body	Try to persuade a smoker to demonstrate the health hazard and dirtiness of smoking by inhaling and breathing out through a white tissue. It is very effective!
Noise pollution—traffice noise	Taping traffic, or measuring on a sound-level meter
Animal and plant life threatened by pollution Man as the cause of pollution	
	Suggested useful books—*Waste Not, Want Not* series by Anne-Marie Constant (Burke Books) and *Dinosaurs and all that Rubbish* by Michael Foreman. The former are quite difficult but are worth considering as they contain a great deal of thought/discussion-provoking material Idea of greed versus need
Success stories where pollution has been stopped and the landscape reclaimed; e.g. sand and gravel pits, old workings ponds canals	These are particularly good as they frequently have 'saved' areas next to polluted ones.
The following are three pieces of writing by children after working through a topic about pollution which included a visit to the canal which ran by the school and the children's homes. 'I saw bottles in the water and they were floating and I can do something about it. I would get them out.' (Erika)	'Pollution must stop otherwise the place will stink of dead fish and stink and stink and the people will move away from the canal.' (Daniel) 'Pollution is rubbish. I saw petrol in the water. We stop by putting our sweet papers in the bin.' (John) In fact he even told his father to pick up a drinks can he had dropped. The message got through!

Geographical work may not always be regarded as absolutely essential to the curriculum in the early years of schooling. It is, however, based upon the real world in which the children themselves live. The local environment provides the experience with which they interpret the world at large through secondary sources. The inclusion of geographical concepts, skills and study methods can contribute to a greater understanding of their world. It can also provide a stimulating context in which language, mathematical and creative development can take place.

7.2 Geography within Environmental Education

John Baines

Over the last fifteen years a new term has been added to our educational language—environmental education. At first sight its meaning seems clear enough, learning about the environment; but that has been going on for a long time in schools under such terms as rural studies/science or environmental studies/science. So why complicate matters with the use of a new term? Many junior school pupils are being introduced to animals in the classroom, growing plants from seed and using their local environment for landscape studies. I have no intention of criticising the many valuable experiences of the environment that children are exposed to as part of their education, but over the last few years there has been an increasing awareness that a new emphasis may be needed.

The way of life we have developed for ourselves threatens the environment which is our life-support system. To keep pace with the demands of a rapidly rising world population and at the same time to raise its standard of comfort, industry has to produce more and more, demanding even more raw materials whose supplies are limited. People and industry require more land area, and therefore agriculture has to become more intensive, using more fertilisers and pesticides which themselves are made largely from finite resources. The quality of the rural landscape is under threat as the stock of wild plants and animals is diminished to allow for more efficient agriculture. Alongside such growth is an accumulation of waste, generally referred to as pollution, which threatens the existence of living organisms including man. Clearly the evidence of danger should not be ignored, for unless man can intervene in this process far more powerfully than he does at the moment, nature may find its own balance through famine, disease and war.

The threats to the environment and the need to develop a way of life that is sustainable have been recognised at a variety of levels from the United Nations with its Environmental Programme to individuals determined to follow a way of life more in harmony with nature. However, recognition of the problems by some does not guarantee a solution, and all environmental conferences have stressed the important contribution of education—environmental education—to the man/environment debate. This brief presentation refers only to education in primary, junior and middle schools.

Defining a problem and realising a need for something to be done about it in school, presents a problem in itself. How does one develop a meaningful course that encompasses the natural, the built and the human environments, a course which requires the teaching of knowledge about the environment, an awareness and appreciation of it and the learning of new attitudes. How much importance should be given to such a course when the public appears convinced that standards in basic skills are not what they used to be? How much time should be given when there are other important issues clamouring for time in the classroom, such issues as development education, health education, humane education, political education, etc?

Environmental education has been introduced in a variety of ways. The curriculum in most primary schools is organised to include a number of clearly defined though overlapping fields of study. Its main concerns are language, mathematics, the creative arts and religious and physical education, but alongside there is usually a less well defined field in which studies loosely termed as 'environmental' may appear. An environmental education course would reflect three common strands:

1. Education in the environment. The environment is a most valuable educational resource particularly for young children who cannot cope with abstract concepts, as well as older ones. They are keen to examine and explore and their immediate and local environments give the opportunity to learn from direct experiences. Such experiences can help with all types of learning including numeracy, creative writing, art and craft work and the development of non-abstract concepts such as the classification of objects and features which are similar but not alike.

2. Education about the environment. We are a part of the environment. As well as providing the basic necessities of life, we use it for recreation and a host of other activities that enrich our lives. The environment provides us with evidence of the wonders of nature and the creative abilities of man. One of the roles of schools is to develop a child's natural curiosity through learning about their environment; a process which will involve seeing the inter-relationships within the web of nature itself and between man and nature.

3. Education for the environment. This third strand is more difficult to work into a school's programme of work because basically it involves the development of an environmental ethic, or a caring attitude towards the environment manifested in our individual and collective behaviour. Although the Rutter report recognises that schools play an important part in the development of attitudes, we are not yet sure how these attitudes are learnt. Indeed exhortation and 'the doom' approach might have produced a contrary reaction, and it may be that awareness and appreciation of the environment through fieldwork or outdoor pursuits are more effective. Teachers of younger children, with fewer timetable restrictions and examination syllabi to work to, are in a better position to develop these activities. Such attitudes must be based on sound information, first-hand experience and personal decision if they are to be lasting.

Two other important aspects of environmental education need to be mentioned as well. It cannot be classified as a subject, like history, maths or geography can. It represents a particular approach to education and is so wide ranging that some schools approach all learning through the environmental theme. Environmental ways of teaching have been summarised as:

1. providing first-hand materials and experience wherever possible;
2. working outside the classroom with minimum fuss;
3. enquiring and exploring, using one's eyes, ears and other senses in both nearby and contrasting environments;
4. training in discussion skills to foster the making of decisions, particularly value judgements;
5. providing for physical contact with plants and animals;
6. making sure children know how to behave in varying environments (codes of behaviour);
7. developing self-reliance and children's ability to organise their own work in the field;
8. allowing for emotional response, while insisting on scientific enquiry;
9. encouraging children to take part in adventurous and enjoyable environmental activities (outdoor education, leisure education).

(From Carson, S. Mc B., *Environmental education: guidelines for the primary and middle years*)

Secondly, environmental education is not solely concerned with the countryside, since it recognises that the rural and urban environments are inextricably linked. There is only one environment, which includes the wilderness at one end of the scale and the giant metropolis at the other. Any course which concentrates on one particular aspect of the environment, cannot be said to represent environmental education.

The National Association for Environmental Education (1976) in its booklet *Environmental education: a statement of aims* states the following for the primary years (5-10):

At the primary stage, environmental education is seen as involving pupils in personal experience of the environment by direct exploration with all their senses, using the school and its immediate surroundings and going further afield when necessary. Such environments will involve both the living environment in small nature reserves, school gardens or in the countryside and the built environment in streetwork. At this stage emphasis should be placed on the development and deepening of concepts. Teachers are expected to use these experiences to develop language in all its aspects, numeracy, scientific methods of enquiry, aesthetic appreciation and creative expression as well as to encourage the development of value judgements and an environmental ethic. Children at this stage should be introduced to the statutory and accepted codes of environmental behaviour.

It continues with a statement for the middle years (9-13).

This represents a starting point, but to satisfy teachers' requests for more specific guidance, Sean Carson, when he was the Hertfordshire County Council Adviser for Environmental Education, produced *Environmental education: guidelines for the primary and middle years*. It suggests suitable content and activities that can be used to achieve the objectives of environmental education, and suitable progression through the different age ranges is indicated.

From these statements it will be realised that environmental education represents an integrated, or as many would prefer to say, non-disintegrated approach to learning in the primary and middle years. In the words of the Director of the Schools Council Project Environment 8-18 it calls for the 'impregnation of the whole of our education by the subject matter, principles, methods and spirit of environmental education'. However, the approach must form a sound basis for the study of individual subjects later on, including geography. It is generally accepted that there are certain geographical skills, concepts, ideas and facts with which it is imperative children should be acquainted. Where geography is not taught as a subject in its own right, it is important that the features mentioned should be taught through the established curriculum.

Elsewhere in this book, is a suggested outline for geographical teaching in the primary and middle years (pp. 13-18). It suggests key ideas, some topics and themes, and some particular activities. It is clear that many of these important aspects are included within environmental education, but each school situation is different and individual teachers will have to plan how they can develop the geographical aspects to make sure there is a sound basis for the children to follow a purely geographical course in later years. However, it is important not to regard environmental education and geography as synonymous,

although they have many concepts, skills and areas of knowledge in common. It would be wrong to try and make either one the complete vehicle for teaching the other. What then is the relationship between geography and environmental education?

Certain topics are likely to be found in both environmental education and geography courses. These include population, settlement, historical landscapes, planning, energy, resources, land-use changes, locational processes, mapping and fieldwork techniques. The Geographical Association Environmental Education Working Group suggested that environmental courses should take cognisance of such themes as:

1. simple systems—food, water, energy cycles;
2. interactions—trade, diffusion, specialisations;
3. environmental controls—temperature, precipitation, competition for land;
4. resource planning—the cost of alternative choices;
5. appraisals and modifications of natural environments;
6. environmental problems—physical, economic, social and moral.

There are also certain key ideas that geographers would like to see introduced including:

1. the broad patterns of the physical world;
2. the inter-relationships of all living organisms including man;
3. landscapes are the product of environmental controls and man's activities;
4. importance to the environmental character of such factors as accessibility;
5. an understanding of cultural landscapes and their ultimate dependence upon the natural world.

Such themes and ideas would need to be included in a manner appropriate to the age range, but if one looks at the performance objectives in environmental education for primary or middle schools (5-12) in the NAEE *Statement of Aims* the common ground is evident.

Performance Objectives in Environmental Education for Primary or Middle Schools (5-12)

Area and Location
Experiences basic orientation within the local and national environments.
Perceives the earth as the home of man but

shrinking in terms of time, distance and limits of resources.

Observes how man uses and influences the environment.

Learns the use to be made of local and world maps.

Atmosphere and Cosmos

Can describe and measure simple climatic factors in the local environment and appreciates their significance for food production.

Recognises the role of the atmosphere in the life of the plants and animals.

Can identify the major climatic and vegetative patterns of the world.

Landforms, Soils and Minerals

Knows that soil is dynamic: (a) it forms; (b) it contains living things and supports plant growth; (c) it erodes or becomes less fertile.

Can identify different soil types.

Sees the interaction between soil and living things.

Understands that mineral resources are limited.

Can point out on a map the general arrangement of landforms in Britain and the world.

Plants and Animals (Biota)

Knows from first-hand experience various kinds of plants and animals in their own environment.

Recognises interdependence among soil, atmosphere, plants (producers), animals and man (consumers).

Knows what is meant by the food chain.

Is aware of some endangered species and measures for their conservation, particularly food species important to man.

Water

Knows the necessity of water for life and its importance as a natural resource.

Knows the water cycle.

Is aware of water pollution.

People

Recognises the varieties and similarities among people.

Knows how people live in and use different environments.

Knows of rural depopulation as a worldwide phenomenon.

Is aware of population growth and its relation to the quality of life.

Social Organisation

Learns individual and group responsibility concerning environment.

Uses environmental experience to gain self-discipline.

Recognises agencies working on environmental problems and recognises international co-operation as a means of solving world environmental problems.

Economics

Relates food, clothing and shelter needs to available resources in various societies.

Recognises the organisation of resources into farming, forestry, fishing, mining, manufacturing, servicing, transportation and communication.

Aesthetics, Ethics, Literacy, Numeracy

Uses environmental experience to acquire basic skills.

Builds a basic vocabulary of environmental terms.

Uses the visual arts and music to describe and interpret various environments.

Develops an appreciation of art and design factors in the built environment.

Built Environment

Recognises different buildings and functional areas in the locality (residential, shopping, work places, leisure provision).

Knows the main local services (police, fire brigade, hospital).

Energy

Recognises manifestations of energy in various forms, and the control of energy by man.

Knows that energy arrives from the sun.

Knows the origin of fossil fuels.

Similarly, the skills developed in environmental education have much to offer the geographer. The enquiry skills are strongly scientific having gained a lot from the approach of science teachers who make a major contribution to environmental education. Environmental education also seeks to develop skills associated with map and photograph interpretation, field studies, observation and recording of landscape features and recording, presentation and interpretation of data. However, there are other concepts and skills and areas of knowledge that do not relate so closely to geography including recognition of plants and animals, outdoor activities, concept of an environmentally ethical lifestyle and ecological balance.

There are few primary and middle schools where geography is taught as a separate subject. More often geography is included as part of an integrated course or one which has topics or themes as its starting point. In these situations, geography should not be forgotten as a sound basis is needed to provide for its future study in secondary schools. The teacher should make sure that the important geographical dimension is woven into the curriculum for these early years. If environmental education is firmly established in the school I hope I have shown that there should be few difficulties.

7.3 Geography within the Humanities

Paul Kelly

Geography in junior, middle and lower secondary schools is often linked with other subjects under the general heading of 'Humanities', 'Social Studies' or 'General Studies'. Such an approach to the curriculum may take a variety of forms ranging from a series of non-sequential topics involving a diversity of subject matter and experiences to a more narrowly defined 'co-ordination' of traditional subjects working to a common theme. The most frequent combinations include geography with history, RE, English and increasingly elements of sociology, anthropology, economics, social psychology, social theory and political ideology. The reasons for grouping these subjects together reflect the many different influences on the school curriculum.

At primary level in particular such schemes are related to child-centred objectives concerned with motivation and learning. It is argued that the curiosity and enthusiasm of young children do not fall naturally within subject boundaries and may even be stultified by any attempt to hedge around with academic disciplines which have been formulated by and for the convenience of adults. The motivation gained by young children following their own interests, albeit under teacher guidance, is fundamental to successful learning. At the early stages of cognitive development the subject label is irrelevant. Within the humanities approach children can be allowed to follow a topic of interest, handle a wide range of sources of information and practise basic skills relevant to a broad spectrum of subjects. In addition to intellectual objectives opportunity may be given for the growth of emotional and motor skills, and geographical ideas may well be placed alongside such apparently disparate subjects as art, drama, mathematics and music.

Middle and secondary schools have also adopted schemes involving some form of integration in their curriculum. An advantage at this stage is that such schemes are a means of bridging the gap between schools. Conventional primary-school practice is for one teacher to be with a class for a whole day. A humanities scheme at middle or lower secondary level ensures that one teacher spends a substantial amount of time with a class, giving some continuity with primary practice, and providing the basis for the development of personal relationships between pupil and teacher. It is the experience of many teachers that this helps to overcome the considerable stress which children may suffer when they transfer from one school to another. The block of time also allows for a more flexible use of teaching staff, rooms and the grouping of lessons.

A third reason for grouping within the humanities is related to the nature of the content of the traditional humanities subjects, and not least to the need to make room in the curriculum for social science subjects. It is often claimed that subjects such as history, RE, English and geography contain large areas of common subject matter in so far as their essential content relates to Man, his nature, ideas, social and political development. There are broad human issues concerning the relationships between individuals, society and environment to which all children should be introduced, and their study requires the conceptual insights of more than one subject. Geography, with its breadth and variety at school level, has traditionally claimed an integrative role in the curriculum and is well suited to play a key role in humanities. Many 'geographical' skills, notably that of graphicacy, are very relevant to history, RE and other social sciences. In the context of man's social development we cannot ignore the influence the physical environment has had on:

1. the way individuals organised themselves into groups—physical geography, settlement, agriculture and industry are relevant geographical themes;
2. the beliefs and values of both individuals and groups. Primitive man related to his environment in terms of fear, ritual and myths, in contrast to the scientific analysis of more recent times. Modern behavioural studies in geography have shown how man's attitudes and values interact with his physical and social environments and so influence spatial patterns.

THE STRUCTURE AND CONTENT OF HUMANITIES COURSES

The variety of approaches to humanities courses is almost as great as the number of schools involved, but some common elements may be identified. The structure of the courses may for convenience be very broadly divided into two: non-sequential and sequential.

Non-sequential work

Non-sequential work generally involves a project-based curriculum, not necessarily arranged in any sequence, and is probably best suited to the 8 to 10+ age group. Self-contained topics are chosen by the teacher or child or combination of both, and skills and concepts are drawn from any subject they feel relevant. The teacher may consider it important that the range of topics covered achieves some balance between broad areas of the curriculum.

An example of work of this nature is given in Figure 7.3, a topic on 'The Street'. The work is suitable for top juniors or middle school pupils of 11-12 years of age and the subject content is largely geography and history. However, skills

and concepts drawn from English, PE, number, art and dance are also introduced. It is not suggested that it is possible or even advisable to attempt all the activities suggested here; the teacher must select according to his own situation and must achieve a balance between the different subject areas.

The topic needs to be started in a lively way, perhaps by a visit from the local Road Safety Officer, or a friendly shopkeeper willing to talk to the children and answer their questions. In this case the teacher had taken a number of 35mm slide photographs of the local street, including some which were unusual views of common features. The children were asked to identify close-up views of a milk crate on the pavement, a rainwater gutter, the royal insignia on a post-box etc. Similarly, street noises were recorded and formed the basis for a 'quiz' enjoyed by the class. Subsequent discussion with the children produced a list of topics which they would like to study. What different types of buildings were in the street? What was the street like 50 years ago? Street furniture. Which shops are used the most? How much litter and noise is there in the street? How safe is the street?

Groups of children visited the street to study their particular topic. Each group was responsible for contributing to a class exhibition of work which became the basis of a class quiz, so encouraging the children to look carefully at what other groups had achieved.

The outline of the topic in Figure 7.3 indicates some of the ways such work can be developed, and also identifies the contribution of different subject areas to the overall topic.

Sequential work

As children grow older they become more able to view their work in terms of organising ideas and it is important to allow for a progression of skills and concepts associated with particular subjects. A sequential curriculum at approximately the 10-13 age range may be based on broad themes but so organised that early learning experiences form the foundation of later ones—in fact that there is a linear development of subject skills.

It is undoubtedly a demanding task to organise a humanities or otherwise integrated programme that will satisfy the requirements of a number of subject disciplines. The planning of such courses needs to be a team effort, and units of work

SUBJECT CONTENT	MATERIALS AND METHOD	PRODUCT
Basic geographical ideas		
Buildings may be grouped according to function	Discuss classification Observe in street	Map of building function; bar graphs; written comment
Shops may be grouped; there is a hierarchy of shops; certain shops are more favourably located due to accessibility	Classify and map street shops; 5-minute count of shoppers entering similar shops, e.g. food shops; play shopping games (Walford[1]) Simulation—locate your own supermarket	Maps of shops; graph of shops and comment; what shops are missing? bar graphs on base map to show which shops are the most popular; discussion
There is flow and density in the movement of people and traffic	5-minute pedestrian count on each side of the street; classify traffic; traffic count	Flow line maps; class display of pictures of traffic types; written reports; where are the lorries coming from? etc.
Man can be responsible for pollution	Compile list of types of litter; collect selected examples; observe and count people who throw litter into the street; photographic record; record noise levels; record different noises; who cleans the streets? research project	Class litter display; photography display; charts; tape-recordings; discussion; written accounts
The street depends on the co-operation of a large number of people	Observe and list aids to road safety; interview crossing keepers/police	Model of street and road signs; report on interviews
Basic historical ideas		
The street is in a process of change through time.	Make a list of building materials and contrast old and new Contrast building methods and styles, e.g. brick bonding, windows etc. How long have you lived in your own house? What alterations have been made? Signs in the street of age—date plates; foot scrapers; post boxes Map of building ages	Class display of building materials old and new—slates, tiles, plastic and iron gutters etc. Histogram to show how long children have lived in their houses Drawings, photographs and written descriptions
The street shows examples of continuity as well as change	The street as it used to be—old maps, photos, interviews with old residents, directories, census records How is the street today the same as it used to be?	Class display of materials Tape recordings of interviews Written descriptions and drawings etc. Display of relevant pictures, drawings; descriptions of buildings, congestion, litter, trades, etc.
Historians work with a variety of source materials	The historian as a detective (see Schools Council *Clues*[2]) Use of first-hand materials—maps, directories, photos, interviews, census material	Display of materials
Historical imagination—what was it like to live in the street 100 years ago	Write a play based on the street 100 years ago—a child pickpocket	Group or class drama
OTHER BASIC SKILLS		
English Transactional	Discussion, oral and written reports Conversations with shopkeepers, crossing keepers etc.	Tapes, reports, class discussion
Creative	Poems about streets and people Descriptive writing of street scenes	Workbook of poetry and writing
Number	Measure dimensions of pavement by trundle wheels or pacing Pedestrian and traffic counts Putting things into sets—traffic, shops etc. Prices of shop goods	Scale map of pavement Graphs Class shop Workcards
Physical Skills	The way people move in the street—walking, running, fast, slow, crowd movements, pushing prams, carrying etc. Children's street games	Individual body movements
Music and Drama	Write and perform music/drama based on London street calls and street markets Simulated street scene—a bank robbery, accident, street traders	Group or class drama
Artistic Skills	Shapes in the street Rubbings of gratings, building materials etc. Paintings, models	Display of various paintings, models, etc.

FIGURE 7.3 An example of non-sequential work: 'The Street' (11-12-year-olds)

Notes: 1. Walford, R. *Games in geography,* 5th ed. London: Longman, 1975.
2. Schools Council. *Clues, clues, clues* (Place, Time and Society series). Bristol: Collins/ESL, 1975.

Basic Themes	Geography	History	English	RE
Term One The School 5/6 weeks	Basic concept of plan Introduction to ideas of time, distance and land use in the context of the school Observation and classification Co-ordinates	History of the school: How do we find out? use of observation, school log books, interviews, etc.	Myself My school	Origins of Religion Animism Superstition Ritual Sacrifice Dreams
The School Neighbourhood 5/6 weeks	Introduction to 1:50 000 O.S map: co-ordinates, direction, symbols	Growth of Barking using local maps, directories and census materials	My neighbourhood	
Term Two Man and Creation 3/4 weeks	Introduction to ideas on the origin of the Earth The Earth in Space Introduction to evolutionary time scale	Introduction to early civilisations: Sumer and Babylon	Space and time travel Myths and legends	Sumer and Babylonian ideas about Creation Biblical account of creation The Jewish Religion
Man and Settlement 6/7 weeks	Origins of early settlement in river basins Fluvial concepts: channel, flood plain etc. Egypt: location; ancient irrigation methods and the Aswan Dam	Ancient Egypt: The Nile, Pharaohs etc. Introduction to Greece and Rome for more able pupils	Magic and Mystery Water	
Term Three Man and Settlement (cont.)	London: site, growth, transport, land-use, docks etc. Communications with rest of Britain: basic atlas work on Br. Isles; continents and oceans Simple perception exercises on the Br. Isles	Britain in the Roman Empire Roman London: forts, every-day Roman life, religion, communications etc.	Animals Friends	Christianity

Pecked lines indicate themes link across subjects

FIGURE 7.4   Outline syllabus of year one Humanities course in a secondary school (based on syllabus of Eastbury School, Barking)

delegated to members of the team for preparation of materials. Ideally a school should contain a geographer whose job is to ensure that within the context of the overall aims of the scheme:

1. objectives specific to the subject are included;
2. geographical content and teaching methods are suitable for all pupils;
3. other members of the teaching team are familiar with the geographical ideas involved in the work, and
4. there is continuity and progression of geographical ideas.

This last objective is one of the most difficult yet important problems. The task is not only to co-ordinate a number of subjects into a theme or topic, but to ensure that each of the participating subject areas maintain a satisfactory sequence of skills and ideas in succeeding topics.

The form of organisation of such courses varies widely. At middle and secondary level it is common for a Head of Humanities or Co-ordinator to plan a programme of work in consultation with specialist teachers in two or more of geography, history, English and RE, with additional elements from the social sciences. In other schemes a single teacher may take the responsi-

bility in the classroom for all subjects, but draw advice and materials from specialist colleagues. The team teaching approach may be adopted to varying degrees, but whatever the organisation the role of co-ordinator would seem to be vital for a cohesive course of study.

Humanities schemes of the sequential type are generally implemented by means of broad 'umbrella' themes which are sufficiently all-embracing to allow for the development of a variety of subject skills and ideas. Many of the themes can be described as aspects of 'Man's interrelationship with his environment', the term 'environment' including both physical and social aspects. Examples of such themes are:

Origin of the Earth
The Earth in Space
The structure of the Earth
Evolution
The Development of Man
Animal societies
Ancient civilisations
Settlement
Primitive societies
Communication
The local community
The local environment

History
1. The local environment provides evidence of both continuity and change.
2. The historian uses a variety of first-hand data to discover the past.
3. Historical factors can help explain the character of an area today.
4. Early civilisations were often closely associated with major drainage basins.

Geography
1. Settlement may be classified according to (a) size (b) function.
2. There were a number of physical and economic factors, and also chance, which determined where early groups settled.
3. Rivers have certain (selected) features, i.e. channelled flow, drainage, floods, sediment transport, which may have important consequences for human settlement and agriculture.
4. Movement of people follows well defined paths in well defined directions and may be concentrated in certain peak hours of the day.
5. Places a great distance apart may be closer together in terms of time.

RE
1. Evidence about the origin of the earth is provided by scientific and religious ideas.
2. Scientific and religious explanations are different in kind.
3. Man has often found a need to explain his origins in religious terms.
4. Creation myths are concerned with expressing religious beliefs.

FIGURE 7.5   Basic ideas in year one Humanities (Eastbury School, Barking)

TOPIC ONE: POWER: DISASTER

The main objective is to explain the diffusion of power in the field of local government. The information provided includes a brief outline of the area which is embraced by Wigan Metro and the departments of the Council. Pupils will use simulated exercises involving a major disaster in Wigan to try to understand the working of various departments within the authority.

The power of the human body is also discussed, e.g. athletics and sport.

TOPIC TWO: VALUES AND BELIEFS

Content	Concept
(a) Money; history of development	
(b) Parts played by different members of the family	Contrasting values in Society
Hierarchy within our own society	
Contrasting study of Eskimo society, their values and beliefs	
(c) Incas	Religious beliefs in other societies
(d) Ancient Egypt, gods of nature	Ancient beliefs
(e) Islam	A modern religion
(f) Christianity	A study of our own society's religion

TOPIC THREE: CONTINUITY AND CHANGE

Content	Concept
Introductory map reading: compass direction, scale, etc.	
Practical map-reading exercise—The Standish Trail	Changing land use in the Standish area
History and growth of Standish with emphasis on the parish church and its changing role in the community	Continuity of worship but changing importance to local community
The place and importance of coalmining in the local area	Changing social and working conditions
Local Transport; case study of canal/railway/road network	Continuity of routes but changing methods of transport

TOPIC FOUR: SIMILARITY AND DIFFERENCE

Content	Concept
(a) Water—where does it originate?	Universal need for water but different distribution methods
Water cycle; man's need for water;	
Taps to wells	
(b) Water supply in history: the Romans, Egypt, China, 18th-century Britain	Different rates of progress in water technology
(c) Water supply today: worldwide; in Britain—recent difficulties and the 1976 drought	Contrast in the distribution of supplies
Importance of water to Nomads in the Monsoon lands	
Attempts to overcome uneven distribution; HEP and irrigation	

TOPIC FIVE: CAUSES AND CONSEQUENCES

Content	Concept
(a) Old Stone Age way of life	Man interacts with his environment
New Stone Age—a contrasting study	
(b) Timechart of selective events in English history	Effects of change in agriculture on man and his environment—both good and bad
The open-field system	
The Enclosures	
Inventions and famous farmers of the 18th-century English Agricultural Revolution	
(c) The Industrial Revolution, especially the Textile industry	Effects of the Industrial Revolution on the people of Britain
(d) Pollution and conservation in the modern world	

TOPIC SIX: CONFLICT AND CONSENSUS

Conflict in Biblical times	Conflict in the Family
Jacob and Esau;	
Joseph and his brothers	
Conflict during the Industrial Revolution:	Conflict in Society
The Luddites	
Modern day conflict, e.g. Northern Ireland	

FIGURE 7.6   Syllabus based on Schools Council, History, Geography and Social Sciences 8-13 Project (mixed-ability secondary school first year, Shevington High School, Wigan)

A Humanities scheme in which a sequential development of subjects is attempted is illustrated in Figure 7.4. The syllabus outline is for the first year of a comprehensive school and shows how work in history, geography, English and RE is related to broad themes. This scheme may be described as 'interdisciplinary' or 'co-ordinated', rather than integrated, as each subject retains its separate identity. All four subjects are taught by class teachers under the leadership of a co-ordinator. As far as possible the work is arranged to facilitate cross-fertilisation of ideas and where there are direct links this is indicated in the scheme by pecked lines between subjects. At the same time forced integrations are avoided; where it is necessary for subjects to go their own way this is shown by continuous lines between subjects. For example, in term 1, RE finds itself unable to contribute to the main theme and retains a distinctive programme.

The three themes in the course are: 'The Local Area'; 'Man and Creation'; and 'Man and Settlement'. Subject departments work within these themes and develop what they consider to be the important ideas and skills relevant to the first year of secondary education, and a summary of these is given in Figure 7.5. The chief integrative influence is perhaps the fact that all subjects are taught by a class teacher who has flexibility in the use of time and can draw together individual threads.

The syllabus shown in Figure 7.6 has been strongly influenced by the work of the Schools Council Project, History, Geography and Social Sciences 8-13. The project produced a framework to help teachers select and structure their own materials. This was achieved in two ways: firstly, objectives relevant to the 8-13 age range were clarified under the headings intellectual skills, social skills, psychomotor skills, attitudes, values and interests. Secondly, seven 'key concepts' were identified to act as organising foci and to guide the teacher in the selection of content. These included communication, power, values and beliefs, conflict/consensus, similarity/difference, continuity/change and causes/consequences.

The school has selected five of these concepts: power, values and beliefs, continuity and change, causes and consequences, conflict and consensus and used them to structure work in history, geography and RE. The course is taught to a mixed-ability secondary school first year using a team teaching approach. Topics three, four and five can be seen to contain a substantial geographical content which form the basis for subsequent specialist geography teaching in year two.

7.4 Project Work for the 5–13s

Roger Cracknell

ORIGIN AND EVOLUTION

The origin of project, topic, centre-of-interest or integrated approaches can be found in the period leading up to 1931. Whilst each term has a slightly different shade of meaning, in practical terms classroom activity is similar today (Rance, 1970). It was the 'centre of interest' that first gained official support in the 1931 Hadow Report on Primary Education, where it was seen as a vehicle of education allowing exploration of the different avenues that diverged from the interest point. It was however recognised that subjects could still provide this starting point for school work. By 1949 a Geographical Association survey was able to report much headway being made by topic approaches. Only half of the 200 schools studied taught geography as a separate syllabus subject. By 1966, however, the situation had changed very little. Half the schools studied by the Plowden team still wrote geography into the timetable as a separate subject, whilst the remainder included geography as part of a combined approach. Since 1966 two surveys have been made that confirm the continuing trend for geography taught as a separate subject to disappear. These are mentioned elsewhere in this book. Geography is now firmly embedded in topic approaches, and it is the relationship between project work and geography that the remainder of this section seeks to examine in more depth.

GEOGRAPHY AND TOPIC WORK

The justification for the treatment of geography through topics has been well documented. A greater concern for the needs and interests of children and the realisation that children do not make divisions between areas of knowledge naturally, have been two most formative principles. But what is project or topic work, and how does it relate to other 'integrated' activity and to geography itself? Much has been written on the relationship between geography and environmental studies, or at least about the definitions of each. The definition of school geography for the 5-13-year-olds is found elsewhere in this book. Environmental studies are based on the direct personal experience of the child within the accessible environment. These may *use* the environment as a *resource* for learning about separate disciplines or school subjects, or as methods of integrating learning, setting out to *ignore* school subject boundaries (Hellyer, 1974).

The essence of project or topic work is that it should arise from the felt needs and interests of the children, and yet be open ended, so that the teacher can feel his way with the class and individual children within it may work through their own schemes (Sadler, 1974). To imply, as the above statement does, that an idea should be both thought up and then developed by the child does not prevent the teacher from creating a situation through stories and pictures, or any other method/medium that may provide the initial stimulation for an idea or topic. Children are less likely to think of 'Explorers' or 'The Romans', than they are other topics such as 'Animals'. Teachers can and do control choice of topic, and indeed they must if they are not to be short of important resource material, through the choice of a particular theme. Topics may or may not use the accessible environment, relying, as they do, very heavily on books and other secondary resource material. The topic approach does not mean that subject disciplines have no value.

PLATE 11. Working from books during a project

simply that a 'pre-disciplinary' approach is more appropriate to young children. Disciplinary studies allowing a deeper insight into various topics are for the later years. The crucial point here is that the fundamental ideas, skills, attitudes and values of the major disciplines can be introduced in a 'pre-disciplinary' way through topics or projects, and in a planned way. A detailed statement regarding ideas, skills and attitudes can be found elsewhere in this book, but these aspects of geographical understanding must be given an opportunity to show themselves in topic work. The contention is that topics must be selected such that the fundamentals of major disciplines, including geography, are presented to children in a pre-disciplinary way during the 5-13 period in a progressively more demanding form.

CHOOSING TOPICS

The comments made above concerning the importance of central ideas, skills, etc., of a subject do not mean a separate treatment of the subject. It simply means that topics should be selected that lend themselves to geographical work in much the same way as others will lend themselves to history or social studies or science. It is not enough that geography should provide only a locational background for other avenues of study; for example, geographical aspects of cocoa do not end when a map has been produced showing the main cocoa-producing areas, and nearest towns. Studies should include reference to the system of cocoa production; conditions of growth; methods of getting the beans to market; the homes of cocoa workers, where they are, and what they are made of. Children could look in detail at the places passed through by a bag of cocoa beans (cartoon bean?) e.g. the market, the port, the town, and also the climate and the landscape. Geography as a study of people and place could thus be covered and the interdependence of Britain and overseas countries emphasised. This should not preclude the study of aspects of other 'disciplines' through this topic. Early methods of transporting the beans (history and science), distances and times between places in Ghana (mathematics); and stories based on market scene/town life (creative writing) could be included. The question is one of balance. A

topic such as eighteenth-century Britain may have less potential for geographical work than a topic on cocoa, or food or homes. Teachers must ensure that children are given ample opportunity to undertake geographical work in topics that lend themselves to the subject, and thus avoid the trap of trying to make work in the subject, where none really exists, as a natural exploration of a particular theme. Towns would be a natural choice for geographical work, fashion would not. The teacher will need to ensure that the child can choose naturally geographical work as a result of stimulus from the school environment which he (the teacher) has arranged. A list of topics through which to emphasise geography is set out below.

For younger children:

Milk	Fish and fishermen
Our school	Food and drink
Homes	Night
On the farm	Autumn (any seasons)

For older children:

Railways	Cities, towns and villages
India	London
Your locality	USA
Britain	Ice and snow (any weather)
Docks	Transport
The seashore	Forests and woodlands
Volcanoes	Aircraft and airports
Cocoa	People at work

A second question is over resources. There is little opportunity to develop map skills or study geographical ideas if there are no maps or textual/visual materials that will give the children the opportunity to progress. A useful section on resources is to be found elsewhere in this book (see Chapter 4 and Appendix 2). Sample studies are particularly helpful, giving detailed coverage of small areas of countries often beyond the experience of most children, and were recommended by the Plowden Report authors.

ORGANISING TOPIC WORK

The way children use books reflects the organisational basis of the topic work as arranged by the teacher. The experience of several observers has been that library books used in topic work often have parts simply copied from them. This is of little value if at the end of the topic the child has progressed no closer towards a greater grasp of central ideas, or an improved ability to undertake certain skills, even though there may have been some increment in the factual knowledge held by the child.

In the classroom situation there is perhaps little to be gained by suggesting a minimum amount of time to be spent on geographical work in a week. Bearing in mind that nearly all geographical work occurs in an integrated form, it would be impossible to measure accurately anyway. Elsewhere a minimum level of progress is stated in terms of geographical understanding of ideas, proficiency of skills, and exposure to attitudes at various stages in the child's progression through the early years of schooling. These aims should be studied, and selected to form termly or half-termly aims. This would be the first step in organising geographical work through projects. The identification of suitable topic themes is the next step, and is followed by a statement of the objectives that will be met through detailed study of the geographical aspects of the topics chosen. Hence:

AIMS
1. To develop an understanding of the fact that there are patterns to the distribution of people in an area. (idea)
2. To help children to use grid references on maps. (skill)

TOPIC
Home and school.

OBJECTIVES
1. Children will be able to identify a pattern to the location of their homes around the school. (idea)
2. Children will be able to relate the locations of their homes to distance from the school. (idea)
3. Children will be able to express the location of homes around the school by using grid references. (skill)

The objectives for each topic will be derived from the aims stated.

By careful organisation of topic work each child ought to attain the objectives (or move closer to attaining them) in each topic with 'geographical' elements. By the end of the term the aims of the geography teaching will have been met (or nearly met) as a result of progress in each topic. The aims will not necessarily be met on the basis of one topic alone, a more cumulative progression towards them is more likely.

A further crucial point, and which forms the next stage of the planning of topic work, concerns the learning experience the child goes through to meet the objective. If the objective in a topic is that all children will 'be able to identify and explain the relationship between school location and the location of homes of children at the school', then each child will need to actually experience seeing the homes (if not placing them) marked on a map in relation to the school and surrounding area, and be given the opportunity to comment—by, say, measuring distances from

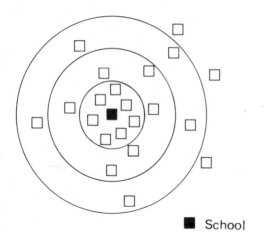

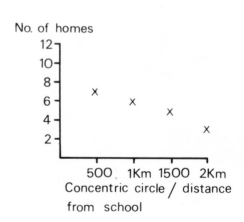

FIGURE 7.7   Location of children's homes

home to school direct, and by road—on the pattern that exists.

LEARNING EXPERIENCES
1. Children will place (or mark) their homes on a large-scale map of the area (or trace overlay).
2. Children will draw concentric circles every 500 metres from the school.
3. Children will count the number of homes lived in by schoolchildren in each concentric circle (see Fig. 7.7).
4. Draw a graph of the number in each circle (see Fig. 7.7).
5. Measure distance from home to school
   (a) direct;
   (b) by road.
6. Using a grid-square overlay, express the location of selected homes by grid references.

This clearly has implications for the organisation of project work. It is apparent that a topic cannot be divided up amongst the class such that individuals can pursue only their own interest. All children in the class must meet the objective, if not together then in rotation (see Fig. 7.8).

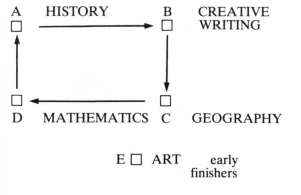

E □ ART   early finishers

FIGURE 7.8

Group A begins with historical aspects of a topic that has been generally introduced to the class as a whole by the teacher. Group B write, Group C look at geography, D at mathematics. At the end of a certain period of time, say 2 hours, the children move around (or the resources move around) such that new experiences, geography, creative writing, etc., are undertaken. In this way the geographical objectives to be covered in the topic can be met by *all* children, not just the

group who happen to have chosen geographical work. The attainment of the central ideas, skills and attitudes inherent in the subject cannot be left to chance.

This problem of organising learning experiences in project work merits further elaboration. We would contend that there are three main ways a topic can be dealt with.
1. Children work individually but covering the same aspects of a topic. The teacher would introduce the topic, and would look at geographical aspects, then historical, mathematical and so on. The links between 'discipline' areas would be strong. The children would have an assignment to cover, and, although this may be to answer the same set of questions using the same resources, they would work as individuals to complete their own assignments. (A variant on this basic theme of all doing the same is for the assignments to be covered by groups of two or three children working together.) Nevertheless, the teacher can control very closely the learning experiences of the children, a major problem perhaps being the need to provide the same or very similar resources for 30-40 children. (Class textbook here?)
2. At the opposite extreme, the children in a class select the aspect of the topic that they wish to study, and do so for the duration of the project, gleaning help from the teacher for new avenues of enquiry once the initial one is exhausted. Although by careful question setting/direction the teacher could ensure a balance of coverage in the topic, this is most difficult to control, and to record experiences enjoyed and progress made. We believe that this approach to geographical understanding, tending as it does to be unstructured, and to present the teacher with considerable planning problems, is best attempted only by the most skilled and experienced teacher.
3. A third approach is that outlined earlier where children work in groups on different aspects of the topic, and rotate after a period of time such that all children become immersed in the aspects of the topic explored by the teacher with the class as a whole at the outset. The demands on resources are not as heavy as in (1) and the teacher can ensure that pre-planned learning experiences can be enjoyed by the children working together intelligently

with the resource material provided in a structured way. Of course in practice there may be circumstances that force modification of the basic plan, and a particular desire of some children to look at an aspect of the project not initially covered by the teacher. The teacher will have to draw up the strategy to be followed with strong regard for his particular class, but we feel the approach outlined above may be a useful starting point, since it allows a minimum amount of work to be covered by all children, and yet can be open ended, allowing the child at the end of the basic work to follow an aspect of the topic he finds most interesting.

Before giving a detailed, worked example of the organisation of a topic, a final point needs making about learning experiences. It makes a nonsense of aims and objectives if the learning experience with which the child becomes involved does not relate to them. If an objective states that children should be able to distinguish groups or types of shops in a small shopping centre, and to identify their location in relation to each other, e.g. building societies together, estate agents, etc., then simply to give the child a town guide and expect him to find out about the locality is clearly not going to bring the child any closer to meeting the objective as stated. We are very cautious about the value of posing a question that simply asks the child to 'find out about', anyway. Whilst some useful factual knowledge may be accumulated, little intellectual growth can be expected in terms of understanding ideas in the subject, or skills of, say, mapwork. If the teacher carefully plans the learning experiences such that they relate to the objectives, then a practical problem can be presented to the child at some future point to assess the degree of understanding and level of skill possessed by the child.

As a conclusion to this section, some examples of structured work in geography are included below. They are placed within the 'project' framework and attempt to illustrate the comments made earlier. They are not intended as complete projects either from the geographical or non-geographical points of view, and to show how the suggestions could be used as a point of departure for work in non-geographical areas some hints for further activity are placed at the end.

AIMS (termly or half-termly)
1. Children will develop a greater awareness of aspects of life in the less developed world.
2. Children will improve their understanding of the notions of distance, locational distribution and relationship in a geographical sense.
3. Children will become more skillful in the collection and analysis of data.
4. Children will become more proficient at map reading.

TOPIC
Food and drink. (In the example below, tea has been chosen as one aspect of this topic through which the aims—and later the objectives—could be met.)

OBJECTIVES
The children will be able by the end of the work to:
1. Recognise that straight-line and walking distances are often very different.
2. Plan the best journey for a plantation worker.
3. Identify a pattern to the distribution of tea bushes.
4. Distinguish climatic conditions in Britain and Sri Lanka based on temperature and rainfall figures.
5. Assess the location of tea collection centres.
6. Read maps using symbols.
7. Calculate map distances.

LEARNING EXPERIENCES

Creating Interest
Children may not show a great deal of interest initially, but a successful way of creating interest is to bring in tea in a packet such that the children can taste it dry, or to bring in some tea as a 'mystery' substance amongst several, or to bring in the plant rather than the crushed product. (The Commonwealth Institute may be able to help here. For address see Appendix 2.)

Activities for younger children.
1. They could begin by considering how many times each day tea is drunk by parents. Results could be expressed pictorially. This could lead to a study of how the vast amounts of tea are shipped. Tea chests may be available.
2. Younger children could also be introduced to the idea that tea bushes have a distributional

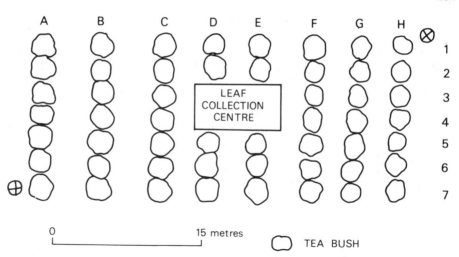

FIGURE 7.9
Leaf collection
centre and tea
bushes

0   15 metres
⬭ TEA BUSH

pattern (rows), and that tea pluckers make a number of long journeys up and down these rows.

(a) A series of exercises could be developed using the rows and columns as co-ordinates (see Fig. 7.9).

(b) Journey distances could be worked out for two 'pluckers' starting at each end. Hence:

(i) How many bushes will each pluck if they work at similar speeds?

(ii) Give the co-ordinate of the closest bush to this point.

(iii) Measurements from the leaf collection centre to various bushes in a straight line, or round the rows can be calculated.

(iv) Work out the best route from bushes H7 and A1 to the leaf collection centre.

Activities for older children

1. A case study of a tea estate in Sri-Lanka could form the bulk of the work for the group. The following acount could set the scene:

We were rising mile by mile and gradually the burning heat relaxed its pressure at the approach to sundown. How quickly the sun slips away. That is the first memory of the tropics. Soon the crickets were shrilling in the grass, and glow worms twinkled by the thousand . . . The road dipped down

towards Kandy, where we stayed the night. From here—twelve hundred feet up—our road led towards the hill station of Nuwara-Eliya, set among the tea estates . . . we continued our journey next day, the constant hairpin bends making the road like a miniature alpine pass . . . I never expected the green hills up country to be so like those of the Lake District. We might have been ascending Newlands or Esk Hause, but for the glory of pink tulip-trees in full bloom, the clusters of huge bats, 'flying foxes', hanging asleep from branches, and the hundreds of thousands of neat, dark tea bushes which suddenly appeared and thereafter dominated the landscape. (From Beddis, R. A. *Asia and North America,* University of London Press, 1969, pp. 104-5.)

2. A further introduction to the area could be given by a look at the climate, especially rainfall and temperature, and by comparing Colombo with London. Figure 7.10 shows graphs of temperature and rainfall for both these places.

Several questions can be asked using the graphs as a basis.

(a) What do the graphs tell you about the amount of rain in each place?

(b) In what ways are the temperatures of the two places similar or different?

(c) What do the rainfall graphs tell you about the amount of water needed to grow tea?

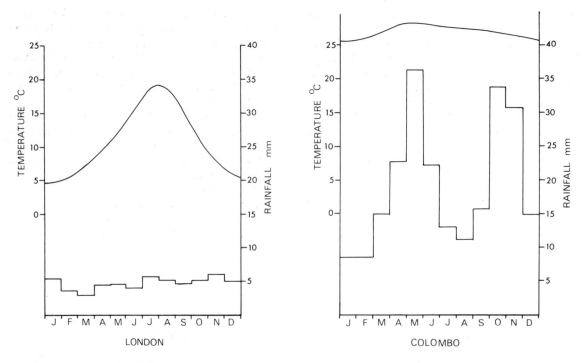

FIGURE 7.10   Temperature and rainfall in London and Colombo

3. Using a large-scale map of a tea estate (Fig. 7.11) a number of activities can take place.
   (a) What symbols are used for a labourer's house; a Hindu shrine; the estate boundary? The teacher could make up many more examples.
   (b) By using the scale to work out distances between various points, some idea of the size of the estate can be gained. Road lengths could be measured.
   (c) The symbol ■ represents the homes of workers. If each of these symbols also stands for 20 workers, then how many workers live on the plantation?
   (d) What evidence is there on the map that the workers may not all be of the same nationality?
   (e) What evidence on the map suggests that before tea can be sold in the shops it has to be processed in some way?
   (f) (i)   Are the leaf collection centres in the best places? Where would you site a new one?
       (ii) Are the schools well placed? Where would you site a new one?

Links with other areas of study
Mathematics: Work could develop using the yields of tea, or trade figures in tea of the tea-producing and consuming nations.
Creative Work: It may be possible for children to model a plantation, or to depict in a piece of work 'early morning' or 'sunset'. They could also try to imagine life working and living within the same area. Children could also in written work describe the climate during the rainy periods.

Topic on 'Time'
(Sarah M. Smith, Farthingsgate Junior School, Scratchface Lane, Purbrook, Waterlooville, Hants.)
The three 9-11-year-old classes of the school followed a topic on time. Each class covered general aspects of telling the time, use of time-tables etc. In addition to this one class prepared a talk/display on the solar system, one on evolution of animals and one on British monarchs which they presented to the other two groups in turn.
   The objectives of the work as a whole were to

enlarge the children's ideas of time and consolidate mathematical work using time. The geographical work, which one class covered, was intended to introduce the children briefly to rocks, to indicate a little of the significance of the fossils they find and to show something of the immensity and wonder of creation.

There were only four weeks available for the topic otherwise far more detail could have been covered. Most of the work in the syllabus (Fig. 7.12) was covered but biological clocks and the 1978 calendar had to be omitted owing to lack of time. This work was carried out in conjunction with normal class work in maths, language, PE, music, etc. When studying evolution with children, especially in such a short period as a

month, it is difficult to convey the slowness of development and change. The ammonite lasted for about 250 million years, primitive worms far longer, while man has only been around for about 1 million years. This is a concept which many junior children are not mature enough to grasp: one can only point out the situation in various ways and hope that if the facts are studied clearly and in chronological order with constant emphasis on the complexity and slowness of change an elementary start on grasping the concept will have been made.

The syllabus shows how each week's work was structured as a unit within itself as far as possible, as well as developing ideas from week to week. The first week's work included a lesson on the

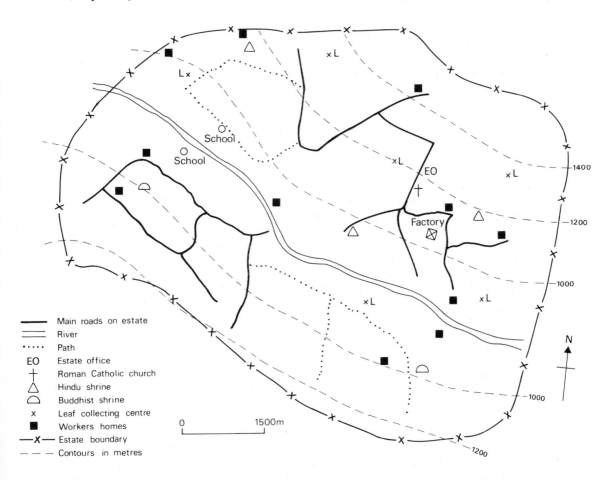

FIGURE 7.11   Map of a tea estate in Sri Lanka

	English (1 hr)	Drama (1 hr)	Maths (1 hr)	Science (1 hr)	Topic (2 x 1 hr)		Art (1 hr)	RE (1 hr)	Craft (1 hr)
Week 1	Origins of names for days of week	'Planets Suite' (Holst) Theme of discovering an unknown planet to Mars	How long is one minute? Timing things	Grow crystals	Origins of Earth from space	Study a crystal or crystalline rock	Make card crystals	Preparing an Assembly on Creation - dance/drama of Genesis story; written work/pictures on wonders of creation and destruction through carelessness, pollution etc. Prayers on creation and our responsibilities towards it.	Making timers (see *Time, Science 5-13*, Macdonald) and Osmiroid Time Cards
Week 2	Origins of the calendar Write one's own calendar poem		Questions on 1978 calendar	Study sediments: chalk, clay, sand	Origins of sedimentary rocks, first life	Day/night Seasons	Illustrate the months using the poem 'January brings the snow'		
Week 3	Write story: The night the clock struck 13	The Creation Story from Genesis	Time zones	Study a fossil	Development of amphibians and reptiles	Own study of amphibians and reptiles including dinosaurs	Illustrate the amphibian or reptile studied		
Week 4	The time machine	↓	24-hour clock and timetables	Biological clocks	Study of evolution post-dinosaurs		Illustrate the animal or bird studied		

Story: *Mary Anning's treasure*, by Helen Bush

FIGURE 7.12   Syllabus for topic on 'Time'

origins of our planet from dust and gas particles to ancient crystalline rocks; crystalline rock samples were studied so the children knew what they were, and epsom salts, sugar and salt crystals were grown from saturated solutions prepared in a variety of ways so the children could see how crystals form and how smaller crystals tend to form more rapidly than larger ones. It was emphasised that this process is much slower inside the earth than in the classroom. The children practised measuring lengths and angles in order to make crystal shapes ranging from cuboid to orthorombic.

The second week concentrated on the origins of sedimentary rocks and experiments were carried out with chalk, clay and sand: which held water? which did water run through most rapidly? etc. The rotation of the earth and its effect on day, night and seasons was discussed and children were given follow-up work to do on their own.

In the third week the work on the earth's rotation was completed through study of Time Zones. The most straightforward way to do this is to start at dawn, 6 a.m. on the international date-line (though not mentioning that term yet). This more or less coincides with the 'eastern' edge of a map and all the children could understand that it was darker and therefore earlier as one went across one's sheet or round the world. I took four stations roughly at 90° of longitude intervals and the children, having been given the times for Fiji, worked out and told me what times to put on the other stations (see Fig. 7.13).

Fiji	New Orleans	London	Calcutta	Fiji
6 am	Noon	6 pm	Midnight	6 am
Noon	6 pm	Midnight	6 am	Noon
6 pm	Midnight	6 am	Noon	6 pm
Midnight	6 am	Noon	6 pm	Midnight

FIGURE 7.13   Time Zones: preliminary chart

PLATE 12.
Some examples of fossils
and rocks displayed during a project

After that the one-hour divisions were added and the Greenwich Meridian occurred as an incidental and most of the children quickly realised how the International dateline worked.

The evolutionary work was continued with the lesson on how some fish evolved into amphibians and later reptiles. Each child then chose a reptile or amphibian to study in more detail on their own: needless to say dinosaurs were the most popular. Finally evolution was brought up to date with each child choosing a mammal or bird to study in detail. The work was presented as a talk and final pictorial display where some effort was made to show the length of each era. The fact that man was squashed into a tiny period showed up well here. The children enjoyed this topic and some good work was produced. Had more time been available I would have spent more time on eventual evolutionary failures, e.g. the ammonite or dinosaurs which are most interesting to consider with this age group. The Genesis Creation story and respect for creation were chosen as an RE theme because I feel if this story is taught in a factual context its value can be appreciated, and not dismissed as total rubbish, but can be discussed.

The story *Mary Anning's Treasure* was chosen because it shows some of the significance of fossils through the story of a famous collector and also it presents the need for constant care in collecting in a lively way.

Further illustrations of topic work can be found in publications by Cracknell (1977, 1979), and the books listed in Appendix 4 may provide some ideas for project work in general.

7.5　The teaching of geography as a separate subject

David Mills

As has been shown in Chapter 1, geography is now taught mainly within a combined study framework in both junior and middle schools and in many of the lower forms in secondary schools. In the view of many teachers this has led to a considerable weakening of the teaching of the subject unless the schemes of work have been properly thought out. Evidence for this was given in *Primary Education in England* (DES, 1978b), which stated 'though good work was being done in some classes, in the majority essential skills and ideas were seldom given sufficient attention; work in geography cannot be soundly based if children are not introduced to the essential skills of the subject' (para 5.136). The main advantage of teaching geography as a separate subject is that it will be more likely to have a properly considered scheme of work and may well also have a trained geographer either to teach many parts of the syllabus or at least to be available to give help and assistance to teachers who might not have had a geographical background. There is also evidence from many secondary schools that integrated schemes of work are effective only as long as the staff who teach them remain the same as those who undertook the original planning. With staff changes some schemes have not been found to be effective and the school has reverted to single subject teaching.

In the previous edition of this handbook a syllabus was given for use in junior schools which still has much to commend it, though it was not devised with ideas, concepts or skills as a basis. The main principles on which it was written were to ensure that within each year group the children would first of all engage in 'local and practical topics'. Included within this were studies of the local environment, mapwork and weather studies. This was then followed by 'extended topics' which included a variety of themes which were largely related to the geography of the British Isles. Finally, there were a series of topics related to 'The World'. The syllabus was based on the still-accepted tenet that the child should be led from the known to the unknown. The syllabus made good use of the case study approach and also attempted to be developmental in that the

difficulty of the topics gradually increased throughout the four years of the junior school. A typical syllabus for first and second-year primary classes in a London school is given below (Syllabus A).

SYLLABUS A
(Craven Park School, Castlewood Road, London, N16 6DH)

First Year (7-year-olds)

Main Theme
The need for shelter.
A.　Homes
B.　Animals' habitats

A.　HOMES
1.　Homes through the Ages:
　　e.g. primitive to modern—caves, huts, wooden, stone, brick, concrete and steel.
2.　Some British Homes:
　　e.g. homes typical of different areas or periods, e.g. Scottish crofts, Tudor thatches, Georgian brick, bungalows, terraced, flats etc.
3.　Some Homes Abroad:
　　e.g. primitive homes of today—Indonesian lake dwellings, Mexican adobe homes, South African kraals, sampans in China. Other homes—Swiss chalets, New York skyscrapers.

B.　ANIMALS' HABITATS
1.　Some British wild animals and where they live, e.g. the fox, deer, badger, rabbit etc.
2.　British farm animals, and their use to man.
3.　Animals typical of other countries and their use to man, e.g. the Polar Bear of the Far North; Elephants of Burma; Camels of the Sahara etc.

LOCAL
1.　Homes:　What our own house looks like.
　　　　　　What type of houses are most of the local houses?
2.　Introducing the plan. Drawing objects from above, e.g. books, chairs, toys. Where is my desk in the classroom; which way do I face?
3.　The school in relation to the rectangle of streets around it.

WEATHER
1. Daily observations of the weather using little pictures or symbols for the sun, rain, snow etc.
2. Summary and presentation at the end of the month, e.g. number of rainy, sunny, windy days etc.

VISITS
Natural History Museum

Second Year (8-year-olds)

Main theme
Man's occupation in supplying our needs.
A. Our food
B. Our clothes
C. Our buildings

A. OUR FOOD
1. Food that is grown, e.g. corn, vegetables, fruit.
2. Food from livestock.
3. Farms exist to supply us with food. How farms in Britain have developed through the ages, e.g. hunting and gathering; the simple plough; strip farming; the 3-field system; Lord and peasant.
   Film: 'Speed the Plough'. Improvements in farming—simply (a) new implements and machinery, (b) new crops, (c) new breeds of animals and (d) crop rotation.
4. Some farms around the world, i.e. the provision of products we cannot grow, e.g. African subsistence agriculture; plantations in Malaya or West Indies; a collective farm in Russia; rice and tea in Asia etc.
5. Transport—beasts of burden—camels, donkeys, horses; ships, early sailing ships, e.g. tea clippers; road, rail and air.

B. OUR CLOTHES
1. What goes to make our clothes?
2. Where do wool, cotton, linen, rubber, leather and man-made fibres come from? Some brief details of their production with detailed account of one, e.g. wool.

C. OUR BUILDINGS
1. What do we build with? e.g. wood, stone, clay, brick, concrete, glass and steel.
2. Relationship between buildings and weather, e.g. roofs.
3. How people have built, e.g. post and lintel, simple arches; methods of building with bricks, i.e. bonds.
4. How people have built in other lands, e.g. Pyramids of Egypt, Stonehenge, Great Wall of China, etc.

LOCAL
1. The River Lee—barge traffic as transport from larger ships. Timber, where does it come from?
2. Land use of local area, e.g. the River Lee and its banks; the factory and timber yard area; residential area; shopping area. Produce a simple land-use map.
3. Plot local roads and shops. Our route to school. Use of scale in classroom and school.
4. Street 'furniture', e.g. drains, manhole covers, lamps. What are local buildings made of on the outside? What is my home made of? e.g. brick, stone, slate, tile, plaster etc.

WEATHER
1. Direction finding and the points of the compass.
2. Temperature, measurement.

VISITS
1. Cutty Sark
2. Commonwealth Institute
3. A farm visit

The main advance which has been made in recent years is the attempt to look more closely at the key ideas and skills and to make the syllabus more clearly developmental. A Working Party set up by the Inner London Education Authority Advisory Panel has produced some guide-lines for 'The Study of Places in the Primary School'. This group was particularly concerned with the need for a genuine intellectual progression in geographical work otherwise there was likely to be a considerable loss of motivation by the children. The group saw place-study as a vehicle for the development of the basic communication skills of literacy, oracy, numeracy and graphicacy. It produced a matrix (Fig. 7.14), which they made clear should not be regarded as a prescriptive syllabus, as each school has its own local potentialities, assemblage of teaching talent, and its own range of children's interests.

In 'The study of places' an important concern has been seen as the need to provide greater 'continuity in the curriculum as children move from one stage to the next'. Continuity is vital on two counts. It enables the teacher to build logically on concepts that the children already have, and offers the children opportunities to use their skills.

The Working Party found it useful to arrange the suggestions in the form of a matrix. Broad age bands have been incorporated into the matrix in an attempt to assist teachers to devise a sequence of learning activities and skill development. The activities and ideas shown in each horizontal

LOWER PRIMARY

Experience		Graphicacy	
Direct	Indirect	Maps	Other Aspects
Direct observation of the immediately accessible environment (i.e. that area normally reached without the aid of transport); the school grounds and the neighbourhood are ideal and sufficient. Such observation will be the basis for much 'labelling' activity, involving the acquisition of vocabulary. Specific destinations or features (e.g. the park, the library, the church) will be more appropriate than more general 'surveys'. Clearly identifiable people in the immediate locality (e.g. lollipop lady, policeman, postman, milkman, bus driver) will provide a basis for discussion, and could also be invited to talk with the children. Recognition and discussion of broad weather categories (e.g. rainy, windy, frosty weather) and seasonal changes can lead to simple scientific investigation and creative work. The children will be indiscriminate 'collectors', both privately and when on class excursions. Some of these collections (e.g. of pebbles, postcards, matchbox labels) may be used as a basis for discussion about places, and provide opportunities for sorting and classifying in various ways.	Stories can be particularly important in extending the children's range of imagining. Whether stories are set in unfamiliar contexts (e.g. the countryside, distant lands, imaginary places) or in familiar environments, they will be a major stimulus to thought and discussion about places. (The stories selected must, of course, be good as stories; ideally they might feature children of the same age range.) Traditional folk-tales from other countries might also be employed. Stories will often provide a basis for discussion, drama and other creative activities. Topic work based upon animals (e.g. polar bears, camels, lions) and their habitats can be a very appropriate way of assisting the children's early awareness of broad global contrasts. There will be opportunities 'to share' the direct experiences of others in the class (e.g. journeys, holidays).	There will normally be little or no formal, systematic 'mapwork': printed maps of any kind will rarely be appropriate. A large-scale map of the local area may be displayed as an element in the room decor, reinforcing the small child's sense of territory. Most representations of place, whether provided by the teacher or produced by the children, will be essentially pictorial, though some will incorporate a 'map' element. Such early spontaneous picture-maps (e.g. 'my house', 'my visit to Granny') should be encouraged. Early 'map' activities will often be based upon imaginative experiences. Stories may contain picture-maps or be the basis for individual or collective pictorial map-making. Such maps may also be derived from pictures. Many simple games involve the representation of routes, destinations and the location of hazards, and provide further opportunities to explore this mode of communication.	Pictures will be a particularly important stimulus for developing ideas about places, and for acquiring vocabulary. Pictures of local places will be as useful as pictures of environments unfamiliar to the children (e.g. mountain scenes, seaside scenes). Aerial photographs of the immediate locality can be a stimulating part of the decor. Films or slide sequences should be very brief. As well as being a source of environmental information, pictures can be employed by the children to communicate their own ideas; they can be encouraged to make pictures of the locality, possibly using cheap cameras. Recording will commonly take the form of simple pictograms (e.g. of weather, jobs, modes of transport) which will start to establish the notion of 'standard symbols' to represent real-world experiences or features. Modelling (e.g. of a farm, a street, a zoo, a village) will also be an important early way of communicating about places. Scale is unimportant, but the recording of the layout of a model can be a useful early approach to the concept of the map.

MIDDLE PRIMARY

Experience		Graphicacy	
Direct	Indirect	Maps	Other Aspects
Observations in the immediate environment will increasingly take the form of small areas. Such surveys will often involve various methods of classification (e.g. of types of buildings, open spaces, traffic). The children's interest in individual environmental detail can be used in the investigation of changes in the locality. Visual 'clues', (e.g. the conversion of houses to offices or shops) can be identified, indicating past and current changes. Simple weather records may be kept over short periods (e.g. two to three weeks); these would not necessarily involve standard measuring units. Organised visits may extend to whole-day explorations beyond the immediate locality but not normally beyond an hour's travelling time. Typical destinations would be a farm, a major open space (e.g. woodland, common, heath), a zoo or a museum. A major objective for such visits is to provide a stimulus for the use of communication skills.	Stories will increasingly be supplemented by 'documentary' material about other environments. This should normally be in the form of sample studies of specific locations (e.g. a farm, a village, a mine, a factory, a port). An emphasis upon families and individuals, preferably named, will add a sense of reality. Such investigations should attempt to bring out the universal nature of human needs and activities (e.g. food, housing, clothing, work, trade) and to establish that all localities contain elements of change. Personal linkages with the wider world (e.g. through travel, relatives in other countries) will also provide opportunities for extending the children's range of imagining. Publicised journeys (e.g. around-the-world yacht race, international sports, royal visits) that have already captured the children's attention may form a starting point for investigations of other countries. The natural interest in spectacular environmental events (e.g. volcanoes, earthquakes, hurricanes, floods), affords another appropriate 'way in' to wider world studies. The emphasis should be upon the impact on people and their responses, rather than on causation. The children's growing awareness of basic global contrasts might be sustained through the discussion of selected stories of exploration. A useful teaching strategy is to invite the children to imagine themselves in another environment, as travellers or inhabitants.	Maps should increasingly complement, but not replace, the pictorial representation of places. Freehand maps (e.g. of the journey to school) should be encouraged; however, by the age of nine there should be a greater use of provided maps. These will normally be in the form of simple duplicated base maps (e.g. local street maps, a farm plan) to which the children can add labels, colours and other information. Map skills appropriate for this age group include the use of colours and symbols, together with keys to explain them. The map languages or codes, however, should preferably not be imposed, but should be devised by the children themselves. The use of simple grids to assist in locating places ('My house is in square B3, the school is in square D5') may be important, possibly through games (e.g. battleships, treasure hunts). 'Imaginative' maps based on stories or ideal layouts for a school, park, zoo, etc. will continue to be important. The study of local and distant places should involve large-scale maps and plans (e.g. the local shops rather than the British Isles, an Indian village rather than India). Grasp of scale should not be a major objective at this stage, a 'subjective' approach to scale (i.e. features recorded on a larger scale) is likely to persist for most children. Early practice in map using should be integrally related to local work, relating map shapes and symbols to features observed in the field. A wide range of types of maps of the locality (e.g. old maps, estate agents' maps, A-Z maps, maps from local newspapers) can be involved, whilst for wider world topics the globe is a most useful adjunct at this stage.	Pictures will continue to be very important. Discussion of a picture will often continue the process of categorising environments (e.g. a: city centre, a village, a port, a harbour, a resort) and the annotation of pictures (e.g. postcards, posters, duplicated sketches) can consolidate vocabulary. A set of slides and/or photographs of the local area is an invaluable resource at this stage, as are large-scale vertical aerial photographs of the area. The children should be encouraged to make as well as to examine pictures of places, both local and distant. Other graphical devices that can be introduced include the histogram (e.g. of a traffic count), the compound bar (e.g. of activities during a day, week or year), the flow diagram (e.g. of milk from cow to classroom) and the section (e.g. of upper floor uses of a shopping street). Models continue to be useful and can now be more closely related to actual places.

UPPER PRIMARY

Experience		Graphicacy	
Direct	Indirect	Maps	Other Aspects
The area used for local study will expand to include locations and networks familiar to the children, involving investigations of journeys and destinations for shopping, recreation and work. The awareness and consideration of live local issues (education *for* the environment) will emerge as an increasingly important element. This will complement the use of the locality for the development of skills (education *through* the environment) and collecting information (education *about* the environment). At this stage there will be more concern for the neighbourhood and townscape as a whole. In weather studies, standard measuring devices may be introduced (e.g. the rain gauge, the thermometer), with a greater emphasis upon averages and generalisations (e.g. seasonal patterns). In addition to day visits, a residential school journey may facilitate elementary comparative studies of different environments. Coast and countryside, river and village all provide opportunities for consolidating map skills in the field. Simple relationships between rock types and scenery (e.g. chalk downland, clay vale) may be introduced.	Several topics or projects of a geographical nature will be undertaken. These will often be selected for their topicality (e.g. the Soviet Union during the 1980 Olympics) or personal relevance (e.g. areas with which children or teachers have links). Geographical topics may be organised around a theme (e.g. mountains), an area (e.g. Canada) or a product (e.g. petroleum). Such topics may include selected contrasting environments within Britain (e.g. a hill farm, a mining town, a fishing port). There will be increasing opportunities for reference to non-school sources of environmental images such as television and the press. An emphasis upon global linkages in trade, tourism and migration will be appropriate. Some systematic support, through one or two selected areas, will be provided for the children's early attempts to sort out the nature of the 'building blocks' of the political map (i.e. district, county or state or province, country and continent) and the physical map (i.e. mountain ranges, plateaux, plains, estuaries, peninsulas and broad climatic types). Simulations and role-play (e.g. the selection of holiday destinations, the routing of a motorway) can be very effective at this stage. Well-chosen stories set in other environments will continue to be the basis for much environmental imagining.	Spontaneous freehand 'map'-making will continue to be encouraged, complemented by an increasing emphasis upon basic map skills. Some children are able to grasp the notion of scale at this stage, but much systematic practice in the measuring of distances and areas is necessary. The ways in which the scale adopted imposes constraints on (i) the area covered by the map and (ii) the degree of detail shown should be explored. There will be a greater emphasis on understanding and using standardised map language (e.g. Ordnance Survey symbols and atlas conventions such as layer tinting). These skills will be most purposefully consolidated if used in the field (e.g. a school journey programme could include an introduction to the points of the compass). Large scales will continue to be dominant in both local and global studies (e.g. a plan of a dairy farm, a plan of a Jamaican plantation, an airport layout), but there will be increasing use of smaller-scale atlas maps in work on journeys and distant locations. Regular use of the atlas will develop familiarity with 'thematic' maps which show one dimension (e.g. relief, political units, rainfall, population). Conventional map grids (e.g. Ordnance Survey four-figure references, latitude and longitude on atlas maps) may be introduced. The design of ideal layouts, possibly linked to the discussion of a local issue, will continue, as will the mapping of stories.	Work will involve much collecting, making and studying of pictures of all kinds, with an emergent emphasis upon the selection of appropriate pictures to represent a local or distant environment. The school journey may provide an opportunity to develop simple transects and cross-sections, whilst the comparative study of places may establish the matrix as a useful way of recording information. The use of relief, rainfall and population maps will afford an opportunity to introduce the isoline concept, which can be employed in local studies (e.g. linking points 5, 10 or 15 minutes away from school) and may involve 'topologically transformed' maps in which the scale used relates not to distance but to some other factor such as travelling time or population size. Work on broad climatic regions (e.g. tundra, desert, rain forest) can involve simple climatic graphs. Conversion graphs (e.g. kilometres/miles, degrees Centigrade/Fahrenheit) may continue to be required. Studies of farming, trade and so on may involve the use of pie diagrams to represent proportions. Other devices include the balance sheet as a way of arranging information (e.g. the costs and benefits of an environmental decision) and the design of publicity materials (e.g. posters, leaflets, newspapers) for real or imagined locations. Vertical and oblique photographs continue to be an important resource and will help the children's understanding of map and townscape. Model making will become increasingly sophisticated and will be linked to specific purposes (e.g. developing an understanding of scale, or designing a redevelopment for the locality).

FIGURE 7.14 The study of places in the primary school

Notes:
1. Available from ILEA Learning Materials Service, Publishing Centre, Highbury Station Road, London N1 1SB.
2. Each idea in the matrix is illustrated in the original publication by a colour photograph of work from ILEA primary schools.

band are *examples* of those considered appropriate and practicable for the age group concerned; the horizontal divisions should be regarded as essentially notional. Clearly much depends on local circumstances, including the enthusiasm and expertise of individual teachers. The allocation of an activity under one specific age range should not be taken as implying that the activity is somehow less appropriate for other age ranges. Nor is the matrix intended to suggest that certain topics, such as homes, transport and deserts, are somehow peculiarly appropriate for particular age groups. *It is the skills and concepts employed, rather than the content area, which should be closely geared to the pupil's age and ability.*

Direct experience

Under this heading the matrix lists examples of the sorts of activity which can use and extend the child's natural curiosity about places—his own neighbourhood and other people's. The matrix emphasises that local environmental work should be a recurring activity throughout the primary school, from simple representations of 'our street' in the infants' school to more systematic surveys of local amentities at the age of eleven.

Indirect experience

Although direct experience is clearly vital, this is certainly not the only environmental experience that should be provided. The appearance on the matrix of an indirect experience column recognises the fact that children have a natural curiosity about distant environments and societies. This interest is reinforced by fragments of information, ideas and insights derived from a multiplicity of sources—family, friends, advertising, stories, comics and the media (especially television).

Although lip service has been paid to the use of the local environment there are still many schools who either do not make use of it at all or whose efforts to utilise the resources are very sporadic. Within any geography syllabus there is a clear need to make use of what children can discover in the field, not only in the area round the school but from evidence collected from work undertaken on school journeys. What is important is that this work should be planned systematically and so can be related to work which follows.

The study of physical geography is also regarded as a very important element though it has probably been rather underplayed until the pupils reach secondary school. This work is also unlikely to be covered unless geography is taught as a separate subject. The study of the landscape and of the factors which cause changes should be an integrated part of the syllabus. Within the 5-11 age range studies in physical geography have traditionally been concerned with weather studies, the study of rocks and fossils, and with some of the more outstanding physical landscapes of the world, e.g. deserts and mountains. These studies are rewarding for younger children and can excite considerable interest, which can then be developed with the 11-13 age range where more emphasis can be placed on the importance of process. It is equally important that children should appreciate the varied landscapes of the British Isles and this can be taught either by fieldwork or by the study of good photographs and texts.

Within the geography syllabus the study of distant areas forms a critical part and can take place from the age of five onwards. A major concern in the teaching of geography has always been with teaching about areas which are unknown to children. This element has always proved to be exciting and worthwhile and must be considered as essential to the syllabus. A major question is 'what areas do I teach?' The teacher concerned with this age range must clearly be selective; he cannot hope to give a world-wide coverage. The selection should be such that it will give the child an awareness of the variety of areas and lives of people who live there. Over the age ranges considered in this book all continents should be covered but the selection should develop from the simple studies undertaken in the infant school to those much more complex with the 13-year-old.

The teaching of mapwork, regarded as fundamental in the teaching of the subject, is also probably taught more effectively if geography is taught separately. The planning of the development of mapwork skills is easier and specific time can be allocated to its teaching. The work which can be undertaken is given in detail in Chapter 5.

Geography in the middle schools overlaps with suggestions for primary and secondary work. The basic essentials remain, however. Conner (1976)

Year	Topic	Assessment Type*	Location	Distance	Distribution	Movement	Change	Scale	Area	Time	Quality	Cost	Density	Height	Gradient	Direction	Accessibility	Systems
ONE	Map Skills	O	X	X			X	X	X	X			X	X	X	X		
	Agriculture I	O	X	X	X			X	X	X			X	X	X			
	Earthquakes, Mountains, Volcanoes	O	X	X			X	X	X	X	X		X	X	X			
	Agriculture II	O		X		X				X	X		X	X	X			X
	Latitude & Longitude	O	X						X							X		
	Agriculture III	F			X		X	X	X	X			X	X	X			
	Routes & Networks		X	X		X											X	
	Towns	O	X	X				X	X	X			X					X
TWO	London	F	X			X	X	X	X		X		X	X		X		X
	Iron & Steel	O	X	X		X	X	X	X	X	X						X	X
	Energy	O	X	X		X	X	X	X	X	X	X	X	X		X		
	Motor Vehicles & Roads	O	X	X		X				X	X						X	X
THREE	Settlement	O/W	X	X		X	X	X		X							X	
	Communications	O/W	X			X	X	X	X	X	X	X	X					
	Map Skills	O/W	X						X	X					X	X		

Syllabus B. Checklist of main ideas covered in years 1 to 3 (11-13-year-olds). (Forest Hill School, London SE23 2XN)
* Assessment Type: O - Objective Test; F - Fieldwork Folder; W - Written Test.

Techniques

Numerical Comprehension	Visual Comprehension	Aural Comprehension	Written Comprehension	Measurement	Correlation	Sketching	Co-ordinates	Cross Sections	First Hand Recording	First Hand Observation	Classifications	Decision-Making	Atlas Use	Synthesis
X	X		X	X	X	X	X	X	X	X	X			X
X	X		X	X	X		X					X		
X	X	X	X	X	X		X						X	
X			X	X	X		X							X
X	X		X				X						X	
	X		X		X	X		X	X	X	X			
X	X		X	X								X		
X	X		X	X	X						X	X	X	X
X	X		X	X	X		X	X	X	X		X	X	X
X	X		X	X	X		X					X		X
X	X	X	X	X	X		X	X			X	X		X
X	X		X									X		X
X	X	X	X	X	X							X		X
X	X			X	X						X	X	X	X
X	X		X	X	X	X	X					X		X

in his investigations into middle-school geography made an analysis of course content when geography is taught an an independent subject (see Fig. 7.15). As can be seen it is very traditional in approach and should be developed with a greater emphasis on ideas and generalisations, problem solving and the discussion of issues, but it can provide a format for development.

Finally, the syllabus used in one London comprehensive school for the first three years of its intake is included (Syllabus B). This syllabus is a good example of one which has been clearly thought out in terms of concepts/ideas, skills/techniques and evaluation.

Year One (9-10-year-olds)
1. The Locality: a simple study of the local environment.
2. We ourselves.
3. Understanding commodities and features of Britain.
4. Some introduction to atlas work and simple scale work, graphic representation, points of the compass etc.
5. Basic mapwork skills.

Year Two (10-11-year-olds)
1. Local Studies: developing an understanding of the local environment.
2. An introduction to fieldwork and fieldwork skills.
3. Weather studies.
4. The British Isles; farming and industry in particular or the occupations of the people.
5. Populations and Trade from abroad: the climates and crops of other areas.
6. Simple atlas work and the development of map reading skills (including contours, scale and using the O.S. map).

Year Three (11-12-year-olds)
1. Local Studies.
2. The British Isles: general geography, industry, occupations—often linking with factors of current interest, e.g. oil shortages, fishing disputes, picture studies.
3. Simple physical geography and geology and the recognition of morphological features.
4. Introduction to other lands: Europe, sample studies of Africa, Australia and the Americas. (Using standard text books, which compare and contrast ways of life in other parts of the world.)
5. Simple weather studies and climates of the world.
6. Astronomy.
7. Fieldwork and fieldwork skills.
8. Atlas and mapwork. Building on the earlier introduction: scale, contours, grid references, distance, direction, latitude and longitude.

Year Four (12-13-year-olds)
1. Fieldwork: more detail and concentration on skills—includes visits to local field study centres.
2. Atlas and mapwork.
3. Vocabulary of physical geography and basic geology, consideration of particular geological areas, e.g. limestone, chalk, earth formation.
4. Regional geography: continents, regions of the Southern Hemisphere, Britain and Europe, the UK and Commonwealth, the world's natural regions, N. America, the Common Market.
5. Work based on textbook courses—
   (i) Longmans—*The Developing World* and *A New Man*
   (ii) *Cole and Beynon—New Ways in Geography*
   (iii) Young and Lowry—*People in Britain* and *People around the World*
6. Local Studies—
   (i) Urban Studies
   (ii) Village Studies
   (iii) Industrial Studies
7. Weather studies, climatology and climatic zones.

FIGURE 7.15   *An analysis of common features of course content, when geography is taught as an independent subject*

(It is important to point out that all schools do not cover all of these topics but that they do cover at least one and often more than one of those listed.) (From Conner, C. 'Geography in the middle school', *Teaching Geography*, 1 (1976), p. 181.)

UNIT TITLE/ TIMING	OBJECTIVES		EVALUATION	RESOURCES	COMMENT
	CONCEPTS/IDEAS	SKILLS/TECHNIQUES			
MAP SKILLS 10 x 70-Min. Periods 7 x 30-Min. H/Ws	Maps as symbols of reality	Identification of map symbols Use of scale Distance Measurement Changing scale Drawing plans	Objective test at end of unit	Workcards O.S. Maps Photos Filmstrip Worksheets Books	
	Height on maps	Map/photo correlation Sketch maps Sketches Mapping contours Hardware contour models			
	Area Direction Location Valleys/slope Maps as permanent records Time distance Cost distance	Measurement of area Judgement and stating of direction 6-fig. grid refs Cross-sections Gradients Observation Recording Classification			Local area
AGRICULTURE I Land Use 6 Periods 4 H/Ws	Variety of agricultural land uses Effect of distance on land use Influences on farmers' decisions	Estimation of area Bar graphs Decision-making	Objective test at end of unit	Worksheets Slides Dice Farm Game	Re-write on card/core system

continued overleaf

UNIT TITLE/TIMING	OBJECTIVES		EVALUATION	RESOURCES	COMMENT
	CONCEPTS/IDEAS	SKILLS/TECHNIQUES			
EARTHQUAKES MOUNTAINS, VOLCANOES 10 Periods 7 H/Ws	Coincidence of earthquakes, young fold mts., volcanoes, plate edges Internal structure of earth Continental drift Causes and prediction of earthquakes Orogenesis—geosynclines vs subduction zones *Modus operandae* of volcanoes Cross-sections Effects of tectonic movements on man	Basic Atlas use (not long. & lat.) Correlation of maps of differing scales Comprehension (written passage) Jigsaw fit of continents Line-graph interpretation Model construction (paper) Comprehension (spoken passage)	Objective test	Film Slides OHP transparencies Books Tapes Workcards Worksheets Atlases Rock specimens	Card/core system
AGRICULTURE II Farms as Systems 6 Periods 4 H/Ws	Farms as systems Physical constraints on agriculture	Comprehension Slide interpretation Estimation of Area Cross-section/map/photo/sketch correlation	Completion of systems diagram for South Down Farm	Books Slides Worksheets Hardware models O.S. maps Photos	Re-write on card/core system
LATITUDE & LONGITUDE 3 Periods 2 H/Ws	Location	Atlas use	Short test on use of atlas	Worksheets Atlases Globe	
AGRICULTURE III Land Use in a Rural area 3 Periods 2 H/Ws	Relationships between 1. Slope and land use 2. Geology and land use 3. Housing & local building materials Influence of London on local work-patterns	Observation Recording Field sketching Map setting	Completion of fieldwork package marked in A-E scale	Books Slides Worksheets Coaches!	Shoreham, Kent

Syllabus B: Year 1 (Forest Hill School),

UNIT TITLE/TIMING	OBJECTIVES		EVALUATION	RESOURCES	COMMENT
	CONCEPTS/IDEAS	SKILLS/TECHNIQUES			

LONDON
 	
12 x 70-Min. Periods
12 x 40-Min. H/Ws
	Location
	Site factors
	Growth
	Residential areas:
	  location
	  density
	  growth/decay
	  quality
	Industrial areas:
	  location
	Service areas:
	  location
	Urban fields:
	  hierachies
	Replanning
	Systems
		Map interpretation
		Measurement of distance
		Crossword
		Map correlation
		Comprehension
		Photo interpretation
		
		Observation
		Recording
			Fieldwork Folder marked on A-E scale	Photos
				Slides
				Workcards
				Books
				
				Coaches!
					Dockland fieldwork

IRON AND STEEL 5 Periods 5 H/Ws	Manufacturing industry as a system Relative location	Map interpretation Decision-making Photo interpretation Comprehension Histogram construction	Objective test	Film Slides Worksheets Workcards Iron & Steel Game South Wales—Mac Unit	

ENERGY:
1. Natural Gas
2. Coal
3. Oil
4. Electricity
 	
12 Periods
12 H/Ws
	Resource:
	  exploration
	  exploitation
	  distribution
	  limitation
	  conservation
	Environmental hazard
	Change/decay
		Map correlation
		Cross-section interpretation
		Slide & photo interpretation
		Graph construction & interpretation
		Atlas use
		Role-play
		Decision-making
			Four objective tests	Films
				Books
				Slides
				Workcards
				Worksheets
				Old trading game
				Atlases
				Video Tape
				Fossils—Coal seam	

continued overleaf

UNIT TITLE/ TIMING	OBJECTIVES		EVALUATION	RESOURCES	COMMENT
	CONCEPTS/IDEAS	SKILLS/TECHNIQUES			
MOTOR VEHICLES & ROADS 5 Period 5 H/Ws	Relative location Importance of industry Systems, Networks Environmental hazards Development Area	Atlas use Graph construction & interpretation Role-play/Discussion Decision-making	Objective test	Film Atlases Books Worksheets	
ROUTES & NETWORKS 3 Periods 2 H/Ws	Detours Accessibility Connectivity	Matrix interpretation		Worksheets Books	
TOWNS 10 Periods 7 H/Ws	Site factors (physical & economic) Growth Size (area & population) Morphology change through time Towns as systems Population density Planning Place-name origin Local historical geography	Jigsaw fit Line & bar graph construction Decision-making	Objective test	Maps Books Workcards Worksheets	Card/core system

Syllabus B: Year 2 (Forest Hill School)

UNIT TITLE/TIMING	OBJECTIVES		EVALUATION	RESOURCES	COMMENT
	CONCEPTS/IDEAS	SKILLS/TECHNIQUES			
SETTLEMENT 12 x 70-Min. Periods 12 x 45-Min. H/Ws	Site factors Urban growth Functional areas Decay/redevelopment Migration from cities Urban fields Hierarchies of service centres	L.U. Map interpretation Photo interpretation Film interpretation Graph construction Model development and criticism	Test (60 mins)	Books L.U. Maps Video tape OHP transparencies Worksheets	
COMMUNICATIONS 12 Periods 12 H/Ws	Types of communication Accessibility Route selection Environmental costs Deviations Change over time Traffic generations Time/cost distance	Matrix construction Role-play Decision-making Map interpretation Map transformation	Test (60 mins)	Worksheets Railway game	
MAP SKILLS 10 Periods 10 H/Ws	Land uses Route location factors Relief	Land-use symbols Land-use map-making Sample analysis 6-Fig. grid refs Map and photo correlation Route planning Problem solving Sketch mapping Distance measurement Contour recognition Transect drawing Profile drawing Measuring gradient Measuring area 1:50 000 map use ¼-inch map use	Test	Maps Photos Workcards Slides	

Syllabus B: Year 3 (Forest Hill School)

8. Evaluation in Geography

John Bentley

Evaluation is an important but often neglected part of the task of teaching. In geography as in all school activities our purpose is to encourage the intellectual growth of children, to stimulate their interests, and to develop their skills of communication. Progress cannot be assumed and we need to be satisfied that the children are improving in these areas. As teachers we are explorers, opening up new areas of potential, and in teaching, as with any successful expedition, there are three essential stages in that journey.

1. There needs to be a clearly defined destination. The start of all teaching is the statement of teaching aims and the clarification of subject objectives.
2. The methods of getting there, the syllabus or scheme of work, must be planned with the objectives in mind and the means of travel, i.e. the teaching methods, identified. Once a general plan is established the teacher can then set out and prepare the individual lessons. Teaching the lessons is not the end of the operation.
3. There is a third and crucial stage; has the purpose of the programme been achieved? The success of a journey is realised only when the destination has been reached and in teaching we need to know when and with what degree of success the stated objectives have been achieved.

Evaluation has both formative and summative functions. Summative evaluation is retrospective, the purpose being to determine the worth and effectiveness of lessons which have been taught. Formative evaluation is forward-looking and the purpose is to gather information which can be used to improve teaching methods and to plan subsequent lessons. Inevitably the results of summative evaluation are used in the process of formative evaluation. In more specific terms evaluation has four principal diagnostic functions which are basic to the teacher's task and these contribute to both the formative and summative roles of assessment and planning.

Assessment in the Cognitive Domain

The measurement of a pupil's progress in factual knowledge and in the intellectual skills of expression, analysis, computation etc. is clearly an important diagnostic function of evaluation. It is an area of principal concern for parents and every teacher is required to provide such evaluation for purpose of report and, of course, for his or her own satisfaction. The measurement of attainment in the cognitive domain also has its controversial uses as a tool in selection procedures. In the typical classroom the daily and weekly monitoring of cognitive growth is aided by simple tests and reading schemes. These measures of cognitive development are generally used for the identification of age-group 'norms'. In the basic skills of literacy and numeracy, standardised tests (e.g. the reading assessment schemes of Schonell or Daniels and Diack) are widely used to measure the relative attainments of children, but standardised tests are rarely used in other subject areas. (The DES survey, *School geography in the changing curriculum* (1974) notes 'that there are no standard procedures for testing achievement in junior school geography' (p. 36).)

Assessment in the Affective Domain

It is in subject areas like geography, history and practical activities, that more emphasis seems to be given to the affective domain which is the area

176

of children's interests, their emotional and social development. In many social science texts concerned with primary education it is attitudes, values and work-habits of children which are emphasised when any comment about evaluation is made. The Schools Council Environmental Studies Project provides typical statements like 'the children were always busy' and 'interest and enjoyment is apparent' (Schools Council, 1972a, Preface). Developments within the affective domain are obviously important aspects of education and, therefore, teachers are expected to assess the child's ability to work independently as well as co-operatively, to assess levels of motivation and enjoyment, and to observe social attitudes and values.

Assessment of Teaching Methods

Evaluation should not be applied only to the work and progress of the pupil. It is equally important that the methods of instruction are assessed. Children reveal their abilities and achievements in their work but it is a simple truth that their work also reflects the quality of the teacher's performance. There is, therefore, a continuing need for teachers to reflect upon the appropriateness, the efficiency and the effectiveness of their teaching methods. When children give wrong or unexpected responses it may be that the questions are at fault and not the answers. The questions and instructions on workcards, the use of visual aids and the general presentation of information are vital skills in the teaching process. They must be continuously and carefully evaluated.

The Assessment of the Teaching Programme

This final diagnostic aspect of evaluation emphasises the necessity of reviewing the total educational experience given to children in the course of a week or a term or longer. Within the scope of geography it is important that during the child's early education topics are so selected that they provide broad geographical perspectives and that they involve the principle skills of graphicacy in progressive sequences. Similarly it is necessary to achieve a balance between subject areas, between class work and group work. There should be a variety of study methods and of types of information, and time spent on practical activities should be sensibly balanced against time spent seated at desks.

Within these four areas outlined above evaluation seeks to monitor the development of children's intellectual performance and social behaviour, and to improve the methods and materials used in teaching. The overall purpose is to create an increasingly effective education. In secondary and higher education public examinations and award-bearing courses have made evaluation an inevitable part of the system. Aims and objectives are clearly stated in the syllabuses, and the quality of performance by teacher and pupils is measured by the number and standard of passes. It is not surprising, therefore, that in these areas of education there are many research reports and books which deal with methods and procedures of evaluation. In *Assessment and the Geography teacher* (Jones, 1979), a useful summary of books on evaluation in geography is provided. Unfortunately, not one of the 22 books listed is principally concerned with geographical work for the 5 to 13 age group. There are two major reasons for this lack of guidance. On the one hand there is the prevailing tradition in primary school teaching that, in areas outside the basic skills of the three Rs, a teacher should be free to pursue topics of interest and activities which are relevant to the particular needs and the local environment of his or her children. This child-centred approach requires a flexibility hard to satisfy in any rigidly-defined syllabus. Then there is the more recent and growing trend towards integrated studies in which geography becomes subsumed under such headings as Humanities, Social or Environmental Studies. Here the emphasis is placed on the inquiry approach (Foster, 1972) and subject boundaries are seen as limitations on the child's sense of investigation and discovery. These integrated multi-disciplinary approaches rely on the individual judgement of the experienced teacher and require less-structured situations. A result of these two developments now commonly practised in the 5 to 13 age range is that the aims and objectives for geography teaching are not expressed precisely but as broad generalisations. (Statements of such broad geographical objectives for younger children are found in DES (1972) and Barker (1974).) It is the lack of specific guidelines which deters evaluation because 'you cannot produce successful evaluation of geographic learning without explicitly stated objectives' (Kurfman, 1971, p. 27).

Of course, there is value in those approaches which allow teachers to use their professional judgement in selecting geographical topics based on the particular needs of their pupils, but there is also a danger in this freedom. The danger arises when teachers rely so heavily on topics of interest that they ignore the need for an overall plan. A topic approach which follows no general scheme of work for the term or, still worse, for the primary school life of the child, cannot be other than aimless. The obvious failings are that broad areas of basic geographic information will be missed out whilst other 'popular' topics will become boring repeats; 'we done Eskimos, Miss!' Moreover, it is evident that in such aimless circumstances little if any thought will be given to the progression of skills and concepts. Unfortunately, there is plenty of evidence that in geography, and in history, this happens all too frequently. The DES Survey *School geography in the changing curriculum* reported that 43% of the junior schools surveyed possessed no scheme of work for geography and combined studies (DES, 1974, p. 38).

8.1 Evaluation Approaches and Methods

In spite of the fact that references are few and that 'there are no standard procedures for testing achievement in junior school geography' (DES, 1974, p. 36), it is possible to follow some simple steps by which teachers can monitor the geographical progress of their children and review their teaching programmes and instructional methods.

STATEMENT OF OBJECTIVES

It should be evident from what has been said earlier that the first and most important step in evaluation is the production of a set of 'explicitly stated objectives' for geographical teaching. This must be done even when the geographical training is pursued as part of an integrated studies approach; indeed in such circumstances the clearer the guidelines the better. Once agreed these objectives can be incorporated into schemes of work which, for each year of school, ensure a progression of skills, knowledge, and understanding. (This may seem an obvious essential, but in support of the DES survey *School geography in the changing curriculum,* only one teacher out of a group of 50 primary school teachers at a recent teachers' centre meeting taught at a school which had a scheme of work for its geography and combined studies.) Each school should be able to produce its own 'core curriculum' suited to its local environment, the needs of its children and the expertise of its teachers. A simple and effective scheme should state for each year of schooling:

1. the principal skills and ideas to be covered and explored;
2. the major places and topics for study, both local and far-away;
3. the range of study methods and the type of source materials and visual aids required.

The drawing up of such a simple scheme helps in the organisation of outside visits and allows better selection of school equipment. Moreover, such a scheme identifies the particular types of equipment that are needed. This is especially true in the purchase of maps. Few schools have sufficient large-scale maps of their own locality and when the occasions for visits arrive there is seldom enough time to obtain large-scale maps of more distant places. Yet of course, that is just the time when maps can be of particular benefit both in the children's preparations for the trip and in their activities whilst on the outing.

KEEPING RECORDS: INTUITIVE ASSESSMENTS

Once the objectives are stated and the schemes have been agreed the simplest and most useful form of evaluation is the keeping of records. Records of an anecdotal nature about each child are a useful means of intuitive and continuing assessment. It may seem an obvious method but it is not commonly practised. A recent DES survey of geography in junior schools (DES, 1974) found that only 8% of schools kept good records

ASSESSMENT - RECORD FOR TOPIC WORK   (Geography and/or. Natural History.)

Autumn/Spring/Summer Term 19 79

NAME: Jon England

Date of birth: Grading of Effort/Achievement - 1 (low) to 5 (high)
4 . 1 . 70

	First half of Term	Second half of Term	
Date(s)	19.3.79	24.4.79	20.7.79
Topic, Work covered, etc.	Work on exercises in "Lets Make Maps" Longmans and "New Ways in Geography" BKI	Group Topic Work "Insects" (Jon, Alistair, Susan, Jane)	
General understanding of facts, vocab. etc.	Steady progress in exercises. Good on scale and grid references. ④	Has little background. Has selected difficult books.	Changed to ③ more suitable reference books.
SKILLS 1. Maps, graphs and diagrams	Has completed exercises⑤ pp. 3-22. All correct on measurements.	Constructing a histogram of insects found.	Good work ④
2. Research - Observation, Data collect.		Rather a slow start.	A bit too ② much copying.
Organisation and presentation of work.	Untidy printing especially with pen. Left hander-has changed to pencil for a while ③	Needs some attention.	Final results ③ show some improvement
Interest and originality etc.	Very keen. Takes book ⑤ home to complete exercises.	Pictures and diagrams are well drawn - written work not given much attention.	
Perseverance, Group co-operation etc.	Has completed work ⑤ ahead of time.	Prefers working on his own - Group worked well with guidance.	
GENERAL COMMENTS	Jon has shown a particular interest in maps. Presentation a little untidy at first.	Jon has produced some interesting maps and graphs, but avoids writing whenever possible. Prefers work on his own. Likes geography!	

FIGURE 8.1

and 18% kept no records of any kind. In situations where records are not kept children can be moved from class to class with nothing to indicate what topics have been studied or what books or maps have been used. If teachers work in such isolation there can be little hope for progression in skill and understanding, and certainly no profitable evaluation of teaching. In most examples of evaluation in geography for the younger age ranges the emphasis is on general appraisals applied to the whole class which record that the children 'enjoyed working together' or that 'the standard of work and display was commendable' or that 'these exercises have been considered "successful" by a number of teachers using them' (Robinson and Jackson, 1978, p. 119). Obviously the general development of children's behaviour and attitudes and the improvements in their presentation of work are significant points for comment, but it is more important to observe the progress of the individuals in a class.

As a general guide for recording the progress and behaviour of each child the teacher can use a check-list of items, or headings under which comments can be made. The following task-list can be used to check off the progress of children in the very early years of schooling. (For the complete check-list see Foster (1972).)

1. Uses school library books well.
2. Understands library classification system.
3. Uses books and maps for finding out.
4. Can tell a simple story.
5. Can write own news.
6. Spells common words correctly.
7. Takes care of property and materials.
8. Clears away spontaneously.
9. Organises time efficiently.
10. Works conscientiously alone.
11. Works co-operatively with a group.
12. Contributes to discussion.
13. Knows days of the week, months of the year.
14. Shows interest in neighbourhood environment.
15. Brings to school things of interest.
16. Shows interest in discovery.
17. Uses spatial terms accurately.
18. Has made some models (a) independently, (b) with a group.
19. Knows the seasons and seasonal activities.
20. Record of any noteworthy achievement.

PLATE 13

This is a typical example of a child's early attempts at visualising accurately elements of the local environment. Lisa (8 years old) lives in a terraced house in South London. Note the conventional 'Play School' style detached house, with its central doorway, windows placed in each corner and the (imagined) chimney pot. The details of flowers and birds are typical of a girl's drawing.

PLATE 14

This map of 'My dream house' was drawn by a 9-year-old boy. It illustrates a transitional stage in the child's understanding of the plan view of maps. Some elements are presented 'as seen' from the child's viewpoint (i.e. egocentrism), whilst others are presented correctly from the bird's-eye viewpoint.

Although this is a general list, teachers can make more specific lists to check the development of particular skills in geographical experiences.

For older children, more use can be made of a record-sheet which can be set out in the way illustrated in Figure 8.1 either on a page of the teacher's record book, or on a card. This latter method is preferable because the cards can be filed for easy reference and, if necessary, passed on as the child moves to other classes. As well as making comments of a subjective nature, the teacher might wish to include a simple grading system to indicate degrees of effort, achievement, interest etc. (see Fig. 8.1).

Under the heading of 'General Comments', two particular aspects of children's geographical work should be carefully observed, graphical work and geographical vocabulary.

Graphical Work

This is a central aspect of geographical skills and the ability to produce and use maps, graphs etc. is clearly related to the child's cognitive development. It is important, therefore, that a teacher

keeps specific records of the child's graphical skills. The following points are listed as a general guide to the evaluation of children's mapwork.

Accuracy and reality of image

Children's early drawings of their home or their route to school contain a great deal of imaginative detail. Initially their observations are inaccurate and fanciful and often reveal a standard image of a 'Janet-and-John' style house (Plate 13). With increasing age and practice in observation the maps and pictures become more accurate, more detailed and proportions become more realistic. Note particularly the style and placing of windows, the form and angle of chimneys, details of doors and gardens etc.

Plan view

The major problem in map drawing for the very young is the understanding required for the 'bird's-eye-view' of the map (Plate 14). This improves with age and practice but it is some time before a consistency of image is achieved. Look especially for the child's representation of cars,

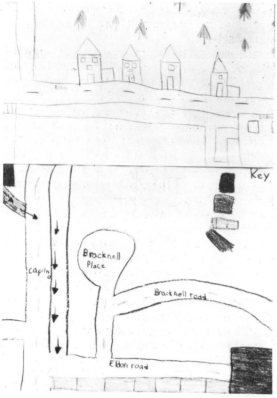

PLATE 15

These are two versions of 'My route to school' drawn by a Canadian child (8 years old). The top one was drawn at the start of a project on maps and the lower one was drawn following the two weeks of classwork. It illustrates a 'before and after' approach to evaluation, and shows the degree of progress by the child in understanding the conventions of maps.

trees etc., which are generally the last things to be viewed correctly.

Neatness and presentation

The early work of children with maps, graphs and cartograms is freehand and set out poorly on the page, often crowded into one corner. The use of the ruler is itself an awkward exercise. As understanding and experience grows the children's work shows marked improvements in layout, neatness and accuracy of representation. The work is presented with greater clarity and sense of proportions and the use of colour becomes more effective. Straight lines are used with greater success. Always difficult but worth encouraging

are the skills of printing and labelling on maps and diagrams.

Key and Scale

The use of a key is initially in the form of listing all the items shown on the map (Plate 15), but with experience the key is used more effectively as a system of classification. Similarly the understanding of relative size and proportions (i.e. scale) is at first largely trial and error and requires considerable use of an eraser. With progressive exercises these abilities in the use of key and scale make obvious development and eventually simple objective testing can be used as a means of evaluating their progress and understanding. E.g. How far is it to A? How many cars are shown on the histogram? What river has the most bridges crossing it? What day has the highest rainfall?

Map Reading and Interpretation

The final stages of work with maps, graphs and diagrams require knowledge of their terminology and conventions and the skills of interpretation, extrapolation and analysis of relationships. At this level the work can be evaluated objectively for there will be right and wrong solutions to the questions. This makes assessment far easier: e.g. exercises on scale, use of symbols, use of index and grid references etc. In observing the progress of the younger children's geographical work the 'before and after' evaluation can be the best and simplest approach. It requires examples of the children's work to be kept over the course of a term or a year, or an exercise to be given at the beginning and end of a scheme of work. In both cases the level of achievement and improvement can be readily observed. It is sometimes useful too, if time allows, to encourage the children to talk about their maps and pictures. In these discussions much can be revealed and what seem to be insignificant squiggles become 'my dad mowing the grass'; such illumination gives the teacher added information in the assessment of a child's understanding.

Geographical Vocabulary

When a teacher selects books for use in lessons, or as reference sources for project work, a criterion for their suitability is the level of reading ability required. Many books designed for younger children are well illustrated but unsuitable because the language used is too difficult.

This is worth particular note in geography because there are many specialist terms which will be unknown to the children. Indeed, an important aspect of the geographical training of the younger age groups is the introduction of new geographical terms. This is certainly necessary in physical geography with words like 'meander', 'erosion' or 'estuary'. The acquisition of new words increases the child's ability to observe and describe accurately. It is also important from time to time to assess the children's understanding of geographical terms like 'valley' or 'town' which are in everyday use. When asked to define such words the children reveal a great deal about their levels of understanding and the accuracy of their geographical concepts (see Milburn, 1972). In some areas of teaching not much time is generally given to the definition of words, yet the few definitions given below illustrate limited concepts which must create some confusion and problems of understanding.

Geographical Term	Definition	Age of Child
Channel	'A thing on the T.V.'	9
Desert	(i) 'A place with no water and surrounded by sand.'	14
	(ii) 'A big very wide patch of sand.'	8
Estuary	'A stray cat or dog.'	10
Hill	(i) 'A hill is a bit of land that is bigger than the rest.'	14
	(ii) 'Quite a big mound of stones.'	8
Town	(i) 'A small amount of houses in the country.'	14
	(ii) 'A busy place with lots of shops and houses.'	8
Valley	(i) 'Something that goes up at both sides.'	7
	(ii) 'A deep drop in rocks.'	8

The introduction and explanation of geographical terms is a necessary element of geographical training and a useful method of evaluating an individual's concept development in geography.

TESTS AND STRUCTURED METHODS OF EVALUATION

Alongside intuitive forms of assessment based on anecdotal records there is an obvious need for more specific and objective diagnostic information. This can be obtained from purposefully designed procedures.

The most widely used forms of evaluation are the end-of-term or end-of-lesson tests. They are quick and effective means of checking on progress. A test has advantages for children because it encourages revision, an important study skill, and the practice of committing things to memory from their own workbooks. And the tidier their books the easier the revision is! There are, however, significant anti-test feelings expressed by some teachers. There are certain drawbacks when a test is seen by the children as a competitive activity and when the fear of being proved inadequate becomes a factor. These aspects result invariably from the wrong emphasis in the classroom; children enjoy quiz-games, and it is with a sense of enjoyment and not of comparison that tests should be used. A simple revision test on the location of places and the use of an atlas, or on the identification of cloud types or on the work of a stream and the annotation of a simple diagram can be planned for say, a 30-minute period. This includes 10 minutes for revision, 10 minutes for the actual test and then 10 minutes for giving the answers and any discussion. The children can mark their own work and even the test itself can be a shared activity between pairs of children. However the real value of this method of evaluation is not for the children, it is for the teacher. The teacher can observe and learn a great deal about the children whilst they are revising and doing the test, and from the results the teacher obtains a necessary guide to their progress and abilities. Most important of all, the teacher can gauge the effectiveness of his or her own teaching methods.

In designing tests and structured methods of assessment the teacher can choose between three basic forms of evaluation: (i) essay-type questions, (ii) interpretation of information, and (iii) objective testing.

Essay-type Questions

The essay question requires the organisation of facts and reasoned discussion. The answer required can be specified as short responses of a paragraph in length or as extended answers of several pages. For the younger age range of the primary school these are unsuitable forms of assessment. However, in later years of schooling, essays are part of the examination system and for the pupils in the early years of secondary school short written responses provide a useful introduction to the formal style of the examination essay. It must be noted that there are problems in assessment and marking because the teacher is evaluating the pupils' powers of expression as well as their factual knowledge. The questions set, therefore, must be explicit about the information required and precise about the length of answer expected.

Interpretation of Information

A second form of evaluation is that based on the interpretation of a given set of data or piece of writing. It could be information in the form of a photograph, a map or a documentary extract. Although the facts would be new to the children the topic would be similar to work done in class, or would require methods of analysis and description already practised, e.g. the construction of a relief profile or a histogram of types of land use. This form of evaluation is very much concerned with the assessment of skills. It is therefore an important area of testing because the skills of observation and graphicacy (i.e. maps and diagrams) are fundamental to a child's progress in geography. One note of caution; there is a problem in providing suitable data for interpretation. If, for example, the teacher wants to use a photograph in a class test then he has to supply one for each child: obtaining 30 copies of one photograph or map can be expensive.

Objective Testing

Objective testing is perhaps the most effective form of assessment for the younger age ranges. The questions require responses limited to a single word or phrase and objective tests are ideally suited to the evaluation of comprehension and specific factual knowledge. Moreover, the marking is precise because answers are either right or wrong and the results are easily classified. The major types of objective testing are True - False statements, Matching, Multiple Choice and Completion of Statement.

As an illustration of the various methods of structured testing read the following description of an imaginary country. Study the passage for three minutes and then, having covered the extract, answer the various types of question set below.

When you have finished and marked your answers it is important to reflect upon the merits and advantages of the different types of test.

The city of Wopakaukin, with a population of 175 000, is the largest settlement in the west of Mainland. It lies near the inland margin of the coastal plain, 200 kms from the sea, and 50 kms from the foothills of the Huegogodon Mountains. These fold mountains are forested and rise in the west to elevations of 325 m..Wopakaukin is 135 m. above sea level. The river Permit flows eastwards from the mountain range and passes through Wopakaukin and across the coastal plain on its way to the Eastern Sea. At the mouth of the river is the port of Calnorth with a population of 230 000. The river used to be the only transport link between Calnorth and Wopakaukin but a major highway was built in the early days of the republic. The only railway in Mainland links Wopakaukin with the small mining settlements of Wellstock and Telenby in the Huegogodon Mountains. For the last 75 years, ores of zinc and silver, mined from zones of igneous rock within the sedimentary rocks of the mountains, have been carried by rail to Wopakaukin. There the people of Telenby and Wellstock exchange their mineral ores for foodstuffs and manufactured goods. Wopakaukin first grew as a bridging point across the Permit River and developed as a local market centre. Later, in the early years of this century, small industries developed based on the metal ores from the west and Wopakaukin became the largest settlement as well as the capital city of Mainland. The revolution in 1967 overthrew the emperor and the seat of government for the new republic was transferred to Calnorth. Only then did the port expand rapidly. New industries were developed in Calnorth, processing the agricultural produce of the coastal plain. The old industries of Wopakaukin also moved downstream to new coastal sites around Calnorth along the estuary of the river Permit. Wopakaukin is no longer the primate city of Mainland but continues to flourish because of the increased trade brought by the new road and the development of tourism. The old city is an attractive centre for visitors with its historic castle and the nearby scenic wilderness of the snow-capped Huegogodon Mountains.

True-False Statements

If the statement is true, circle the T. If the statement is false, circle the F.

1. T F Wopakaukin is the capital of Mainland.
2. T F Telenby is a settlement based on forestry.
3. T F The Permit river flows westwards.
4. T F The railways link Calnorth and Wellstock with Wopakaukin.

Completion of Statements

1. The Permit river flows into the ....
2. The revolution in Mainland was in ....
3. The width of the coastal plain is ....
4. The city of Wopakaukin originated as a ....

Matching Statements

All the following terms on the left need to be matched with the appropriate locations or features listed on the right. Draw a line to make the correct pairings.

Capital city	Wopakaukin
Mining settlement	Huegogodon Mountains
Igneous rocks	Calnorth
Tourist centre	Coastal plain
Folded sedimentary rocks	Metal ores
Modern industry	Wellstock
Agricultural produce	Permit Estuary

Multiple Choice

Underline the correct answer.

1. The Population of Calnorth (in thousands) is
   273   237   167   230
2. The distance of Wopakaukin from the sea (in kilometres) is 250   150   200   175
3. The Huegogodon Mountains were formed by
   ....Volcanic activity
                                      folding
                                      faulting
                                      all of these
4. It is possible to transport metal ores from the mining settlements to Calnorth by..............
   .... road
                                      road and rail
                                      river and road
                                      rail

Interpretation

From the information presented in the extract, produce an annotated sketch map of Mainland.

Essay-Type Questions

1. What have been the three major phases of economic development in the growth of Wopakaukin? Give your answer in less than 100 words.
2. What have been the two significant changes in the development of Mainland since the revolution?
3. Discuss the extent of the relationship between the physical features of Mainland and its economic activities.
4. 'Transport is the basis of growth'. Discuss this statement with reference to any *one* settlement of Mainland.

When you have assessed your answers it should be evident that the various types of questions test quite different areas of knowledge and ability. The objective questions test facts, whilst the essays require, in addition, significant skills of interpretation, judgement and expression. It is also important to note how accurately and objectively the answers from the different types of questions can be marked. The grading of essays takes longer and relies more on intuitive assessment. All these factors need to be borne in mind when an examination or a test is being prepared.

STANDARDISED TESTS OF BASIC SKILLS IN GEOGRAPHY

From the evidence of national surveys as well as personal experience it is clear that in the majority of primary schools there is no systematic evaluation of progress in geography. In the main this is because geography is seldom taught as a separate subject and very few schools have considered it necessary to produce explicit objectives for geography with younger children. Furthermore, many teachers have preferred to place their emphasis on the development of social skills, attitudes and values. Although these are disappointing explanations there are some grounds for excuse in that there have been no standard procedures for testing achievement in basic geographical skills. This situation has prevailed for many years but the recent publication of two standardised series of tests should encourage systematic evaluation of children's progress is basic geographical skills.

The Richmond tests (Hieronymus *et al.*, 1974) were developed in America and have been modified for use in the UK. There are five areas of tests: vocabulary, reading comprehension, language skills, work-study skills and mathematics skills. It is the section on work-study skills that tests map-reading, the interpretation of graphs and tables and knowledge and use of reference materials.

The other series of tests have been produced at the Institute of Education at the University of Bristol and are published as the *Bristol Achievement Tests* (Brimer, 1974). They have been constructed to produce balanced measures of basic skills and concepts in school achievement. The five levels of Study Skills Tests cover the social and scientific studies area of the curriculum. Level 1 is for the age range 8.0 to 9.11; level 5 is for the age range 12.0 to 13.11.

The great advantage of these tests is that they provide, by multiple-choice objective questions, standardised scores and thus a foundation for establishing norms of achievement for given age groups.

CONCLUSIONS

The geographical skills and concepts ideas that are explained in this book are too important to be left to chance development. They are essential attributes for an individual's achievement, satisfaction and participation in a complex world. Until recently there has been 'no hard and fast body of knowledge . . . expected of the junior school leavers' in geography (DES, 1974, p. 48). There is evidence that work in geography suffers from a surfeit of loosely structured projects and a belief that a flexible multi-disciplinary approach can operate throughout a school without plan or co-ordination. Since education is a process of growth, in geography, as in all areas of the curriculum, we must plan for and assess that growth. Therefore, schemes of work are most necessary, specific geographical objectives must be clearly stated, especially so in topic work, and evaluation is essential (Salmon and Masterson, 1974).

The stages of evaluation are:

1. State the geographical objectives.
2. Plan the scheme of work and then prepare the lessons that will achieve those objectives.
3. Observe and evaluate, by the methods outlined,
   (i) The children's intellectual and social development;
   (ii) the instructional methods, equipment and materials used.
4. From the evidence gained, think again about the plans for next time.

Evaluation is continuous as well as esssential, and for any teacher the end-of-term report will invariably read 'could do better'.

References

(Note: See also Appendixes 1, 2 and 4 for other useful books and articles)

Anderson, E. W. (1969) *Hardware models in geography teaching* (Teaching Geography Occasional Papers, No. 7). Sheffield: Geographical Association.

Archer, J. E. and Dalton, T. H. (1970) *Fieldwork in geography*, 2nd ed. London: Batsford.

Balchin, W. G. V. and Coleman, A. D. (1965) 'Graphicacy should be the fourth ace in the pack', *Times Educational Supplement*, 5th Nov; reprinted in Bale *et al.* (1973), pp. 78-86.

Bale, J., Graves, N. and Walford, R. (1973) *Perspectives in geographical education*. Edinburgh: Oliver and Boyd.

Barker, E. (1974) *Geography and younger children*. London: University of London Press.

Bayliss, D. G. and Renwick, T. M. (1966) 'Photograph study in a junior school', *Geography*, 51, 322-9; reprinted in Bale *et al.* (1973), pp. 119-30.

Beddis, R. A. (1968) *A technique of using screen and blackboard to extract information from a photograph* (Teaching Geography Occasional Papers, No. 3). Sheffield: Geographical Association.

Blachford, K. R. (1972) 'Values in geographical education', *Geographical Education*, 1, 319-30.

Blaut, M. and Stea, D. (1974) 'Mapping at the age of three', *Journal of Geography*, 73, 5-9.

Bradshaw, M. J. *et al.* (1978) *The earth's changing surface*. London: Hodder and Stoughton.

Brimer, A. (ed.) (1974) *Bristol achievement tests*. London: Nelson.

Brown, J. Hume (1976) *Elementary geographical fieldwork*. Glasgow: Blackie.

Buttimer, A. (1974) *Values and the teaching of geography*. Washington: Association of American Geographers, Commission on College Geography, Resources Paper, No. 24.

Bruner, J. S. (1963) *The process of education*. Cambridge, Mass: Harvard University Press.

Calder, N. (1972) *Restless earth*. London: BBC.

Carnie, J. (1972) 'Children's attitudes to other nationalities', in Graves, N. J. (ed.) *New movements in the study and teaching of geography*. London: Temple Smith, pp. 121-34.

Carson, S. Mc.B. *Environmental education: guidelines for the primary and middle years*. Hertfordshire County Council.

Catling, S. J. (1978) 'Cognitive mapping exercises as a primary geographical experience', *Teaching Geography*, 3, 120-23.

——. (1979) 'Maps and cognitive maps: the young child's perception', *Geography*, 64, 288-96.

——. (1980) 'Map use and objectives for map learning', *Teaching Geography*, 6, 15-17.

Cole, J. P. and Beynon, M. J. (1969) *New ways in geography*. Oxford: Blackwell.

Coley, J. A. (1975) 'Geography in middle schools', *Teaching Geography*, 1, 65-7.

Collis, M. (1974) *Using the environment (Science 5-13)*, books 1 to 4. London: Macdonald Education, for Schools Council.

Conner, C. (1976) 'Geography in the middle school', *Teaching Geography*, 1, 178-82.

Cowie, P. M. (1978) 'Teaching about values in public schools', *Geographical Education*, 3, 133-46.

Cracknell, J. R. (1974) *A study of the changing place and nature of geography and methods of teaching the subject in elementary and primary schools of England and Wales from 1870-1974, with reference in particular to the 7-11-year age group*. Unpublished MA dissertation, University of London.

——. (1977) 'Key ideas for the junior school', *Times Educational Supplement*, 25 March.

——. (1979) *Geography through topics in primary and middle schools* (Teaching Geography Occasional Papers, No. 31). Sheffield: Geographical Association.

Crisp, T. (1974) *Food and farming (People and places, 1)*. London: Nelson.

Daugherty, R. (1980) 'Integration through key concepts: key to what?', *Teaching Geography*, 5, 134-5.

David, E. (1940) 'Children's maps: an experiment', *Geography*, 25, 86-9.

Department of Education and Science (1967) *Children and their primary schools* (Plowden Report). London: HMSO.

——. (1972) *New thinking in school geography* (Education Pamphlet, No. 59). London: HMSO.

——. (1978a) *Curriculum 11-16: Geography* (HM Inspectorate Geography Committee, Working Paper), Birmingham: DES.

——. (1978b) *Primary education in England.* London: HMSO.

Fenton, E. (1966) 'Teaching about values in the public schools', in Fenton, E. (ed.) *Teaching the new social studies*. New York: Holt, Rinehart and Winston, pp. 41-5.

Foster, J. (1972) *Discovery learning in the primary school*. London: Routledge and Kegan Paul.

Freeman, T. (1971) *The writing of geography*. Manchester: Manchester University Press.

Hellyer, M. J. (1974) 'Geography in environmental studies, in Long, M. (ed). *Handbook for geography teachers*. London: Methuen, pp. 78-86.

Hieronymus, A. N. *et al.* (1974) *Richmond tests of basic skills*. London: Nelson.

Holmes, D. (after A. Holmes) (1976) *Elements of physical geology*. New York: Nelson. (Original more readable, i.e. *Principles of physical geology.*)

Jones, M. (1979) *Assessment and the geography teacher* (Bibliographic Notes, No. 4). Sheffield: Geographical Association.

Kent, W. A. and Moore, K. R. (1974) *An approach to fieldwork in geomorphology: the example of North Norfolk* (Teaching Geography Occasional Papers, No. 20). Sheffield: Geographical Association.

Kurfman, D. G. (ed.) (1971) *Evaluation in geographic education: the 1971 yearbook of the National Council for Geographic Education*. Belmont, California: Fearon.

Long, M. (1953) 'Children's reactions to geographical pictures', *Geography*, 38, 100-107.

Long, M. and Roberson, B. S. (1966) *Teaching Geography*. London: Heinemann.

Milburn, D. (1972) 'Children's vocabulary', in Graves, N. J. (ed.) *New movements in the study and teaching of geography*. London: Temple Smith, pp. 107-20.

Ministry of Education (1967) *Primary education in Wales* (Gittins Report). London: HMSO.

Morris, J. W. (1972) 'Geography in junior schools', *Trends in Education*, No. 28.

National Association for Environmental Education (1976) *Environmental education: a statement of aims*. Birmingham: NAEE.

Pattison, W. D. (1964) 'The four traditions of geography', *Journal of Geography*, 63, 211-16.

Piaget, J. and Inhelder, B. (1956) *The child's conception of space*. London: Routledge and Kegan Paul.

Prior, F. M. (1959) *The place of maps in the junior school*. Unpublished dissertation for the Diploma in the Psychology of Childhood, University of Birmingham.

Purton, R. W. (1970) *Surrounded by books*. London: Ward Lock.

Rance, P. (1970) *Teaching by topics*, 2nd ed. London: Ward Lock.

Roberson, B. S. and Long, M. (1956) 'Sample studies: the development of a method', *Geography*, 41, 248-59.

Robinson, R. and Jackson, J. (1978) 'Town growth and the measures of distance', *Teaching Geography*, 3, 116-19.

Rushby, J. G. *et al.* (1967-9) *Study geography*, books 1 to 5. London: Longman.

Sadler, J. E. (1974) *Concepts in primary education*. London: Allen and Unwin.

Salmon, R. B. and Masterson, T. H. (1974) *Principles of objective testing in geography*. London: Heinemann.

Sandford, H. A. (1972) 'Perceptual problems', in Graves, N. J. (ed.) *New movements in the study and teaching of geography*. London: Temple Smith, pp. 83-92.

——. (1974) 'Atlases', in Long, M. (ed.) *Handbook for geography teachers*. London: Methuen, pp. 184-7.

——. (1978) 'Taking a fresh look at atlases', *Teaching Geography*, 4, 62-5.

——. (1979) 'Things maps don't tell us', *Geography*, 64, 297-302.

——. (1980) 'Map design for children', *Bulletin of the Society of University Cartographers*, 14, 39-48.

——. (in prep.) 'Directed and free search of the school atlas map'.

——. (in prep.) 'Towns on maps'.

Satterly, D. J. (1964) 'Skills and concepts involved in map drawing and map interpretation', *New Era*, 45, 260-63; reprinted in Bale *et al.* (1973), pp. 162-9.

Schools Council (1972a) *Environmental studies project: case studies*. London: Hart-Davis.

——. (1972b) *Environmental studies project: starting from maps*. London: Hart-Davis.

——. (1972c) *Environmental studies project: teacher's guide*. London: Hart-Davis.

——. (1973) *Environmental studies project: starting from rocks*. London: Hart-Davis.

——. (1975) *Place, time and society 8-13*. Bristol: Collins-ESL.

Scott, N. and Lampitt, R. (1967) *Understanding maps*. Loughborough: Ladybird Books.

Smith, D. L. (1978) 'Values and the teaching of geography', *Geographical Education*, 3, 147-61.

Sorrell, P. (1978) 'Map design with the young in mind', *Cartographic Journal*, 11, 82-90.

Unesco (1974) *Declaration on education for international understanding*. Paris: Unesco. (Available free in the UK from the Department of Education and Science.)

Watson, J. W. (1977) 'On the teaching of value geography', *Geography*, 62, 198-204.

Weyman, D. and Wilson, C. (1975) *Hydrology for schools* (Teaching Geography Occasional Papers, No. 25). Sheffield: Geographical Association.

Appendix 1. A short bibliography of post-1970 articles on primary and middle-school geography

Carter, D. 'In Kentish Hop-gardens. Junior pupils' perceptions', *Teaching Geography*, 5 (1980) 105-7.

Catling, S. J. 'The child's spatial conception and geographic education', *Journal of Geography*, 77 (1978) 24-8.

——. 'Foundations for primary and middle school geography', *Classroom Geographer*, Nov. (1978) 3-8.

——. 'Whither primary geography? Reflections on the HMI report, *Primary Education in England*', *Teaching Geography*, 5 (1979) 73-6.

Cracknell, J. R. 'Geography in junior schools', *Geography*, 61 (1976) 150-56.

——. 'Putting geography back into the primary school curriculum', *Teaching Geography*, 4 (1979) 115-16.

Crawford, C. 'The delimitation of urban zones—field-work for middle school pupils', *Classroom Geographer*, February (1977) 8-11.

Dark, A. 'Time and place in Harrow', *Teaching Geography* (1978) 169-70.

Dillon, M. A. 'The teaching of geography in primary schools in the Republic of Ireland', *Geographical Viewpoint*, 6 (1977) 36-48.

Emery, J. S. *et al.* 'Environmental Education: the geography teacher's contribution', *Journal of Geography*, 73 (1974) 8-18.

Fahy, G. 'A suggested schedule of work for first-year post-primary students', *Geographical Viewpoint*, 4 (1975) 39-45.

Jex, S. 'Urban field studies in a primary school', *Teaching Geography*, 4 (1979) 148-52.

Kravitz, B. 'Teaching primary children the location of neighbourhood services', *Journal of Geography*, 70 (1971) 411-14.

Mines, K. '"Off-site"—studying the urban landscape in the primary school', *BEE*, 74 (1977) 5-12.

——. 'This Poplar where I live'. *BEE*, 100/101, August/Sept. (1979) 17-23.

Newsome, D. 'Mounds of earth: the discoveries of M2 children', *Teaching Geography*, 2 (1976) 60-63.

Oaks, S. M. 'A hydrology project in the primary school', *Geography*, 59 (1974) 65-7.

——. 'Junior schools volcano project', *Teaching Geography*, 1 (1976) 134-6.

Oxfordshire Advisory Group on middle school geography. 'Geographical ideas and skills: an Oxfordshire group report', *Teaching Geography*, 4 (1978) 12-13.

Quirk, B. and Trim, V. 'Childspace: Piaget and cognitive geography', *The Southampshire Geographer*, 10 (1978) 9-17.

Rawling, E. 'Middle school fieldwork: two approaches', *Teaching Geography*, 3 (1977) 3-8.

Rowley, A. and Spencer, I. 'Introducing weather study to primary school children', *Weather*, 25 (1970) 96-7.

Sabaroff, R. E. 'Orienting the child to his world', *Journal of Geography*, 69 (1970) 410-14.

Saxby, W. J. 'Recent developments in geography curricula in New South Wales', *Geographical Education*, 2 (1976) 511-22.

Schneider, D. O. 'The performance of elementary teachers and students on a test of map and globe skills', *The Journal of Geography*, 75 (1976) 326-32.

Stedman, K. 'Mapwork in the middle school at the general planning level', *Classroom Geographer*, October (1979) 18-19.

Tanner, R. 'Resources supplement: Primary fiction with an urban bias; Primary environmental education books; Primary workcards, worksheets, packs; Primary teachers' books for environmental education', *BEE*, 74, June (1977) 13-20.

Teasdale, J. C. 'Rivers: a project undertaken by a junior school class', *Geography*, 58 (1973) 351-4.

Thake, J. 'Child's play? Mapping concepts for 7-9-year-olds', *Classroom Geographer*, May (1977) 3-12.

Appendix 2. Resources

Resources available for schools are probably more numerous than is often realised and they are still often available free, or at only a nominal charge. A comprehensive list is not included in this handbook, not only for reasons of size, but also because there are already several publications which list resources available, costs, addresses etc. Schools are recommended to keep an index of resources which may be consulted when the need arises. This appendix offers suggestions of what might be included and also lists a number of reference books which might be useful as the basis of a staff reference library. Locally, information and resources may be obtained from, for example, teachers' centres, reference libraries and information centres, town halls, museums, local newspapers and travel agents.

Reference Books

Berry, P. S. *Sourcebook for environmental studies.* London: George Philip, 1975.

Council for Environmental Education. *Directory of centres for outdoor studies in England and Wales,* 2nd ed. London: Council for Environmental Education, 1973.

Department of Education and Science. *The environment: sources of information for teachers.* London: HMSO, 1979.

Department of Education and Science. *Museums in education* (Education Survey, No. 12).

Hancock, J. C. and Whiteley, P.F. *The geographer's vademecum of sources and materials,* 2nd ed. London: George Philip, 1978.

Long, M. (ed.) *Handbook for geography teachers.* London: Methuen, 1974.

Museums and galleries in Great Britain and Ireland. Dunstable: ABC Travel Guides Ltd., 1978.

Treasure chest for teachers, 8th ed. Kettering: Schoolmaster Publishing, 1975.

Bibliographies

Brewer, J. G. *The literature of geography,* 2nd ed. London: Bingley, 1978.

Geographical Association. *Bibliographic notes* series. Sheffield: Geographical Association, 1979 -.

Lukehurst, C. T. and Graves, N. J. *Geography in education: a bibliography of British sources, 1870-1970.* Sheffield: Geographical Association, 1972.

Dictionaries and Gazetteers

Monkhouse, F. J. *A dictionary of geography,* 2nd ed. London: Arnold, 1972.

Moore, W. G. *A dictionary of geography.* London: Black, 1976.

Moore, W. G. *The Penguin encyclopaedia of places.* Harmondsworth: Penguin, 1971.

Stamp, L. D. and Clark, A. N. (eds.) *A glossary of geographical terms,* 3rd ed. London: Longman, 1979.

Periodicals

Classroom Geographer (Published by Brighton Polytechnic, Falmer, Brighton.)

Geography (Published by the Geographical Association, 343 Fulwood Road, Sheffield S10 3BP; subscription (1980/81) £9.30 per year.)

Teaching Geography (Published by Longman for the Geographical Association; subscription (1980/81) £9.60 per year. Subscription to both *Geography* and *Teaching Geography* is £14 per year.)

Geographical Magazine (Published by I.P.C. Magazines, King's Reach Tower, Stamford Street, London SE1 9LS.)

National Geographic (Published by the National Geographic Society, Washington, DC 20036.)

ORGANISATIONS

This is a brief list only. Other organisations providing educational materials may be found in, for example,

The geographer's vademecum of sources and materials (see above).

Advisory Centre for Education, 18 Victoria Park Square, London E2

Association of Agriculture Farm Study Scheme, Victoria Chambers, 16/20 Strutton Ground, London SW1P 2HP

British Airports Authority, 2 Buckingham Palace Gate, London SW1

British Airways, Victoria Terminal, Buckingham Palace Road, London SW1W 9SR

British Broadcasting Corporation, School Broadcasting Council, The Langham, Portland Place, London W1A 1AA

British Gas Corporation, 326 High Holborn, London WC1V 7PT

British Rail
LMR, Euston Road, London NW1 1HT
SR, Waterloo Station, London SE1 8SE
WR, Paddington Station, London W2 1HA

British Steel Corporation, Information Officer, 151 Gower Street, London WC1E 6BB

Centre for World Development Education, 128 Buckingham Palace Road, London SW1W 9SH

Commission of the European Communities, 20 Kensington Palace Gardens, London W8 4QQ

Commonwealth Institute, Kensington High Street, London W8 6NQ

The Conservation Trust, 246 London Road, Earley, Reading, Berks, RG6 1AJ

Embassies of various countries will often provide educational resources; addresses in the London telephone directories.

The Geographical Association, 343 Fulwood Road, Sheffield, S10 3BP

George Philip Group, 12-14 Long Acre, London WC2E 9LP

High Commissions of Commonwealth Countries; addresses in the London telephone directories.

Independent Broadcasting Authority, 70 Brompton Road, London SW1

Information and Documentation Centre for the Geography of the Netherlands, Geografisch Instituut van de Rijksuniversiteit, Heidelberglaan 2, Utrecht, Netherlands

National Audio-Visual Aids Centre, 254 Belsize Park, London NW6

National Coal Board, Hobart House, Grosvenor Place, London SW1 7AE

Ordnance Survey, Department No. 32, Romsey Road, Maybush, Southampton SO9 4DH

Petroleum companies often supply educational aids: addresses in London telephone directories and *The geographers vademecum.*

Port of London Authority, World Trade Centre, Europa House, East Smithfield, London E1

Royal Town Planning Institute, 26 Portland Place, London W1N 4BE

The Schools Council, 160 Great Portland Street, London W1N 6LL

Society for Academic Gaming and Simulation in Training and Education, Centre for Extension

Studies, University of Loughborough, Leicester-shire

Town and Country Planning Association, 17 Carlton House Terrace, London SW1Y 5AS

Unesco, 7 Place de Fontenoy, 75700 Paris, France

AUDIO-VISUAL AIDS

A large number of organisations produce audio-visual aids useful in the teaching of geography. A selection of these are listed below, but further information is available in, for example, *The geographer's vademecum of sources and materials* (see above). Filmstrips are now often produced to accompany books; publishers' catalogues should be consulted for details of these. Lists of filmstrips and slide sets received by The Geographical Association (and which may be borrowed by members) are published in *Geography* and *Teaching Geography*.

Aerofilms Ltd, Gate Studios, Station Road, Bore-hamwood, Herts, WD6 1EJ

Audio-Visual Productions, Hocker Hill House, Chepstow, Gwent, NP6 5ER

Common Ground Filmstrips, Longman Group Ltd, Longman House, Burnt Mill, Harlow, Essex, CM20 2JE

Educational Productions Ltd, Bradford Road, East Ardsley, Wakefield, W. Yorks., WF3 2JN

Focal Point Filmstrips Ltd, 251 Copnor Road, Ports-mouth, PO1 2BR

Gateway Educational Media, Waverley Road, Yate, Bristol, BS17 5RB

National Audio Visual Aids Library, Paxton Place, Gipsy Road, London SE27 9SR

The Slide Centre, 143 Chatham Road, London SW11 6SR

Visual Publications, The Green, Northleach, Chelten-ham, GL54 3EX

Appendix 3: Guide to the selection of an Atlas for young children

Herbert A. Sandford assisted by Gerald Young

Not all teachers have the opportunity to see a full range of atlases and it is hoped that the following guide will help towards an initial selection before requesting inspection copies. Atlases vary greatly, serve many purposes and can be regarded from many points of view. It is therefore necessary to limit this analysis to a few characteristics. The results of a growing body of research underpin the methods of analysis. There is no implication that any one atlas is better than another. In this analysis (tabulated below) the atlases are merely described and individual teachers may judge their suitability for their own purposes.

Date: The date (Column D) is that of the latest copy supplied by the publishers.

Viewing Area (Column E): This is the largest spread of material that the child is normally required to scan. A large area of map is difficult to scan but does enable the map maker to show the whole of a continent on a single opening of the atlas.

Indexes (Columns F and G): There are very divergent views on indexes or gazetteers and so these are described fairly fully. 'I' shows the presence of an index, the suffix 's' being added if a significant proportion of the placenames are omitted. Pupils usually begin to learn the use of atlas co-ordinates by means of a letter/letter or letter/number system (indicated by 'l') or even by compass direction ('c') but sooner or later most pupils will be taught the geographical co-ordinates. These may appear in the index with both degrees and minutes, degrees and

fractions of a degree, or simply to the nearest degree: the smallest unit employed is indicated as '''', or '0'. A 'p' shows that only the page is given.

Pages (Column H): This shows the number of pages devoted to teaching the child how to use the atlas. This is generally present as a distinct 'learning programme' but may continue through the atlas, this continuation being shown by a plus sign. Column I gives the total amount of teaching material in the atlas, including the learning programme but excluding the index.

Regional content (Columns J, K and L): These state the percentages of the atlas, exclusive of learning programme and index, that concern the home region (British Isles), the continents and the world. Most teachers would prefer a fairly full treatment of the home lands but may or may not prefer continental maps to world ones.

Types of maps (Columns M, N, O and P): This material is broken down according to whether it is political, physical, general or thematic. These terms have their usual meanings when applied to conventional atlases. Political maps are coloured country by country and physical maps are coloured according to the relief. They commonly exist as complementary pairs side by side and *both* are likely to show the main rivers, towns and railways. There has been a tendency in recent years for these pairs of maps to be replaced by a single 'politico-relief' or general map. This economy essentially involves adding all the desired 'political' information on to a map coloured according to its relief, this

GUIDE TO THE SELECTION OF AN ATLAS FOR YOUNG CHILDREN

A	B	C	D	E
	PUBLISHER	TITLE	DATE	VIEWING AREA cm
1.	Bartholomew	* *First Atlas of the Environment*	1980	27 x 20
2.	,,	* *Second Atlas of the Environment*	1977	28 x 28
3.	Bartholomew/Holmes McDougall	*Our World[1]*	1978	30 x 22
4.	,, ,, ,,	*Problems of our Planet*	1977	30 x 21
5.	Cassell	*First School Atlas*	1973	25 x 21
6.	,,	*World Study Atlas[2]*	1978	26 x 20
7.	Collins	*New Clear School Atlas*	1976	20 x 15
8.	Collins-Longman	*Atlas One[3,4]*	1980	25 x 21
9.	,, ,,	*Atlas Two[5,6]*	1980	25 x 21
10.	Franklin Watts	*The Basic Atlas*	1976	26 x 19
11.	Hamlyn	*Boys' & Girls' Atlas*	1975	32 x 31
12.	Macdonald	*Maps of Many Lands*	1976	27 x 21
13.	Nelson	*Junior Atlas[7]*	1975	28 x 21
14.	,,	*Atlas 80[8,9,10]*	1978	27 x 20
15.	Oxford	*First Atlas[11]*	1979	47 x 32
16.	Philips[12]	*First Venture Atlas*	1973	23 x 19
17.	,,	*Venture Atlas*	1979	26 x 22
18.	,,	*Middle School Atlas*	1978	26 x 22
19.	,,	*Visual Atlas*	1978	21 x 18
20.	Schofield & Sims	*Our World[13]*	1976	29 x 23
21.	Usborne	* *Children's Atlas of the World*	1979	41 x 26
22.	Wheaton	*Primary Atlas[14]*	1976	29 x 22
23.	,,	*Atlas for the Middle School*	1979	27 x 21

Notes
*Atlas or general maps of environmental (landscape) type, ie. showing both landform and land cover. The Bartholomew's environmental atlases (1 and 2) are integrated with a complete set of environmental globes, wall maps, overhead projector transparencies and work pads.
1. Also sold under the title *Exploration Universe*.
2. Can be used with *Development Books 1 and 2*.
3. Can be used with *Atlas One Workbook*.
4. Also *First Atlas for Irish Schools*.
5. Can be used with *Atlas Two Workbook*.
6. Also *Second Atlas for Irish Schools*.

F	G	H	I	J	K	L	M	N	O	P	Q	R	S	T	U	V	W	X	Y	Z
INDEX		PAGES		CONTENT %										INDICES						
				ATLAS region			ATLAS mode				HOME REGION format			(Low) 0 to 9 (high)						
		learning programme	teaching material	home region	continents	world	political	physical	general	thematic	maps	pictures	text, etc.	density	generalisation	metrication	picture difficulty	realism	quantifiability	integration
Is	1	16+	39	31	51	18	0	0	80*	20	72	19	9	1	2	9	1	8	1	2
I	1	3	37	35	49	16	6	6	61*	27	99	0	0	2	3	9	-	8	6	0
		0	52	40	5	55	4	4	0	92	64	30	6	3	5	7	3	5	3	5
		0	64	3	41	56	0	0	0	99	55	25	20	1	7	8	4	2	5	9
		7+	26	43	10	47	11	26	0	63	71	25	4	1	3	5	3	5	6	0
I	0l	0	59	28	27	45	5	2	23	70	57	42	1	2	3	5	2	5	6	3
I	1	0	50	20	64	16	20	16	48	16	99	0	0	7	2	2	-	5	8	0
Isc		4	33	24	56	20	39	0	20	41	99	0	0	1	4	9	-	6	5	1
I	0l	2+	64	35	41	24	10	20	23	47	95	5	0	3	3	9	9	7	6	1
I	p	0	80	15	81	4	6	0	44	50	60	23	17	1	3	5	0	3	1	0
		10	60	3	84	13	0	0	83	17	50	38	12	0	8	5	0	0	1	1
		2	26	0	99	0	0	0	99	0	85	15	0	0	7	-	0	1	0	0
I	1	3+	48	23	42	35	39	28	0	33	76	10	14	3	2	5	6	6	3	0
I	1	1	49	27	57	16	38	19	2	41	99	0	1	3	2	9	-	4	6	1
		5	20	91	8	1	18	18	9	55	93	7	0	-	-	9	4	3	1	0
		3+	35	48	8	44	9	25	25	41	74	18	8	2	3	9	3	5	6	0
I	0l	0	43	14	60	26	9	2	58	31	99	0	0	1	2	7	-	5	6	0
Is	0l	3	34	33	41	26	9	10	43	38	99	0	0	1	2	7	-	5	6	2
I	0l	2	47	22	62	16	24	23	37	16	99	0	0	5	3	6	-	5	8	0
		2	46	53	6	41	16	7	0	77	56	18	26	2	7	9	2	3	5	2
I	0l	28	58	7	86	7	6	0	94*	0	99	0	0	1	2	8	-	7	1	0
		2+	37	42	29	29	26	3	0	71	67	29	4	0	6	9	3	4	5	0
I	1	4+	44	43	39	18	8	5	30	57	79	7	14	3	3	7	6	5	6	0

7. Can be used with *Junior Atlas Workbook* and *Workbooks 1 to 3*.

8. Can be used with *Atlas 80 Workbook*.

9. Also *Atlas of Scotland*.

10. Can be used with *Atlas of Scotland Workbook*.

11. Can be used with *First Atlas Workbook*.

12. Local supplements available for Cornwall, Ireland, Northern Ireland, S. E. Scotland, S. W. Scotland and Wales.

13. Can be used with *Checkpoint*.

14. Can be used with *Primary Geography Cards*.

A, B, C . . . . . . .Z for explanation see text

being by altitude colours and/or relief shadow. It is an advantage for physical and human geography to be brought together in this way though it does result in a map that is more difficult to read and interpret. There is a new development in general maps. These rely upon shadow effects to indicate the relief and the maps are coloured according to the natural and man made use of the land, that is, they show land *cover* as well as land *form*. These have been styled 'environmental' and are indicated by an asterisk. Thematic material includes climate, population, products and so forth. In the strict sense, political and physical maps are thematic although the common use of this term excludes them.

Home region format (Columns Q, R and S): These show the extent to which pictures, text and diagrams supplement the maps.

The indices (Columns T to Z) are on a 10-point scale, 0 (low) to 9 (high). The presence of a dash indicates that the index is inapplicable or else that complete objectivity could not be obtained.
Density (Column T): Children find it very difficult to read maps that are densely covered with names but too few may give a very false impression if many town stamps are also omitted. The Index of Density will provide some guidance.
Index of Generalisation (Column U): Many atlases, especially for young children, are highly generalised: coastlines are smoothed and many mountains, islands and lakes are omitted. This makes the map simpler to use but gives a false representation of reality.
Metrication (Column V): Only complete metrication is scored as 9 in Column V.
Pictures (Column W): Difficult pictures (9 in Column

W) are monochrome, high altitude, vertical photographs while easy ones are coloured paintings of close-up familiar objects.
Realism (Column X): This describes the extent to which the maps provide a realistic visual impression of the landscape. An obscure gradation from one altitude colour to another, the use of relief shadow, showing land cover in addition to land form and retaining the earth's natural complexity all add to realism. Such maps, however, may not be easy to read.
Quantifiability (Column Y): The Index of Quantifiability describes the ease of measuring altitude, distance, direction and so forth. This is facilitated by a low degree of generalisation and also by bold altitude colours unobscured by relief shadow. Realism, however, is low.
Integrated Studies provision (Column Z): The last column shows the extent to which the atlas provides for integrated studies by including less traditional material, material on religion, history, science and so forth. Such atlases remain, of course, predominantly geographical in the usual sense.

An example in the use of the Guide might be helpful. If one's priority is for an atlas for teaching integrated studies by topics, a glance down Column Z might suggest *Problems of our planet*. Looking along the line to Column P it is seen that the treatment is entirely thematic, well suited to project and topic work in I.D.E.

Note: The assistance of Mr. Gerald Young, Head of Geography at Prince Rock Secondary School, Plymouth, is gratefully acknowledged in the compilation of the analytical table.

Appendix 4. Books for teachers and children

1. BOOKS FOR TEACHERS (in addition to those mentioned in the text and listed in the References section)

General
Bailey, P. *Teaching geography*. Newton Abbot: David and Charles, 1975.
Department of Education and Science. *Teaching of ideas in geography* (HMI Matters for Discussion Series, No. 5). London: HMSO, 1978.

Physical geography and Weather studies
Bradshaw, M. J. et al. *The earth's changing surface.* London: Hodder and Stoughton, 1978.
Dury, G. H. *The face of the Earth.* Harmondsworth: Penguin, 1970.
Francis, P. *Volcanoes.* Harmondsworth: Penguin, 1976.
Geographical Association. Teaching Geography Occasional Papers:
21. Anderson, E. W. *Drainage basin instrumentation in fieldwork.* 1974.
23. Mottershead, R. *Practical biogeography.* 1974.

25. Weyman, D. and Wilson, C. *Hydrology for schools.* 1975.
29. Simmons, R. L. and Mears, J. K. *Landscape drawing.* 1977.
Haddon, J. *Local geography in towns.* London: Philip, 1971.
Hanwell, J. and Newson, M. *Techniques in physical geography.* Basingstoke: Macmillan, 1973.
Hoskins, W. V. *The making of the English landscape.* London: Hodder and Stoughton, 1955.
Martin, G. and Turner, E. (eds) *Environmental studies:* Leicester: Blond, 1972.
Perry, G. A., Jones, E. and Hammersley, A. *Handbook for environmental studies,* rev. ed. London: Blandford Press, 1971.
Meteorological Office. *Course in elementary meteorology,* 2nd ed. London: HMSO, 1978.
Thornes, J. B. *River channels.* Basingstoke: Macmillan Educational, 1979.
Trueman, A. E. *Geology and scenery in England and Wales,* rev. ed. Harmondsworth: Penguin, 1971.
Schools Council. *Out and about: teachers' guide to safety on educational visits.* London: Evans/ Methuen, 1972.

Urban fieldwork

Briggs, K. *Fieldwork in urban geography*. Edinburgh: Oliver and Boyd, 1970.

Bell, S. and Williams, M. *Using the urban environment*. London: Heinemann Educational, 1972.

Scoffham, S. *Using the school's surroundings: a guide to local studies in urban schools*. London: Ward Lock, 1980.

Games and simulations

Davison, A. and Gordon, P. *Games and simulations in action*. London: Woburn Press, 1978.

Taylor, J. and Walford, R. *Learning and the simulation game*. Milton Keynes: Open University Press, 1978.

Walford, R. *Games in geography*, 5th ed. London: Longman, 1975.

Sources of simple simulations may be found in the following books:

Cole, J. P. and Beynon, N. J. *New ways in geography*. Oxford, Blackwell, 1968-70.

Dalton, R. *et al. Simulation games in geography*. London: Macmillan, 1972.

Durham Geography Study Group. *Games and simulations in geography teaching*. Durham Education Committee, 1973. (Booklet, resource list and nine games.)

Haigh, J. M. *Geography games*. Oxford: Blackwell, 1975.

Rolfe, J. *et al. Oxford Geography Project* (Books 1, 2 and 3) rev. ed. Oxford: Oxford University Press, 1979.

Schools Council. *Games and simulations in the classroom (Time, Place and Society: a project booklet)*. Bristol: Collins/ESL, 1975.

Walker, M. *et al. Location and links - Books 1 to 5*. Oxford: Blackwell, 1973.

Models

Bayley, T. *Model making in cardboard*. Leicester: Dryad Press, 1964.

——. *The craft of model making*. Leicester: Dryad Press, 1966.

Sutton, H. T. *Models in action*. London: Evans, 1972.

——. *Teaching with models*. London: Evans, 1975.

Case Studies

Palmer, J. A. *Chivenor follow-up: farm visits as a starting point for the development of environmental studies with primary school children of different ages*. London: Association of Agriculture, 1979.

Project work

Culling, G. *Projects for the middle school*. Woking: Lutterworth Press, 1972.

Fellows, M. S. *Projects for schools*. London: Museum Press, 1965.

Haggit, E. *Projects in the primary school*. London: Longman, 1975.

Hoare, R. J. *Topic work with books*. London: Chapman, 1971.

Rance, P. *Teaching by topics*, 2nd ed. London: Ward Lock Educational, 1970.

2. TEXTBOOKS AND CLASS REFERENCE BOOKS

General

Bateman, R. and Martin, F. *Steps in geography* (series). London: Hutchinson, 1980- .

Bowler, L. and Waites, B. *Exploring geography* (series). Huddersfield: Schofield and Sims, 1979- .

Catling, S., Firth, T. and Rowbotham, D. *Outset geography* (series). Edinburgh: Oliver and Boyd, 1981- .

Cole, J. P. and Beynon, N. J. *New ways in geography* (series). Oxford: Blackwell, 1969-72.

Elliot, G. *Oxford new geography* (series). Oxford: Oxford University Press, 1980- .

Evans, H. *The young geographer* (series). Exeter: Wheaton, 1971-8.

Renwick, M. and Pick, W. *Going places* (series). Sunbury-on-Thames: Nelson, 1980- .

Greasley, B. *et al. Harrap's basic geography* (books 1 to 3 and teaching guide). London: Harrap, 1979.

Williamson, J. and Meredith, S. *The children's book of Britain*. London: Usborne, 1980.

Introductory mapwork

Collins-Longman. *Atlas One* and *Atlas One workbook*. Glasgow/London: Collins-Longman, 1980.

Gregory, O. *Making plans*. Oxford: Oxford University Press, 1978.

Harris, P. C. and Giffard, E. O. *Let's make maps: a pre-atlas workbook*. Glasgow/London: Collins-Longman, 1980.

Marchington, T. *Reading maps*. London: Macdonald, 1972.

Myatt, J. and Payne, H. C. *Mapping out geography* (series). Edinburgh: Oliver and Boyd, 1970-72.

Oxford first atlas and *A first atlas workbook*. Oxford: Oxford University Press, 1979.

Case studies

BBC school pamphlets.

Beddis, R. A. *Focal points in geography* (Case studies 1 to 4). London: University of London Press, 1967-73.

Burrell, E. R. and Hancock, J. *A sample geography of Western Europe*. London: Methuen, 1972.

Hutson, A. B. A. *Sample studies around the world*. London: Allman and Son, 1970.

Johnson, R. *Farms in Britain*. London: Macmillan, 1970.

——. *Mines and quarries in Britain*. London: Macmillan, 1971.

Rushby, J. G. *et al. Study geography* (Stages 2 to 5). London: Longman, 1967-9.

Wheeler, K. E. *et al. Studies in agricultural geography*. London: Blond Educational, 1970.

Physical geography

Atherton, M. and Robinson, R. *Water at work (Study the Earth* series). Sevenoaks: Hodder and Stoughton, 1980.

Bailey, B. *The weather*. London: Macdonald Educational, 1974.

Bodin, S. *Weather and climate in colour*. Poole: Blandford Press, 1978.

British Museum (Natural History). *The succession of life through geological time*.

Calder, N. *Restless earth*. London: BBC, 1972.

Corretti, G. *Let's look at planet Earth*. Hove: Wayland, 1979.

Dineley, D. *Rocks*. London: Collins, 1977.

Dobson, F. R. and Virgo, H. E. *The elements of geography in colour*. London: Hodder and Stoughton, 1974.

Ellis, C. *The pebbles on the beach*. London: Faber, 1965.

Geological Museum. *The story of the Earth*. London: HMSO, 1972.

Giles, B. *Weather observation*. Wakefield: EP Publishing, 1978.

Hamilton, R. *Fossils and fossil collecting*. London: Hamlyn, 1975.

Holford, I. *The Guinness book of weather facts and feats*. London: Guinness Superlatives, 1977.

Ingle, R. *Guide to the seashore*. London: Hamlyn, 1969.

Kirkaldy, J. F. *Fossils in colour*. London: Blandford Press, 1970.

——. *Minerals and rocks in colour*. London: Blandford Press, 1963.

Ladybird Books, Series 737, *Leaders:* No. 1. *Water;* No. 23. *Air;* No. 27. *The stream;* No. 33. *Mountains*. Loughborough: Ladybird Books, 1973-7.

Ladybird Books, Series 536, *Nature*, No. 17. *Our rocks and minerals*. Loughborough: Ladybird Books, 1966.

Lines, C. J. and Bolwell, L. H. *Discovering your environment* (series of 10 books). London: Ginn, 1968-71.

Lloyd Davies, M. *Lowlands; Mountains and hills; The coast*. London: Muller, 1977.

Lucas, A. and D. *Focus on oceans* and *Focus on water*. London: Methuen, 1976.

Macdonald First Library, No. 37. *Rocks and mining;* No. 39. *Rivers and river life;* No. 47. *Mountains*. London: Macdonald Educational 1971, 1972.

Macdonald Starters series, No. 34. *Rivers*. London: Macdonald Educational, 1971.

Milburn, D. *A first book of geology*. Oxford: Blackwell, 1967.

Newing, F. E. and Bowood, R. *The weather*. Loughborough: Ladybird Books, 1962.

Nuffield Junior Science. *Autumn into winter*. London: Collins, 1965.

Price, B. *The weather*. London: Macdonald Educational, 1972.

Ryan, P. *The ocean world*. Harmondsworth: Penguin, 1973.

Sauvain, P. A. *Practical geography, Book 3. Man and environment*. Amersham: Hulton Educational, 1971.

Schmidt, S. *Discovering the oceans*. Guildford: Lutterworth Press, 1974.

Science and your surroundings series:
 Nicholls, A. *On the road*. Aylesbury: Ginn, 1971.
 Wigley, H. *Piece of waste ground*. Aylesbury: Ginn, 1970.

Scorer, R. and Wexler, M. *A colour guide to clouds*. Oxford: Pergamon Press, 1964.

Scott, J. *Fun with meteorology*. London: Kaye and Ward, 1975.

Smith, A. J. *Geology*. London: Hamlyn, 1975.

Tyler, J. and Watts, L. *The children's book of the seas*. London: Usborne, 1976.

Waters, D. *Sea coasts (On location series)*. London: Mills and Boon, 1979.

Whitten, D. G. A. *Rocks, minerals and crystals*. London: Hamlyn, 1976.

Wilkes, A. *Usborne first travellers* series: *Mountains; Deserts; Jungles*. London: Usborne, 1980.

Wilson, F. and Mansfield, F. *Spotters' guide to the weather*. London: Usborne, 1979.

Woodcock, R. *Mountains* (Macdonald New Reference Library, No. 26). London: Macdonald Educational, 1980.

Woolley, A. *et al. Guide to minerals, rocks and fossils*. London: Hamlyn, 1974.

Yonge, C. M. *The seashore*, rev. ed. *(New naturalist* series). London: Collins, 1966.

Human and Economic Geography and Stories of other countries

Appiah, P. *Tales of an Ashanti father*. London: Andre Deutsch, 1967.

Birch, C. *Chinese myths and fantasies*. Oxford: Oxford University Press, 1961.

Bothwell, J. *India*. London: Franklin Watts, 1979.

Clare, R. *A railway junction (Look inside* series). Basingstoke: Macmillan Education, 1979.

Clare, R. *Towns and cities (Meet the World* series). London: Arnold, 1979.

Cranfield, J. and Buckman, D. *Coal (World resources* series). Hove: Wayland, 1978.

Crisp, T. *People and places* (series). London: Nelson, 1974-5 (Titles include: *Food and farming; Towns; Fuel and power; Industry*).

Downing, C. *Russian tales and legends*. Oxford: Oxford University Press, 1956.

Finlay, W. *Folk tales from the North*. London: Kaye and Ward, 1968.

Fordham, D. *Eskimos (Surviving people* series). London: Macdonald Educational, 1979.

Graham-Cameron, M. *The farmer*, 2nd ed. Cambridge: Dinosaur Publications, 1980.

Gibberd, V. *Buildings and backgrounds*. Cambridge: Dinosaur Publications for the National Trust, 1979.

Hale, D. and Vickers, M. *Coalmining* and *Iron and steel (People and progress* series). London: Arnold, 1979.

Haviland, V. *Favourite fairy stories told in Spain*. London: Bodley Head, 1966.

Hayes, J. *Food and farming* and *Villages, towns and cities (Down to earth* series). London: Hutchinson, 1980.

Moore, W. G. *Man and his world: food*. Amersham: Hulton Educational, 1976.

Pick, C. C. *Oil and machines*. Hove: Wayland, 1979.

Pollard, M. *My world*. London: Macdonald Educational in association with Unicef, 1979.

Rivers of the World series. Hove: Wayland (Includes:

Douglas, G. *The Ganges,* 1978; McConnell, R. *The Amazon,* 1978.).
Unesco. *Folk tales from Asia for children everywhere.* (Sponsored by the Asian Cultural Centre for Unesco.)
Williams, T. and A. *A motorway (Look inside* series). Basingstoke: Macmillan Education, 1979.
Wright, J. A. *Problems in world farming (Living in the modern world* series). London: Hodder and Stoughton, 1976.

3. SCHOOLS COUNCIL PROJECTS RELEVANT TO PRIMARY AND MIDDLE-SCHOOL GEOGRAPHY

Environmental Studies 5-13

This was established to help teachers use the environment systematically to provide experiences which help the progressive development of a child's skills and concepts throughout his primary school career and beyond. Environmental studies was defined not as a 'subject' but as an approach to learning which leads to the progressive development of attitudes and skills required for the observation, recording, interpretation and communication of scientific, historical and geographical data.

Materials are published by Hart-Davis Educational (see under Schools Council 1972a, b, c, 1973 in References section), and a 16mm colour film is available from the National Audio-Visual Aids Library (address in Appendix 2).

History, Geography and Social Sciences 8-13

The aim of this project was to produce material for use with 8-13-year-olds, whether the three subjects were taught separately or in some combination. Emphasis was laid on helping teachers to develop procedures and materials appropriate to their own situations rather than producing a standard set of materials.

Materials are published by Collins Education, Westerhill, Bishopriggs, Glasgow G4 0NB and ESL, Waverley Road, Yate, Bristol BS17 5RB, under the series title *Place, Time and Society,* and include handbooks for teachers and pupils' packs.

Science 5-13

This project was established to consolidate and extend the work on primary science teaching initiated by the Nuffield Junior Science Project. The main work of the project has been to identify objectives for guiding pupils' education through science, to relate them to stages in pupils' educational development and to exemplify ways in which these objectives might be achieved. The aim of the development work has been to assist teachers to help children, through discovery methods, to gain experience and understanding of the environment and to develop their powers of thinking effectively about it.

The published materials, which are intended to be source books from which teachers can draw materials to suit their own circumstances, are published by Macdonald Educational, 49 Poland Street, London, W1A 2LG.

Index